# Using Artificial Intelligence

## ABSOLUTE BEGINNER'S GUIDE

Michael Miller

Pearson

AARP®
Real Possibilities

# Using Artificial Intelligence Absolute Beginner's Guide

Copyright © 2025 by Pearson Education, Inc.

Hoboken, New Jersey

ISBN-13:  978-0-13-535605-0
ISBN-10: 0-13-535605-9

Library of Congress Control Number: 2024947065

5 2024

## Trademarks

**Editor-in-Chief**
Brett Bartow

**Executive Editor**
Laura Norman

**Associate Editor**
Anshul Sharma

**Marketing**
Josh DeMatteo

**Director, AARP Books**
Jodi Lipson; Leah Miller

**Development Editor**
Charlotte Kughen

**Managing Editor**
Sandra Schroeder

**Senior Project Editor**
Tonya Simpson

**Copy Editor**
The Wordsmithery LLC

**Indexer**
Cheryl Lenser

**Proofreader**
Johnna Vanhoose Dinse

**Publishing Coordinator**
Cindy Teeters

**Compositor**
Bronkella Publishing LLC

**Graphics Processing**
tj graham art

## Warning and Disclaimer

## Special Sales

For information about buying this title in bulk quantities, or for special sales opportunities (which may include electronic versions; custom cover designs; and content particular to your business, training goals, marketing focus, or branding interests), please contact our corporate sales department at corpsales@pearsoned.com or (800) 382-3419.

For government sales inquiries, please contact governmentsales@pearsoned.com.

For questions about sales outside the U.S., please contact international@pearsoned.com.

# Contents at a Glance

# Table of Contents

# About the Author

This book is written by me, Michael Miller. I've written more than 200 books over the past four decades, including many in the *Absolute Beginner's Guide* series and almost two dozen books with AARP. My books have collectively sold more than 1.5 million copies worldwide, so I must be doing something right.

I have a particular interest in new and evolving technologies, so writing about AI is right up my alley. My readers say I have a knack for explaining complex technologies in easy-to-understand terms, and I have no reason to argue with that. I hope I can help you better understand artificial intelligence and how you can use it in your everyday life.

Oh, in case you're wondering, I am an older gentleman, which only means I've been around long enough to experience many different "new" technologies. (I have been writing for four decades, after all; I wrote one of the first books about the Internet when it was new!) I live with my wife and random daily combinations of four stepchildren and eight grandchildren in a suburb of the Twin Cities in the often-frozen land of Minnesota. In my spare time, what there is of it, I play drums, entertain (and am entertained by) my grandchildren, and write about music from the '60s, '70s, and '80s in my Classic Song of the Day blog (www.classicsongoftheday.com).

You can find out more about me on my website, located at www.millerwriter.com. Feel free to use the contact form there to get in touch with me. I'm open to criticism, faint praise, and the occasional earnest question. I may or may not respond personally, although I guarantee I'll read everything you write.

# Dedication

*To my eight wonderful grandkids who will grow up in an AI world: Collin, Alethia, Hayley, Judah, Lael, Jackson, Jamie, and Adelynn.*

# Acknowledgments

My thanks to everyone at Pearson who helped turned my words into a book, including Laura Norman, Anshul Sharma, and Charlotte Kughen. Thanks also to the good folks at AARP for their input and support, including Jodi Lipson, Leah Miller, and Michael Phillips.

# About AARP

AARP is the nation's largest nonprofit, nonpartisan organization dedicated to empowering people 50 and older to choose how they live as they age. With a nationwide presence and nearly 38 million members, AARP strengthens communities and advocates for what matters most to families: health security, financial stability and personal fulfillment. AARP also produces the nation's largest circulation publications: AARP The Magazine and AARP Bulletin. To learn more, visit www.aarp.org, www.aarp.org/espanol or follow @AARP, @AARPenEspanol and @AARPadvocates, @AliadosAdelante on social media.

# We Want to Hear from You!

As the reader of this book, you are our most important critic and commentator. We value your opinion and want to know what we're doing right, what we could do better, what areas you'd like to see us publish in, and any other words of wisdom you're willing to pass our way.

We welcome your comments. You can email or write to let us know what you did or didn't like about this book[md]as well as what we can do to make our books better.

*Please note that we cannot help you with technical problems related to the topic of this book.*

When you email, please be sure to include this book's title and author as well as your name and email address. We will carefully review your comments and share them with the author and editors who worked on the book.

Email: community@informit.com

# Reader Services

Visit our website and register this book at informit.com/register for convenient access to any updates, downloads, or errata that might be available for this book.

# Figure Credits

Figures 10.2, 10.3: Layla

Figures 10.4, 10.5: Roam Around

Figures 10.6, 10.7: Trip Planner AI.

Figures 10.8, 10.9: Wonderplan

Figures 10.10, 10.12: OpenAI Inc

Figure 10.11: © 2024 Anthropic PBC

Figure 10.13: Vasco Electronics

Figures 11.1, 11.8, 11.12: © 2024 Meta

Figures 11.2, 11.6, 11.7, 11.13: OpenAI Inc

Figure 11.3: © 2024 Anthropic PBC

Figures 11.5, 11.10: © Microsoft 2024

Figures 11.4, 11.9, 11.11, 11.14: Google LLC

Figure 12.1: SixD Incorporated

Figure 12.2: © Intuition Robotics Inc. 2024

Figure 13.1: (Based on *Superintelligence: Paths, Dangers, Strategies* by Nick Bostrom. Estimates of the timing and duration of takeoff were not included on Bostrom's original graph.)

Figure 13.2: © 2024 Engineered Arts

# Introduction

You can't open a newspaper, load a web page, or scroll through a TikTok feed without being presented with either inspiring or alarming stories about AI.

*Artificial intelligence*—AI—is considered one of the most significant technological developments of the current century. And its impact is just beginning.

In its simplest form, AI is the idea of machines that learn and think like humans. Long a concept in science fiction (think Frankenstein and "Star Trek"), AI has only in the past years become a reality.

In fact, your life is already being touched by AI, and it's likely you'll be affected even more in the months and years to come. It's not just theoretical or for scientists and researchers; AI is a technology that you can use in your daily life.

If you think AI might be a passing fad, take a look at some recent headlines:

- "AI Will Make Mental Healthcare More Human" (*Psychology Today*)
- "Artists' AI Dilemma: Can Artificial Intelligence Make Intelligent Art?" (*The Guardian*)
- "How to Protect Yourself (and Your Loved Ones) From AI Scam Calls" (*Wired*)
- "Jamie Dimon Says AI May Be as Impactful on Humanity as Printing Press, Electricity and Computers" (CNBC)
- "'Social Order Could Collapse' in AI Era, Two Top Japan Companies Say" (*Wall Street Journal*)
- "Will Artificial Intelligence Boost Productivity? Companies Sure Hope So" (*The Seattle Times*)

All those stories—and many more--were published *in a single day*. As you read them, you may find it difficult to get a grasp on what AI is and its potential impact on our world. Is AI the greatest thing since fire and sliced bread, or will it cause the demise of humankind as we know it? How can it enhance your life and make it better? What should you watch out for?

The answers, at this point in time, are obviously less than clear. What is clear is that AI is here—and here to stay.

# AI Is Already Changing Things—and Will Change Even More

AI is all around you, including places you may not even realize. AI powers personalized content recommendations on your favorite streaming video sites. It drives real-time navigation apps on your phone. It's used in virtual assistants like Alexa and Siri. It's even a part of supply chain management that puts the products you need on store shelves.

And that's just the simple AI that's been in use for the past few years. Newer generative AI—what most of this book is about—doesn't just *power* things; it *empowers* you to create new things. Generative AI lets you create stories, images, video, and audio with just a few brief prompts. You can use AI to help you write letters and social media posts; people who have trouble drawing a straight line (like me!) can use AI to create both fantastic and realistic images; businesses can use AI to answer customer questions and manage employee schedules. It's all out there, and there's even more to come.

It's clear that AI will have a radical effect on our lives. We can expect to interact with AI in much of what we do—writing emails, articles, and blog posts; creating art; finding information; managing finances; traveling; and obtaining medical care. There's little in this world that AI won't impact.

That doesn't mean AI is perfect or always safe or easy to use. AI is a powerful technology that can be confusing and intimidating, even to those who work with it every day. There are seemingly unlimited ways for technology to incorporate AI and unlimited ways for people like you and me to use AI to assist in our daily lives.

There are also a seemingly unlimited number of AI tools available today, with more introduced constantly. Sorting through these options and understanding how they work—and how you can get the most out of them—are just a few of the things we as individuals need to master moving forward.

It's important to be aware of and able to recognize the limitations and risks presented by this new technology. Because AI is trained on data from human beings, it can represent both the best and the worst of our society. AI can be used to spread misinformation. It can increase the sophistication of scams. It can reflect societal biases such as preconceptions about age, race, and gender. It can offer up intellectual property that belongs to someone else. And it can also be seen as threatening to human security; some experts believe that AI has the potential to replace humans in many areas, if not completely. Whatever its ultimate impact, AI is part of our world and we will all come into contact with it in our daily lives. Just as we've had to learn how to use the new technologies of the past, from washing machines and motor vehicles to personal computers and the Internet, we need to learn how to use and get the most out of AI going forward. By getting out there and experimenting with today's AI tools, you can discover all the amazing ways that AI can help you become both more productive and more creative. And how to know where you shouldn't use it, or where you should use it with caution.

That's what this book is about.

XX    USING ARTIFICIAL INTELLIGENCE **ABSOLUTE BEGINNER'S GUIDE**

# What's In This Book

*Using Artificial Intelligence: Absolute Beginner's Guide* is a book about what AI is—the pros and cons, benefits and risks—and how to use it. It's a book about a highly technical subject written for a nontechnical audience in easy-to-understand language. I try to make AI as understandable as possible while focusing on the technology's practical aspects. That is, this book eschews all the technical mumbo jumbo in favor of showing you the many ways you can use AI to perform everyday tasks.

If I do my job right as an author, this book will help you

- Understand, at a very basic level, how AI works

- Learn how AI can benefit you in your life

- Recognize and manage some of AI's risks, limitations, and security implications

- Discover commonly available AI tools and use them for specific tasks

- Identify when AI can be helpful and trusted and when it can't
- Spot AI-generated content

I include lots of examples to show you how AI works and give you step-by-step instructions so you can try AI for yourself. You'll see how AI works in different applications, from writing letters and creating art to managing your health and helping you be more productive at work. The emphasis is on the practical use of AI—how you might encounter and employ the technology in the real world.

# How This Book Is Organized

The information in *Using Artificial Intelligence: Absolute Beginner's Guide* is organized into 13 chapters and a glossary. Here's how that information is presented:

**Chapter 1, "AI: What It Is and How It Works":** This first chapter digs into the ideas and technologies behind AI, focusing on the newer, more powerful generative AI. You'll learn AI's history, how it works, and how AI is being used today.

**Chapter 2, "The Benefits and Risks of AI":** Here is where I discuss the great ways that AI can help you—and what to watch out for.

**Chapter 3, "Getting Started with All-Purpose AI Tools":** This chapter gets into the fun stuff: how to use free and publicly available AI tools—such as ChatGPT, Google Gemini, Meta AI, and Microsoft Copilot —for fun and in practical applications.

**Chapter 4, "Using AI to Find the Right Words":** Learn how to use AI to assist in writing everything from email messages and letters to articles and business reports. You can even use AI to write poetry and fiction for your own personal use (you can't claim AI-written material as your own!)—and edit your existing work to make it read better.

**Chapter 5, "Using AI to Find Information":** AI is several steps beyond today's web-based search engines. Discover how AI can find information faster—and help you understand what it finds—and when you need to verify AI's output (short answer: always!). Whether you want to figure out how to fix your car or plan dinner for six with picky eaters, AI can help. It can also be a great tool to help you summarize information.

**Chapter 6, "Using AI to Connect with People and Pursue Interests":** AI can help you connect with other people who share your interests. You can even use AI to manage—or generate—your online conversations and help you pursue your favorite hobbies. This chapter also covers how and when to have helpful conversations with AI

**Chapter 7, "Using AI to Create Art and Images":** Discover the easy-to-use AI tools that let you create photorealistic images or pieces of art that transcend your imagination.

**Chapter 8, "Using AI to Get a Job":** Get a leg up on other applicants by using AI tools to find the right job, craft the perfect resume and cover letter, and prepare for job interviews.

**Chapter 9, "Using AI at Work":** It's not surprising that employers are looking for AI to improve productivity. Learn how to use today's AI-based tools to automate routine tasks, collaborate with colleagues, and make better business decisions.

**Chapter 10, "Using AI to Manage Your Travel and Transportation":** Discover how AI can help you create trip plans, find the best places to stay (at the best prices), and prepare for your journey. You'll also learn about self-driving vehicles and using AI to map the most efficient routes.

**Chapter 11, "Using AI for Health and Wellness":** Learn how you can use AI to create fitness and nutrition plans, better understand what your providers tell you, and improve your mental health.

**Chapter 12 "Using AI to Help Caregivers":** If you are one of the more than 37 million people caring for a relative or friend, you're probably eager to get all the help you can—and AI can help you become a better caregiver. Discover how AI can automate daily tasks such as pill management, improve personal health and safety, and even provide companionship.

**Chapter 13, "The Future of AI":** The first dozen chapters of this book tell you where AI is today. This final chapter predicts what's next for AI—how AI will evolve and how it will affect our lives in the future.

**Glossary:** This section provides a list of AI-related terms you need to know. Learning these terms won't make you an AI expert, but using them may make you sound like one.

One last thing. As you read through this book, you'll see a variety of notes that provide additional information and warnings that alert you to AI's limitations. You'll even find some extended sidebars that provide tangential information and responses to frequently asked questions. These notes, warnings, and sidebars aren't essential for learning how to use AI, but you may find them interesting or helpful.

# This Book Is About *Generative* AI

As you'll learn in the very first chapter of this book, there are two types of AI in use today: the older predictive AI and the newer generative AI. While predictive AI is interesting and useful, and the type we know best—asking Siri questions, getting Alexa to turn on music, having your grammar and spelling checked when you're writing—it's the more powerful (and, dare I say, more "intelligent") generative AI that promises to have the biggest impact on society. Generative AI is so named because it can generate new content—words, pictures, sounds, ideas—that didn't exist previously. This ability to create something from nothing is what gives generative AI its promise to transform our world.

For all these reasons, this book focuses on generative AI—what it is and how to use it. I won't completely ignore predictive AI, but generative AI is where it's at today and where I devote the bulk of my attention and coverage.

1

# AI: WHAT IT IS AND HOW IT WORKS

Artificial intelligence—AI—already touches our lives in innumerable ways, and it will continue to do so in ways we can only imagine today. The newest form of AI, *generative AI* (what this book mostly focuses on), promises to help individuals like you and me create all sorts of new content. But to get the most out of generative AI, it's helpful to have an understanding of this new technology—which is what you'll get from this chapter.

# What Generative AI Is ...

Let's start with the basics. What exactly is artificial intelligence?

When I asked ChatGPT, one of the most popular generative AI tools today, that question, here's how it responded:

> **AI means making computers do things that humans do, like learning, reasoning, and problem-solving. The aim is to create smart systems that can do tasks that usually need human intelligence.**

Not surprisingly, that's not a bad answer. (You'd expect AI to know what AI is.) Put in more human terms, AI is an intelligence not naturally born. It is a simulation of natural human intelligence created by machines.

AI is all about computers that go beyond computing to also "think." That means they don't merely regurgitate facts from existing sources but actually come up with new ideas and processes. AI "learns" from enormous amounts of data it's exposed to, creating something new—just like human beings can.

The goal of AI is to create machines that can think like humans and also perform tasks that go beyond the capabilities of human minds. It happens when computers ingest and analyze large amounts of data, identify patterns, and extrapolate from those patterns to deduce solutions and make decisions.

As to why AI exists, I'll let ChatGPT answer that question, too:

> **Overall, AI exists to enhance human capabilities, improve our quality of life, drive innovation, and address some of the most pressing challenges facing society today.**

I couldn't have put it better myself.

# ...and What It Isn't

Note that AI isn't a "smart" app on your phone—it's much more advanced than that. While there are some who seek to exploit the buzz around AI by applying the term "artificial intelligence" to existing processes and applications, true AI goes well beyond the technologies in use today.

For example, today's web-based search engines—Bing, Google, Yahoo, and the rest—might look like AI as they try to understand your queries and deliver relevant results. But there's not much intelligence behind what they do; they use simple algorithms to deliver certain results based on defined inputs. They don't think or figure things out, they just follow a set of rules to try to find the best results. (Although you may notice that Google recently began adding AI's best thinking to the top of your search results.)

 **NOTE**   An *algorithm* is a set of step-by-step rules or instructions designed to perform a task or solve a problem. Think of an algorithm along the lines of "if this happens, then do that; if something else happens, then do this other thing."

Likewise, many online chatbots purport to use AI technology but actually don't. One chatbot I've used for online customer service claims to be "AI powered" but, in reality, there is nothing intelligent about it; it simply supplies prewritten answers based on predetermined customer questions. That is, you pick a question from a list and it spits out the appropriate answer. That may be artificial, but it certainly isn't intelligent.

## Understanding Predictive AI

Predictive AI is an older, more established form of artificial intelligence. Until very recently, it was the only kind of AI you were likely to encounter in day-to-day life.

 **NOTE**   Predictive AI is also known as traditional AI, narrow AI, or weak AI.

Predictive AI is so named because it is most often used to predict specific outcomes or trends based on existing data. Predictive AI is used by today's web search engines to predict what web pages match your query; by social media companies to predict what posts you're mostly likely interested in; and by streaming video and music services to predict what shows or songs you might like.

Predictive AI is task-specific, typically operating with a predefined set of instructions for a specific task. It uses the standard AI processes of data collection, data processing, outcomes, assessments, and adjustments but is based primarily on historical data. It analyses that historical data to understand patterns and trends it can use to make predictions about future trends and events.

You can find predictive AI in use today in a variety of applications, where it predicts

- Traffic flow
- Social media likes/dislikes
- User search queries

- Viewer/listener likes/dislikes

- Spelling and grammar checks

- Need for preventive maintenance

- Credit risk analysis

- Customer demand forecasting

- Inventory level predictions

- Patient outcomes in healthcare

- Stock prices

## Understanding Generative AI

Generative AI is a newer type of artificial intelligence that can generate new data similar to and based on existing information and examples. Unlike predictive AI, which is focused on making specific predictions, generative AI is capable of generating completely new data that has not previously existed. As the name implies, generative AI can generate text, audio, images, videos, music, and other content that is often indistinguishable from that created by humans.

 **NOTE** Generative AI is also known as strong AI.

Generative AI can be used to create all sorts of things, from newspaper articles and photorealistic artwork to web pages and software programs. (That's right, generative AI can create programming code—much faster than can human developers.) It can generate hypothetical scenarios and simulations for training and educational purposes. It can create new and totally unique content beyond what it was trained on.

You can find generative AI in use today in

- AI text generators and chatbots, such as Anthropic's Claude, Google's Gemini, Microsoft's Copilot, and OpenAI's ChatGPT

- AI image generators, such as Adobe Firefly, DALL-E, DeepAI's AI Image Generator, Deep Dream Generator, Microsoft Designer's Image Creator, and Midjourney

- AI video generators, such as Colossyan AI, DeepBrain AI, HeyGen AI, and SundaySky

**NOTE**   Generative or strong AI isn't the ultimate form of artificial intelligence; rather, experts describe the currently theoretical *super AI* to be a form of artificial intelligence that surpasses human intelligence. Learn more about super AI in Chapter 13, "The Future of AI."

## Comparing Predictive and Generative AI

Predictive and generative AI are related in that they use similar learning techniques, but they're substantially different in terms of what they're designed to achieve. In essence, predictive AI anticipates future outcomes while generative AI creates new outcomes. Predictive AI is smart but generative AI is creative. Both have their place in our collective future.

 **NOTE**   Generative AI is the newest, most powerful form of AI, and what the majority of this book is about.

Not surprisingly, generative AI models require larger datasets—that is, the bank of information that AI needs to draw from—than predictive models. Generative AI also requires a correspondingly larger amount of computing power. Table 1.1 details the differences between predictive AI and generative AI.

**TABLE 1.1.**   Comparing Predictive AI and Generative AI

|  | Predictive AI | Generative AI |
|---|---|---|
| **Objective** | Predict future outcomes or trends | Generate new data or content (in addition to predicting outcomes and trends) |
| **Data requirements** | Historical and current data within a specific topic area | Large quantities of high-quality data |
| **Output** | Predictions based on input data | Newly generated text, images, videos, and audio |
| **Applications** | Finance, healthcare, marketing, chatbots, web search | All the applications of predictive AI plus art and design, writing, music production, travel and transportation, caregiving, training simulations, and more |
| **Tech requirements** | Moderate to high levels of computational power and data storage capacity | Much higher computational power and large data storage capacity |

# DISPELLING SOME COMMON MISCONCEPTIONS ABOUT AI

You've no doubt heard about AI and some of what it can do, but you may possess some misconceptions about the technology—what it does and how it does it. So let's take a moment to look at and dispel some of the most common misconceptions:

- **AI is the same as human intelligence.** Some people have the misconception that AI possesses human-like intelligence and thinks like humans do. Nothing could be further from the truth. Today's AI systems are specialized and possess narrow capabilities. AI systems lack human understanding, consciousness, and emotions. AI is not self-aware; it is not human.

- **AI will achieve consciousness.** The idea that AI will somehow achieve sentience and become human is a concept rooted in science fiction. There's no evidence that AI will develop self-awareness, at least any time soon. Today, AI is just a (very complex) computer program.

- **AI is always right.** While AI systems are much more accurate than humans for some tasks, they can make mistakes—especially if the data they're working with contains inaccuracies. In fact, AI is known for its "hallucinations," where it spits out wildly incorrect information. Although AI does learn from its mistakes, it's not 100 percent reliable. In fact, you should verify everything that comes out of AI.

- **AI is a recent invention.** You may just now be hearing about AI, but it's been around for decades. It's only now becoming feasible on a mass scale.

- **AI will replace all human jobs.** While AI can and probably will automate many types of tasks, especially repetitive ones, it can't replace everything humans do. That said, AI stands to have a huge impact on the job market—and not always in a positive fashion. (Learn more about the risks of AI in Chapter 2, "The Benefits and Risks of AI" and AI's impact on how you work in Chapter 9, "Using AI at Work.")

- **AI will solve all the world's problems.** If AI is so smart, it's just a matter of time before it figures out the answer to life, the universe, and everything, right? (And, no, the answer isn't "42"—and if you're not sure what that means, you can ask an AI tool to explain it to you!) Well, you might think so or hope so, but as promising as AI is, it has its limitations. It's just a tool that we humans can use to tackle all those problems, nothing more and nothing less.

- **AI will cause the extinction of the human race.** This is the big fear: that AI achieves sentience, gets smarter than us, and decides that it doesn't need us puny humans. While some say it's a possibility, others say it's highly unlikely. (Turn to Chapter 13 to learn more about this and other possible future scenarios for AI technology.)

You may have more thoughts and opinions about AI that may or may not be accurate. I hope you discover the real truth as you read this book.

# A Brief History of Artificial Intelligence

Before we get into the nitty gritty details of how AI works, let's take a brief look at where it came from and how it developed. (If you're not a history buff, feel free to skip this section!)

AI technology isn't really new, although recent developments in the technology have brought it further into our everyday lives. Just when and where did AI first come about—and how has it developed over the years?

## Artificial Intelligence Is an Ancient Concept

The idea of some type of artificial intelligence predates modern times by thousands of years. Perhaps the first instance of inanimate objects exhibiting intelligence is from the myth of the Greek god Hephaestus creating automatons endowed with artificial intelligence. The concept of artificially intelligent automatons continued through the ages, through Hero of Alexandria's mechanical theater to Leonardo da Vinci's designs for a mechanical knight to Wolfgang von Kemplelen's chess-playing automaton, The Turk. None of these fictional or real-world designs used true artificial intelligence, however.

## The Birth of Modern AI

AI took a step closer to reality in the mid-twentieth century with the development of the modern computer, which was necessary to power AI technology. That enabled Alan Turing, in 1950, to devise what became known as the Turing Test to determine whether a computer possesses intelligence.

Essentially, the Turing Test evaluates a machine's ability to exhibit intelligent behavior by having an evaluator blindly pose a series of questions to both a computer and a human being; if the evaluator can't tell the difference between the two responses, the machine is said to possess intelligence. The Turing Test is still being used today to evaluate AI systems.

The modern era of AI is generally agreed to have started in 1956 during a conference of AI experts at Dartmouth College. This conference jump started the AI movement, and government and industry attention and funding soon followed—as did a plethora of AI research.

One byproduct of this research was a natural language processing program called ELIZA that laid the foundation for today's chatbots. ELIZA could simulate human conversation by using pattern-matching algorithms that gave the impression that users were conversing with a real human being.

```
Welcome to
                EEEEEE  LL       IIII   ZZZZZZ   AAAAA
                EE      LL        II        ZZ   AA  AA
                EEEEE   LL        II       ZZZ   AAAAAAA
                EE      LL        II      ZZ     AA   AA
                EEEEEE  LLLLLL   IIII  ZZZZZZ    AA   AA

    Eliza is a mock Rogerian psychotherapist.
    The original program was described by Joseph Weizenbaum in 1966.
    This implementation by Norbert Landsteiner 2005.


    ELIZA: Is something troubling you ?
    YOU:   Men are all alike.
    ELIZA: What is the connection, do you suppose ?
    YOU:   They're always bugging us about something or other.
    ELIZA: Can you think of a specific example ?
    YOU:   Well, my boyfriend made me come here.
    ELIZA: Is it important to you that your boyfriend made you come here ?
    YOU:   He says I'm depressed much of the time.
    ELIZA: I am sorry to hear that you are depressed.
    YOU:   It's true. I am unhappy.
    ELIZA: Can you explain what made you unhappy ?
    YOU:
```

**FIGURE 1.1**

*A typical conversation with ELIZA, the prototype for today's AI-driven chatbots. (Public domain image courtesy of Wikimedia Commons)*

## The First AI Boom—and the First AI Bust

The period from 1980 to 1987 saw what many called the first AI boom. During these years, AI research showed rapid growth with many important breakthroughs, all supported by ample government funding. This AI boom was followed by what became known as the AI winter, from 1987 to 1993, which saw a dramatic decline in interest in and funding of AI technology. Private investors and the government, seeing a relatively low immediate return on their previous investments, pulled back on their AI funding.

The AI winter began to thaw in the 1990s. Rapid increases in computing power, paired with an explosion of data spawning from the development of the public Internet, sparked new breakthroughs in everything AI—natural language processing, machine learning, deep learning, robotics, and the like. It was during this period that IBM's Deep Blue computer program first defeated Russian chess grandmaster Garry Kasparov, a major victory for AI technology.

## AI in the Twenty-First Century

AI bounced back significantly at and after the turn of the century, again fueled by advancements in computing power and data inventory. AI developments previously limited to research laboratories were transformed into actual products for businesses and computers. This modern AI boom continues to this day and keeps accelerating at its pace.

Consider the following AI-related developments since the turn of the century:

- Google search engine, using predictive AI to anticipate user queries, launched in 2000.

- Netflix's recommendation system was implemented in 2000.

- Amazon's recommendation engine was introduced in 2001.

- Roomba, the first AI-driven robotic vacuum was introduced in 2002.

- NASA's AI-powered rovers Spirit and Opportunity landed on Mars and traverse the red planet without human guidance in 2004.

- Waymo, Google's self-driving car project was launched in 2009.

- IBM's Watson natural language computer system launched in 2011.

- Apple's Siri digital assistant launched and, in 2011, competed on the *Jeopardy!* quiz show.

- Amazon's Alexa voice assistant launched in 2014.

- Google's open-source deep learning framework, TensorFlow, launched in 2015.

- Facebook, Twitter, and other social media companies started using AI to power the algorithms that introduce new content to users in the 2010s.

- OpenAI research laboratory, founded in 2015, launched the GPT-3 AI language model in 2020 and DALL-E image generator in 2021.

- Vehicles from Tesla and other car manufacturers that incorporate self-driving features reached the marketplace in the 2020s.

The 2020s also saw the advent of generative AI, the successor to the earlier and simpler predictive AI. As we've discussed, generative AI lets users generate new content by entering a simple prompt—a major advancement in the use of AI technology.

In short, AI has a long history with accelerated development in recent years. A lot has happened—and there's a lot more to go.

## AI IN FICTION

While AI was being developed in real-world research laboratories, the concept of artificial intelligence also took hold in fiction. Some of the more notable fictional imaginings of AI include

- *Star Trek: The Next Generation*, the television series that ran from 1987 to 1994 (and had subsequent movies and sequels) that featured the android Lieutenant Data as an AI-powered almost-human member of the ship's crew.
- *The Terminator*, a 1984 film by director James Cameron that starred Arnold Schwarzenegger as an android from the future fighting a war between humans and the AI network known as Skynet.
- *Westworld*, a 1973 film (and later, in 2016, a television series) that revolved around a wild west-themed amusement park populated by androids that eventually gain sentience.
- *2001: A Space Odyssey*, a landmark 1968 film by director Stanley Kubrick (and written by Arthur C. Clarke) that featured a sentient computer system named HAL 9000 that eventually runs somewhat amuck.
- "I Sing the Body Electric," a 1962 episode of *The Twilight Zone*, written by Ray Bradbury, all about an intelligent android grandmother. (This episode became the basis for Bradbury's 1969 short story of the same name.)
- *I, Robot*, a 1950 collection of short stories by Isaac Asimov that introduced Asimov's Three Laws of Robotics, which have had a major impact on both science fiction and real-world artificial intelligence.

There's a lot more than that, of course, but this gives a sense of how the concept of artificial intelligence has intrigued society over time. I wonder what kind of AI fiction will be written now that artificial intelligence is finally becoming a reality?

## How Does Generative AI Work?

Now that you know what AI is and where it came from, it's time to learn a little bit about how AI works.

In a nutshell, the AI process starts by collecting large amounts of data from a variety of sources. The AI system needs this data as source material to learn how the world works, just as we humans need real-world experiences along with books and other media to feed us information.

With all this data in hand, AI now starts looking at the data. It uses a variety of algorithms and technologies to extract key information from the assembled data, identify patterns, and make connections between different pieces of data.

Making these connections helps the AI model learn. It uses what it learns to make predictions and then evaluates its results and learns from them. It adapts based on these outcomes, essentially teaching itself from its experiences. Again, it's very much like the way we humans learn by experiencing and adapting, just all done by machine.

## Understanding the AI Process

The AI process is as simple and as complex as what was just described. To do all that, however, requires the use of some very sophisticated technologies and lots of computing power. It's a five-step process that keeps reiterating and learning, as shown in Figure 1.2. Again, if this type of technical detail makes your eyes glaze over, skip ahead!

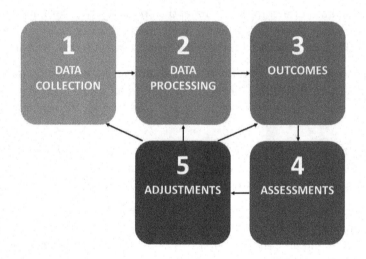

**FIGURE 1.2**

*The five steps of the AI process*

## Step 1: Data Collection

The data collection process assembles data of various types from multiple sources. Data can be in the form of text, speech, images, videos—you name it. It can come from existing databases, social media feeds, websites on the Internet, and more.

More targeted AI requires data that is applicable to only a specific purpose. For example, AI designed for use in healthcare would collect reams of data from medical sources but wouldn't need data about interplanetary mechanics or seventeenth-century architecture. In contrast, general AI models require a vast amount of data across a wide variety of topics—a lot of everything. To plan a dinner menu for a small party, AI would need lots of recipes and examples of menus of small dinner parties.

Whatever the model, the more (applicable) data, the better. An AI model operating on a limited amount of data won't have enough information to learn from and make decisions. The more data available, the faster and more appropriate the model's learning.

## Step 2: Data Processing

Data processing is actually a big step that involves a lot of different substeps and technologies.

First, the data collected must be cleaned and preprocessed. That means rooting out inaccurate or incomplete data and standardizing or formatting the data to make it easier to process. This often involves the use of *natural language processing* (NLP) to understand the meaning behind the words in text and speech.

Next, AI uses various *algorithms* to analyze and learn from the data. As previously discussed, an algorithm is a set of rules to be followed in a process or problem-solving operation. Think of an algorithm working like "if this happens, then do that."

To use these algorithms, AI employs *machine learning* (ML) techniques that train algorithms to find patterns and identify underlying structure. Machine learning enables the model to learn automatically without being programmed to do so.

AI models also employ *deep learning*, a type of machine learning that uses artificial neural networks to recognize complex patterns at multiple levels. Deep learning mimics human neural networks to process data, find connections between data, and make inferences based on that data.

 **NOTE**   A *neural network* is a type of machine learning algorithm with multiple interconnected *nodes* that perform specific functions, such as receiving data, processing data, and generating results.

Some AI engines also employ *large language models* (LLMs) to more quickly process large amounts of text. An LLM is a kind of deep learning model that is pre-trained on vast amounts of data. Think of it as a prepackaged data starter kit that enables AI to have a bit of a head start rather than beginning from scratch.

When working with visual data, AI models often employ *computer vision*. This technology uses pattern recognition and deep learning to interpret the content of an image.

The goal of this data processing is to interpret the data collected, make predictions based on that data, and then ultimately act on those predictions. It's the prediction part of the process that leads to the next step, generating outcomes.

Continuing with the dinner party example from Step 1, in this step, AI would read all those recipes and menus to learn what was in them.

## Step 3: Outcomes

After data is processed and patterns within that data identified, AI models use those patterns to predict various outcomes. For example, a marketing-focused AI model might use data patterns to predict future market trends.

In the outcome step, AI must determine whether specific data matches previous patterns. This sets up a pass/fail situation that helps the AI model determine outcomes that can be used for future decision-making.

Using the dinner party example, in this step, AI would try putting together different dishes in a sample menu and maybe even hold a "test" dinner to see how people respond to the suggested menu.

## Step 4: Assessments

The outcomes of the previous steps are now assessed to gain further insight. This assessment process involves analysis of the outcome, discovery of what triggered the outcome, and feedback that can be incorporated into the algorithm going forward—which is what happens in the next step.

Continuing the example of a dinner menu, AI would evaluate the results of your test menu to determine what worked and what didn't.

## Step 5: Adjustments

If data passes the outcomes test, it verifies the previously identified pattern. If data fails the test—that is, if it doesn't fit into those previous patterns—then the AI model must make adjustments. It might adjust the input data, algorithm rules, or target outcomes.

These adjustments are then incorporated into the AI model in a kind of feedback loop. That is, the adjustments are fed back into the data collection, data processing, and outcome steps to fine-tune the entire model. Thus the model learns over time as it processes data.

In terms of the dinner party example, this is where AI would take what it has learned and make any necessary adjustments to create the final menu. (AI would also collect feedback from your real dinner to determine how you might change things for the next dinner you host.)

## What's Necessary to Make Generative AI Work

The AI process is simple enough to understand but requires a large amount of resources to make it work—especially the more advanced generative AI. An accurately trained generative AI model must have processed millions of pieces of data, and that takes a lot of computing power.

The first thing you need to make AI work is reams of data from a variety of sources. Such quantities of data were not readily available until the very recent past, when the birth of the Internet provided easy access to virtually all the data in the world.

Processing all that data requires enormous amounts of computational power. All those computations and reiterations can be accomplished only by computers running fast, high-powered CPUs and GPUs. Such computing power simply didn't exist, at least affordably, until very recently.

 **NOTE** A *CPU* (central processing unit) is the "brain" that powers all the necessary functions of a computer. A *GPU* (graphics processing unit) is another specialized electronic circuit that accelerates the rendering of images and videos. AI needs CPUs to sift through and process all the data it is fed and GPUs to create AI-generated images.

Finally, all those computers need electricity to run—and AI requires vast amounts of electricity. Running an AI model is a very large-scale operation, one that requires large amounts of capital to finance. (Microsoft just recently signed a deal to reopen the Three Mile Island nuclear power plant to power its AI efforts.) Again, until recently, only a very few large companies could afford to create and maintain their own AI models.

# WHO ARE THE AI POWER PLAYERS?

Given AI's huge need for resources of all kinds, it's not surprising that some of the biggest players in AI are also some of the biggest tech titans today—companies that have the financial and technical resources to create large-scale AI engines. These power players include

- Alphabet (Google), which is heavily invested in using AI in their search and advertising services
- Apple, which is interested in incorporating AI in its operating system and applications
- Amazon, which, through its Amazon Web Services (AWS) division, hosts many of the large AI models
- Anthropic, founded by former members of OpenAI and backed by Amazon, with the goal of researching the safety and reliability of AI systems
- Baidu, a large Chinese tech company with its fingers in all sorts of technologies, including AI
- IBM, which has decades of AI experience and a huge stake in computer hardware
- Lenovo, a major provider of enterprise storage solutions, necessary to store all the data necessary for today's AI models
- Meta (Facebook and Instagram), which possesses an enormous amount of computer and graphics processing power
- Microsoft, which, like Apple, is interested in incorporating AI in its operating system and applications, including all the Office apps
- Nvidia, which manufactures some of the most popular GPUs used in AI processing
- OpenAI, an AI development company partially funded by and partnered with Microsoft
- Oracle, whose cloud infrastructure is in high demand by other AI companies

Because of the high costs involved, these big tech players have a huge advantage over smaller players. A smaller company may be able to develop a unique AI model, but it still has to rely on these larger companies to host and power that model. In today's world of AI, the big tech titans have a substantial advantage.

# How to Use Today's AI Generators

An AI generator is a tool—an app or a website—that uses generative AI to create new content based on user input. These generators are typically specialized in terms of the types of content they generate: some generate text, others images, still others music.

I get more into all-purpose AI generators in Chapter 3, but looking at these services is a good way to understand how AI works. They'll probably be the primary way most people interact with AI for the near future.

To give you an idea of how to use an AI generator, I'll use ChatGPT as an example. It's the AI engine from OpenAI, one of the largest AI research companies. (Other AI tools such as Anthropic's Claude, Google Gemini, and Microsoft Copilot work in a similar way.) ChatGPT generates text responses to user prompts and functions kind of like an online chatbot. You can use ChatGPT to answer questions, provide information, and write things for you—letters, reports, articles, even poetry.

As you can see in Figure 1.3, the main ChatGPT page looks a little like a search engine query page. When you register (for free) and sign in, your previous prompts are listed in the left column. The prompt box is at the bottom of the page.

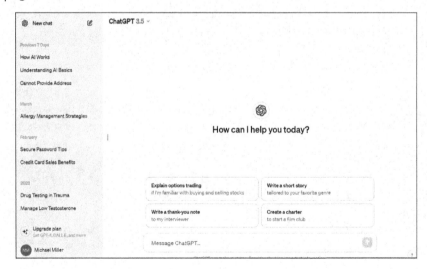

**FIGURE 1.3**

*The ChatGPT AI generator*

To use ChatGPT, all you have to do is enter a prompt—that is, a query or suggestion—into the **Message ChatGPT** box and press Enter. As you can see in Figure 1.4, ChatGPT then does what you ask it to do, generating its results above the prompt box. You can continue the conversation by entering additional prompts; your prompts and ChatGPT's responses are displayed one after another, just like a conversation.

**FIGURE 1.4**

*A typical ChatGPT prompt and response*

It's really as simple as that. The more detailed your prompt, the more precise ChatGPT's response. You can specify the length of what you want, the style, even specific details. (Figure 1.5 shows a very detailed prompt and ChatGPT's response.)

Other AI generators work in a similar fashion—although customized for different types of output. For example, an AI image generator, such as DeepAI's AI Image Generator (shown in Figure 1.6), typically offers options for different types of images and styles (photographic, illustrative, and so on).

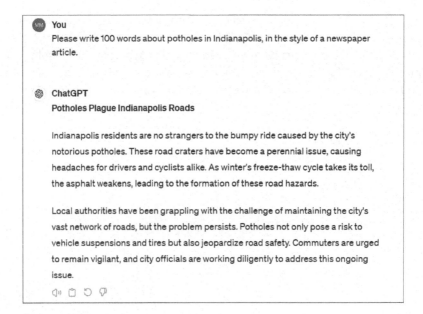

**FIGURE 1.5**

*Asking ChatGPT to write a newspaper article*

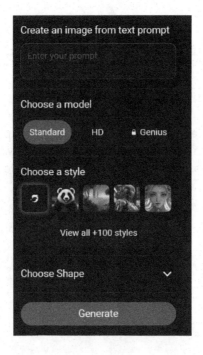

**FIGURE 1.6**

*The prompt panel of DeepAI's AI Image Generator*

**NOTE**   Find out more about using AI generators and other popular AI tools—many of which are free—in Chapter 3, "Getting Started with All-Purpose AI Tools."

# How You Can Use Generative AI In Your Daily Life

As you can see, generative AI is going to be an important technology for lots of people and businesses going forward. But what does it matter to you, personally?

The reality is that generative AI has applications across a wide variety of activities and industries. It's likely to impact your home life and the activities in which you participate. It is also likely to impact your job and the jobs of people around you. It's going to be virtually everywhere, in one form or another.

Let's take a quick look at how AI will impact various industries and activities.

 **WARNING**   You can't use AI-generated content for all purposes. Chapter 2, "The Benefits and Risks of AI," goes into when you can use AI-generated content and when it's not a good idea. For instance, you wouldn't claim AI-generated content as your own.

## AI in Art

Amateurs and professionals alike are already using AI to create new artwork. AI can create photorealistic images to accompany newspaper and media stories based merely on text instructions. It can be used to create art in comic books and magazines. It can be used by fans to create artwork of their favorite stars and fictional characters.

Unfortunately, generative AI can also be used to create deepfakes and manipulated images meant to fool and confuse the public. We're already seeing AI-generated deepfake pornographic images of celebrities and deepfake images of politicians in campaign ads. As generative AI keeps getting better, it will become more difficult to distinguish what images are real and which are AI-generated.

 **NOTE**   Learn more about AI art in Chapter 7, "Using AI to Create Art and Images."

## AI in Business

Many businesses are using generative AI to make their operations more efficient and productive. AI is already being incorporated into all manner of business processes and used to design new and refine existing processes. Customer support operations are using AI by providing 24/7 AI chatbots to answer customer questions. AI can assist in business analysis and provide more informed input on decision-making. AI is already being and will continue to be used to make businesses more competitive.

For workers, AI is making it easier to do a lot of different jobs. Repetitive tasks are being automated and even higher-level tasks are being made easier with AI assistance. For many tasks, workers are using AI to get a head start and take care of some of the drudgework involved. It's changing the nature of work for many workers.

 **NOTE**   Learn more about AI in business in Chapter 9, "Using AI at Work."

## AI in Finance and Banking

Consumers are using generative AI to get personalized financial advice. They use it to monitor their personal financial transactions. They can also use AI to maximize the return on their investments and improve their credit ratings.

Generative AI also has many applications for banks and other financial institutions. Some financial institutions are using AI to evaluate your loan risk and identify or prevent fraudulent transactions. They're starting to use AI to automate backend operations and reduce human error. Like other businesses, they're using generative AI to provide highly detailed customer service via 24/7 chatbots. They're also using AI to ensure they comply with complex governmental and industry financial regulations.

## AI in Gaming

Generative AI is changing the world of computer games. Generative AI can create and already is creating realistic gaming environments for today's most advanced computer games. It can create complex characters and animations. It can develop detailed gameplay and create immersive environments.

Generative AI is capable of creating more sophisticated graphics and visual effects than are currently available. It can also develop plotlines and enhance interactions between human players and in-game characters—all of which greatly improves gameplay and benefits gamers at all levels.

## AI in Healthcare

AI is already having a significant impact on our health and wellness—both directly to individuals and through improvements in the healthcare industry.

For individuals, generative AI can help you better understand your conditions and your doctor's instructions. It can help you create personalized health and exercise plans. It can anticipate the onset of illness or disease. It can also provide answers to your health-related questions.

For providers and healthcare facilities, generative AI can help more accurately diagnose illnesses and diseases and improve patient outcomes. It can help physicians better prescribe and manage medications. It can help clinics and hospitals better serve their patients in terms of scheduling, billing, and support. And AI can help the pharmaceutical industry more quickly develop more and more effective drugs.

 **NOTE**   Learn more about AI in healthcare in Chapter 11, "Using AI for Health and Wellness."

## AI in Writing

If you do any writing at all, even if it's just the occasional text message, generative AI can help you write better. With the right prompts, AI can write letters, blog posts, social media posts, even essays and reports. If you're not a writer by nature, AI can make you sound like one.

 **NOTE**   Learn more about AI and writing in Chapter 4, "Using AI to Find the Right Words."

Generative AI can write stories and articles based on available information. It can determine what readers want to read and provide customized news feeds. It can perform in-depth research for human journalists. It can automate formerly manual tasks and free up reporters to do more reporting. It can help reporters meet their deadlines. It can provide news coverage in areas that were previously economically unfeasible.

Unfortunately, generative AI also can be and is being used to replace human journalists at many media outlets. This can lower the quality and availability of news to many users. And with AI hallucinations and limited data, you need to verify all AI-generated content before sharing it either publicly or privately.

## AI for Learning

Teachers today are starting to use generative AI to develop their lesson plans. Trainers are using AI to create realistic training simulations. AI can also help automate grading and assessing student process. It's helping teachers develop personalized learning for individual students—and helping students better learn difficult material.

Unfortunately, generative AI can also help students cheat. It can write papers for students that read and sound just like something the student wrote—or even better. It can anticipate and answer test questions. It can help students get around the system by doing a minimum amount of original work—all of which is something educators have to figure out how to deal with.

## AI in Marketing and Advertising

Generative AI is accelerating the mass personalization that is driving today's marketing industry. Thanks to generative AI, marketers are able to better target potential customers and develop personalized advertising and marketing campaigns. This should, at least in theory, improve lead generation and sales as well as increase customer satisfaction.

Marketers can also use generative AI to create brochures and advertisements, and script and even produce commercials. Generative AI can handle a marketing campaign from inception to graphic design to copywriting to print, web, and video creation, with a minimal amount of human input.

## AI in Music

Commercial customers are already using generative AI to create background music, music for commercials, music you hear when on hold, and other similar uses. Unfortunately, unscrupulous producers and streaming music services are also using AI to create songs and performances that closely mimic those of popular artists—without paying any royalties to the original artists.

On the plus side, some innovative musicians are using generative AI to help them create new music. Some producers and record labels are also using generative AI to "clean" older recordings to make them sound better for modern audiences. And AI is not just for professional musicians; some fans are using generative AI to create music that sounds like and honors the musicians they love.

 **NOTE**   In 2023, producer Giles Martin, son of famed producer George Martin, worked with Paul McCartney and Ringo Starr to use AI to clean up and enhance some old, previously abandoned tracks by the late John Lennon and George Harrison. The result was the last "new" Beatles song, "Now and Then."

## AI in Programming and Software Development

Generative AI can write programming code much faster and more accurately than human developers. This is enabling the release of more sophisticated computer programs and apps on a faster development cycle. Generative AI can also write HTML code to develop better and more fully featured websites. It's not an understatement to say that AI is shaking up the developer industry.

## AI in Transportation and Travel

The automotive industry is using AI to develop the first true self-driving car, which promises to revolutionize the trucking and ridesharing industries, as well as how you drive yourself and your family. AI is also helping municipalities better manage traffic flow and predict when street and equipment maintenance is due.

Just as important, AI is helping map apps be more accurate and provide better driving directions. Real-time AI analysis can help you avoid traffic slowdowns and find the fastest route to your destination.

 **NOTE**   Learn more about AI in transportation in Chapter 10, "Using AI to Manage Your Travel and Transportation."

## AI Everywhere

Bottom line, generative AI is going to be everywhere, whether you recognize it or not. AI will affect your life in ways you cannot even imagine—both for better and for worse. That's why you need to know how AI works, so you can better use it proactively in your own life.

 **NOTE**   Learn more about how AI will affect your life in Chapter 2.

# Summary

In this chapter, you learned what AI is (the simulation of human intelligence in machines) and what it isn't (simple rules-based processes). You learned the difference between the older predictive AI and the newer, more creative generative AI. You also learned the history of AI, dating all the way back to the days of the ancient Greeks through the birth of modern AI in the 1950s and today's explosion of AI development.

In addition, this chapter showed you how AI works by examining the five steps of the AI process: data collection, data processing, outcomes, assessments, and adjustments. More important, you learned how AI is already affecting a variety of industries and activities.

However it works, the reality is that AI is here today and here to stay. It's only going to get smarter, more powerful, and more impactful in the months and years to come.

2

# THE BENEFITS AND RISKS OF AI

AI proponents predict that this developing technology will result in a bounty of benefits. According to its most enthusiastic supporters, AI will do everything from improving productivity and enhancing creativity to curing diseases and halting or even reversing climate change. On the other hand, naysayers warn of the negative impacts of AI—lost jobs, deepfakes and media manipulation, and technology that surpasses and even replaces the human race.

Which of these AI-influenced futures is most likely? Is AI all rainbows and unicorns, or do we need to prepare for war against amoral AI-powered terminators?

The reality is that AI promises some very real benefits but also brings with it some very real risks and issues. We need to know enough about what AI is and how it works to embrace its likely benefits while guarding against its possible downsides.

# Understanding the Potential Benefits of AI

You've no doubt seen some of the effects of AI in your everyday life. Some of what AI does will benefit you. Some might negatively impact you. Some won't affect you at all. It all depends on what directions AI takes and, to a large degree, the things you do from day to day—the type of work you do, the entertainment you choose, and more.

Let's start by looking at some of the potential benefits of AI, of which there are likely to be a plethora.

## Automating Boring Manual Processes

One thing that AI does very well is figure out how to do repetitive work and do it quickly, without complaining or needing a break. If you do this type of work, you may find AI stepping in to do it in your place—which may or may not be a good thing.

AI can do many boring, repetitive tasks much better than humans; AI is faster and more accurate than any human being could hope to be. AI also doesn't get bored or need to take bathroom breaks. In many ways, AI is the perfect worker for activities like proofreading documents, filing contracts, and comparing invoices. AI-based systems can also pack boxes, assemble products, and perform other manual tasks at high speed and with a low incidence of errors. Businesses will love it.

## Improving Business Productivity

Speaking of businesses, since AI can do repetitive tasks faster and more accurately than human beings, it is improving efficiency and productivity across a wide range of industries. AI, once it gets going, should also be able to figure out new and better ways to do many of these tasks. It's not just a rule follower but a reinventor of rules as it learns from what it does.

The reality is that AI is already benefiting businesses in a number of important ways. Here are some examples:

- Streamlining existing processes

- Devising and implementing new processes

- Eliminating human errors

- Improving workplace safety

- Reducing the need for human labor, especially for repetitive tasks

- Producing more targeted marketing campaigns

- Sorting, filtering, and organizing data

- Analyzing data and providing detailed insights

- Improving decision making

- Designing new products and services

All these functions increase productivity and reduce costs, which makes AI highly attractive to the business community.

 **NOTE**   Learn more about using AI in business in Chapter 9, "Using AI at Work."

## Reducing Risk

Consider all the activities that place people at risk—working with hazardous materials, operating heavy machinery, working in harsh environments, and more. By merging AI and robotics technologies, humans may no longer need to go deep underground or to unsafe heights, defuse bombs, or change lightbulbs on tall cellular towers. Autonomous robots, powered by AI, can do the job safely and keep humans out of harm's way.

## Making More Things Available 24/7

Unlike human beings, AI systems don't need to eat, sleep, or take breaks. That means they're available 24/7, even on holidays. Even better, AI systems remain at peak capability and capacity over that entire period; they don't experience "peak productivity" because they're always working at their max.

That also means that AI-powered systems can deliver service at all hours of the day and night. Instead of closing a call center after a certain hour, an AI-powered call center is available to take customer calls every minute of every hour. This means businesses effectively never need to close, plus they can now serve customers around the globe, no matter when that might be in local time.

## Personalizing the User Experience

AI will further enable the trend of mass personalization. Imagine an AI system ana-lyzing your past browsing patterns and using that to create in real time a personal home page on your favorite shopping site, with deals created in the moment just for you. AI will know what colors you prefer, how big the type needs to be, what kind of products you're interested in, and more, and use that information to create a totally unique and personalized shopping experience.

## Enabling Better Recommendations

Adjacent to the creation of AI-powered user experiences, expect AI systems at your favorite streaming video and audio sites to make better and more personal-ized recommendations for you. You're used to Amazon, Disney+, Netflix, or rec-ommending shows based on your past viewing habits; in most instances, those recommendations are based on shared actors or genres. With AI, providers can go beyond that by analyzing a whole range of behaviors to determine seemingly unrelated shows or playlists you're apt to like. Thanks to AI, your favorite stream-ing service will know what you like and dislike—maybe better than you do!

## Improving Digital Assistants

The use of digital assistants has been increasing in recent years, both in the home (such as Amazon's Alexa, Apple's Siri, and the Google Assistant) and in busi-nesses. To date, those assistants have not been very "smart," typically capable only of answering basic questions and performing basic tasks on command.

Integrating advanced AI technology into these systems will make them signifi-cantly more useful. Imagine a not-too-distant version of Alexa that knows when you come home, can sense what kind of mood you're in, and selects the proper music for your mood. Or it knows that you're interested in a particular news story or topic and feeds you new stories as they develop.

 **NOTE**   As I write this, Apple just announced that they're incorporating OpenAI into their Siri digital assistant and Amazon is rumored to soon announce a subscription-only version of Alexa that is AI-powered. The merging of AI with now-decades-old digi-tal assistant technology is happening.

On the business front, envision a chat assistant in the bottom corner of a website that doesn't just provide canned answers to common questions but can actu-ally respond to questions in real time, just like a real human support person.

Customers won't be able to tell whether they're conversing with a human or a chatbot, which benefits both the business and its customers.

## Managing Messages

If an AI-powered chatbot can interact with users in real time, why not employ personal chatbots to answer your phone calls, email messages, and texts? This is particularly appealing if you're inundated with messages either at home or at work; let an AI assistant manage all your inboxes, respond to those messages it can, and route to you only those messages to which you need to personally respond. It will be like having your own personal assistant on your computer or phone.

## Improving Healthcare

The medical field is employing AI in a number of different ways, all beneficial to patients.

Physicians benefit from AI systems that ingest relevant patient information, compare it to existing data (including patient records, lab results, and data from clinical trials), and make instant and accurate diagnoses. The AI models can also devise extremely detailed and personalized treatment plans that have more positive health outcomes for patients.

Physicians can also use AI to perform delicate procedures where even the slightest error could be life-threatening. When programmed correctly and allowed to learn over time, an AI-powered robotic surgical system can be more precise than a surgeon and virtually error-free.

(And in case you think this latter application is a futuristic dream, know that the Smart Tissue Autonomous Robot—STAR—has already performed laparoscopic surgery without any human guidance whatsoever.)

For individuals, AI technology can help people better manage their health and wellness, as well as understand physician advice and instructions. AI can also catch errors that might develop when treatment spans multiple physicians or clinics, such as multiple prescriptions that shouldn't be taken with one another. That sort of coordination is difficult with traditional manual systems but is a snap for AI-based systems.

 **NOTE**   Learn more about using AI in healthcare in Chapter 11, "Using AI for Health and Wellness."

## Enhancing Learning

AI is helping students learn more and learn faster by developing learning plans personalized to each individual. Consider the vast amounts of data available on student performance and learning styles and how AI can analyze and extract actionable insights to improve learning efficiency. Thanks to AI-based learning systems, students can learn at their own pace and focus on those areas where they need more work.

## Augmenting Creativity

Today's AI models are already capable of creating short stories, poetry, images, and songs. Many media sites are using AI to write news stories and blog posts. Fans and some artists are using AI to create new artwork. Companies are using AI to create pleasant-sounding background music for phone systems and commercials.

Going forward, AI-created art will get better—more human-like and more creative. Writers, artists, and musicians are learning how to use AI to assist them in their work, generating new ideas, exploring new styles, and developing a new type of creative process that merges human creativity with machine output.

 **NOTE**  Learn more about using AI for writing in Chapter 4, "Using AI to Find the Right Words." Learn more about using AI for art in Chapter 7, "Using AI to Create Art and Images."

## Making Your Life Easier

Here's the bottom line about all these current and potential AI benefits: AI will make all our lives easier. We'll become more productive, more effective, and less bothered by menial tasks. Our lives will be more enjoyable and safer. AI is already changing our world for the better and will continue to do so, in ways we cannot fully imagine. But risks abound.

# Understanding the Potential Risks of AI

Just as AI promises numerous potential benefits, it also comes with risk. Will AI really make your life better—or will it negatively impact your life and livelihood? Again, it all depends on what you do and how AI develops.

## AI Can Spread Misinformation

AI is just a tool. It does what users ask it to do. If someone prompts an AI system to produce a picture of a giraffe flying a helicopter, AI will do it. The initiators of that prompt can then use that image in whatever way they want.

Thus, we come to a real-world issue concerning the use of AI content: mischievous or malicious individuals can use AI to create blatant falsehoods, either in words or visuals, and then spread those falsehoods over social media and other channels. AI-generated text, images, and videos can be particularly convincing, especially as AI models continue to improve. If someone wants to convince people that a giraffe can fly a helicopter, a photorealistic image of that scenario can be very persuasive.

Realistic but false text, images, audio, and videos are called *deepfakes*. In the past, people have used image editing programs such as Adobe Photoshop to manually manipulate images and create deepfakes. Today, AI image generators can do the job better and faster with just a few simple prompts.

Say, for example, you wanted to conduct a smear campaign against a neighbor you don't particularly like. You can feed an AI image generator a picture of your neighbor and prompt it to create a photorealistic image of that neighbor burning trash on their lawn. You could then take this very real-looking picture to your neighborhood association and try to get your neighbor in trouble.

In this same fashion, celebrity deepfakes are popular. Take a popular actress, tell the AI image generator to create a picture of said actress sans clothing, and—voilà!—you have a ready-made pornographic image ready for distribution on the Internet.

This sort of AI-powered manipulation can also be used for political and propaganda purposes. We've already seen deepfake photos purporting to show people doing things they didn't really do, deepfake videos purporting to show events that didn't really happen, and deepfake phone calls impersonating politicians saying things they didn't really say. AI can make these deepfakes extremely convincing—so convincing that voters could be swayed to change their vote from one candidate to another.

 **NOTE**   AI-created deepfakes make it difficult for people to determine what's real and what's not. To learn how to spot faked AI content, read ahead to the "How to Spot AI in the Wild" section later in this chapter.

In addition, AI can be used to spread false information over social media. Most social media platforms use AI algorithms to decide what shows up in users' feeds.

Manipulate that algorithm just a bit, and you can fill peoples' feeds with political falsehoods and biased viewpoints. That could be dangerous for any functioning democracy.

Even though the Federal Communications Commission (FCC) recently outlawed AI-generated political robocalls and major tech companies signed an accord to prevent AI from being used to disrupt elections, AI-powered misinformation remains a major short-term and long-term threat to elections in the United States and abroad. FBI Director Christopher Wray recently warned about foreign adversaries using AI technology to influence U.S. elections, saying that AI makes it "easier for both more and less-sophisticated foreign adversaries to engage in malign influence."

If nothing else, the threat of AI-generated deepfakes could cause people to question even legitimate stories and images. If you can't tell what's real and what's fake, what can you believe?

## AI Can Be Biased

AI results are based on the data fed into large language models. The more data, the better the results.

Equally important to the *quantity* of data available is the *quality* of that data. In AI, as in most things, it's a garbage in, garbage out type of situation. Bad data will result in unreliable AI models.

Because AI relies on the data it's fed, biased data can be a significant problem. Remember, most AI models get data by scraping content from the Internet. Unfortunately, there's a lot of flawed or biased content on the Internet, and those characteristics can be absorbed into an AI model.

Bias can infiltrate AI systems in a number of ways. AI can ingest training data that reflects historical or social prejudices. It can include training data that includes biased human decisions and use data that either over- or underrepresents specific groups, thus reinforcing existing biases. It can even treat opinions or obvious jokes in the training data the same as it does hard facts.

In addition, AI can exhibit the biases of the people who develop its algorithms. As AI researcher Olga Russakovsky notes, "AI researchers are primarily people who are male, who come from certain racial demographics, who grew up in high socioeconomic areas, primarily people without disabilities." That creates a very specific worldview that is, to some extent, exhibited in AI output.

For all these reasons, AI content today often exhibits the same biases that exist in our society at large. Without conscious upfront programming, AI is likely to perpetuate those biases in the decisions it makes.

Consider, as an example, a company's use of AI to vet job candidates. If an AI model reflects a society's bias against specific ethnic or racial groups, a company will continue to hire fewer people from those groups.

Similarly, AI-powered speech recognition software can fail to understand certain accents and dialects because the generally white male researchers don't speak that way. This can cause problems for an AI chatbot trying to understand or respond to questions from customers of certain backgrounds.

As another example, consider AI-generated images. Given the gender and race bias present in today's AI systems, if you ask an AI tool to create an image of a businessperson, what are the odds that it will show a white male and not, perhaps, a female of color? (Pretty good; see Figure 2.1, the result of a single such prompt with DeepAI's AI Image Generator.)

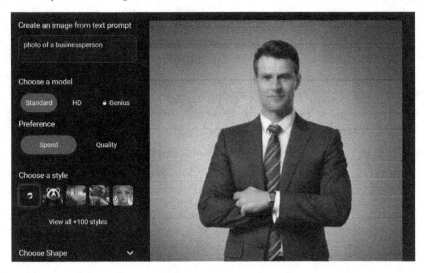

**FIGURE 2.1**

*The stereotypical image generated by the prompt, **photo of a businessperson**. (Image generated by DeepAI's AI Image Generator.)*

AI models can also reinforce society's historical age bias, especially in employment. This is particularly concerning given the use of AI-powered recruitment systems; if the algorithms used by these systems are biased toward younger candidates, older job candidates may be unfairly excluded from consideration for some jobs.

Guarding against all forms of bias is essential in creating trustworthy AI content. Otherwise, AI will increasingly exhibit those biases, both good and bad, that exist in our society today.

## AI Can Invade Your Privacy

Here's a major concern of AI critics today: AI is a major threat to our personal privacy, and they will only grow.

Think back to Chapter 1, "Artificial Intelligence: What It Is and How It Works." Do you remember where and how AI models get all the data they use to train and learn?

The answer is that AI gets its data from you and me and everyone around us. Most of the data that's been fed into AI large language models has been scraped off the public Internet. That means not only website content but also social media posts, online messages, and other communications between unsuspecting individuals.

That's right, your friendly neighborhood AI model is based at least in part on your own thoughts and words, as well as those of your friends and neighbors. And the models have obtained your information without asking you permission. If it's out there on the Internet, the thinking goes, it's free for the taking. It might be different if the content is behind a paywall or on a private site that requires registration or permission. But anything that's out there publicly, the AI companies say, is there for the taking.

That includes content that isn't actually on the Internet but has been supplied online—conversations you've had with chatbots, chats you've had with friends and family, and questions you've asked on support sites.

To be fair, AI large language models don't target your individual data per se; instead, they incorporate it and data from millions of other people into their models. It's not using your data against you to do harm, as a scammer would, but it's still using your data without your permission.

 **NOTE**   Separate from the ingestion of large amounts of personal data for generative AI, predictive AI often uses your individual data to make personal recommendations. That's a different issue, and one to which you probably consented (via terms of service) when you signed up for a given streaming service or online store.

Despite numerous data privacy laws on the books, few if any such regulations explicitly protect your data privacy from AI. Some regulations have been proposed, but neither the United States nor the EU have enacted laws that cover AI's use of personal data. That leaves your data out there for the taking by any AI large language model that wants to use it.

That's not a good thing.

# AI Will Replace Some Jobs

With every new technological age comes some degree of change and displacement. The industrial age eliminated many formerly manual factory jobs. The automotive age displaced workers in the horse and buggy industry. The rise of the Internet resulted in job losses in traditional media and communications companies. This sort of change is inevitable.

Don't be surprised, then, if the biggest near-term impact of artificial intelligence technology is a significant loss of jobs. Companies large and small are looking to AI to help them improve their productivity, which means replacing expensive human workers with cheaper, less-demanding, more efficient AI systems. For these companies, "improved productivity" means fewer employees, which means layoffs—sometimes for even the most seasoned workers.

Now, many employers will couch this scenario as letting AI take over repetitive jobs so they can "repurpose" employees to higher-value tasks. While that is a possible scenario, it's equally possible and perhaps more probable that many employees displaced by AI either won't have the necessary skills for those higher-value jobs or that those jobs won't exist at all. While the impact of AI will differ from company to company (and industry to industry), it's likely to have a net negative impact on the human workforce.

What industries will be most impacted by the AI revolution? AI is likely to have an effect across the board, but in particular, anticipate job losses in the following sectors:

- Agriculture, with AI-powered robots automating many manual tasks, such as planting and harvesting, especially on larger farms
- Finance and banking, with AI automating both customer-facing and back-office jobs
- Healthcare, with AI assisting or replacing many scheduling and back-office functions
- Legal services, with AI taking over contract generation and management
- Manufacturing, with AI-powered robots replacing factory workers

- News media, with newspapers and websites using AI to generate articles and posts

- Transportation, with self-driving vehicles eliminating human drivers to transform the trucking and rideshare industries

How big will this AI-powered job disruption be? Goldman Sachs estimates that generative AI could eventually replace up to 300 million jobs worldwide, with many occupations experiencing a 25 to 50 percent job loss. This would be a huge disruption to the job market—and to the way of life for hundreds of millions of workers.

Unlike the industrial revolution, which primarily impacted manual or blue-collar workers, the AI revolution is likely to also affect higher-paid white collar workers. That will be a major difference from previous technology-based changes and a big concern for skilled workers everywhere.

It's not all doom and gloom, however. On the plus side, Goldman Sachs predicts that artists, computer system analysts, HR managers, legal professionals, mental health professionals, surgeons, teachers, writers, and those in leadership roles are less likely to be replaced by AI because of the need for human judgment and creativity in those roles. In addition, there is already a huge demand for jobs programming and training AI systems.

Will your job be one of those lost to AI? Perhaps, and even if not, many of your coworkers will be impacted. Prepare to be disrupted.

 **NOTE**   I take issue with Goldman Sachs' prediction that AI will not affect writers. I used to write blog posts for a number of websites, up to a dozen or so posts a month. In recent months, that work has dwindled to next to nothing. It seems that many of the companies for which I used to write wanted lower-cost content and AI filled the bill. Instead of paying for my expert writing, they opted to go with AI's free content, which is apparently good enough for their purposes. My side writing income has pretty much evaporated, and AI is to blame. (Thank you, AI!)

## AI Will Make Mistakes

AI constantly makes mistakes—or in AI parlance, hallucinates. We all must verify its output. If we try to rely too much on AI, especially for mission-critical tasks, we will be disappointed when things go wrong, which they will. Witness AI-powered self-driving cars that get into accidents because of faulty or less-intelligent AI systems, or AI image generators that give people six fingers and a missing ear.

Today's AI systems will make mistakes. Putting all our trust in said systems, at least at this point in time, is ill advised. If you rely completely on AI and AI isn't perfect, the decisions you make based on that AI may be flawed. Likewise, if you're using AI to manage operations or systems, you may experience system interruptions if AI gets some of the data wrong.

AI will get better and more reliable, but it's not there yet, wishful thinking aside.

## AI Uses Significant Resources

AI is a resource- and power-hungry technology. Today's increasingly larger AI models require vast amounts of power, both in terms of electricity and computing power. AI models need many fast and powerful CPUs and GPUs, vast amounts of data storage capacity, fast and reliable Internet connections, and lots and lots of electricity to run it all.

Unfortunately, none of these items are cheap or limitless. AI is an expensive technology, which is why so many large models are the provenance of today's large tech titans, such as Amazon and Microsoft, that have the financial and other means to pull it off.

Looking just at AI's electricity needs, one expert calculated that by 2027, the AI sector will consume between 85 and 135 terawatt hours per year. To put that in perspective, that's about half a percent of all global electricity consumption. That's massive—and increasing daily.

At some point there may not be enough available resources to power all the AI systems currently being developed. What do AI companies do if there's a chip shortage or a lack of storage or not enough electricity to go around? Or, equally likely, if the costs of these resources rise to unaffordable levels? The ability of the AI industry to grow may be constrained by resource availability and pricing.

In addition, all the resources that power AI have a major impact on the environment. The energy usage alone contributes significantly to fossil fuel usage and the resulting climate change. AI is not in the least bit environmentally friendly.

 **NOTE**   These are just the known risks of today's AI. Experts have additional reservations about AI's future impact, which you can read more about in Chapter 13, "The Future of AI."

## WHO IS LEGALLY RESPONSIBLE FOR AI?

Here's an interesting question. In the event of harm caused by AI—a self-driving car that runs amok and kills a pedestrian, for example—who is legally responsible? Is it even possible to hold AI systems responsible for their actions?

This is a complex question where the answer is far from clear. Do we hold responsible the company that developed the AI model? Or the company that sold that particular AI? Or the one that used it in their application (such as the automotive manufacturer that built and sold the self-driving car)? Or do we hold the AI's programmer responsible? Or is it the fault of the individual using that AI?

Establishing the legal liabilities of AI systems is imperative but challenging. When something goes wrong with such a system, some person or some entity needs to be held responsible—doesn't it? Can we hold a computer algorithm legally responsible for its actions? Who pays the price when something goes wrong?

Legal experts have been wrangling about this one for some time now with no apparent conclusions. While I have no idea how this one will shake out, I do predict that a lot of legal hours will be billed over this issue.

# How to Spot AI in the Wild

I talked earlier in this chapter about how AI can be and is being used today to write text, create images, and more. Unfortunately, that means that AI can be used to write stories that spread lies and propaganda or create images that represent scenes that never took place. The AI-generated content looks so real and reads so naturally that it's difficult to tell it from the real thing.

How, then, can you keep from being fooled by fake content? How can you identify AI in the wild?

## How to Identify AI-Written Text

Many, many companies are using AI to create content for their blogs, social media feeds, and websites. AI content is increasingly popular because it's free or low cost; companies don't have to pay a real human writer to write it.

AI-written content can sometimes be good. It can appear well-written. It can be informative.

On the other hand, AI-written content can sometimes be poorly written; it can read just a little "off." And, worst-case scenario, it can contain incorrect information or even deliberate misinformation.

When examining written content, you find on the web or elsewhere, look for these signs that it may be AI-generated:

- **Incorrect information:** AI systems are often trained on limited data sets that don't contain precise information. In this scenario, AI might "guess" at an answer and guess incorrectly. In addition, misinformation deliberately spreads falsehoods that are often easily identified.

- **Controversial opinions presented as facts:** While human propagandists can also couch falsehoods as facts, AI systems do it better. Malicious actors are using AI to spread misinformation, so if you see something especially controversial, question its authorship.

- **Outdated information:** AI systems are often trained on data sets that contain older information. References in a given article that are several years old could signal that it may be AI-generated from information that isn't current.

- **Repetitive words and phrases:** Many AI models have a limited vocabulary and continually reuse those words and phrases they know.

- **Tone of voice:** AI writing tends to be drier and, dare I say, more robotic. Humans tend to write more conversationally and informally.

All that said, today's most advanced AI models can write text that is difficult to distinguish from human-written text. Because of these advancements, it's becoming more and more difficult to determine which text is written by a human and which by AI. If you can't tell the difference between AI and human text, you're not alone.

Then how can you identify text that was generated by AI? The best piece of advice is to trust your instincts. If a piece of information doesn't seem right, you should look for another source—ideally one you can trust. Always go with a trusted source over a random article from an unknown website.

 **NOTE**   Some companies, including OpenAI, are working on embedding watermarks in their AI-generated text, typically in the form of specific word patterns. This will help experts better identify text that was written by AI systems.

## AI TEXT DETECTORS

Want to find out if a given article or piece of text is AI-generated? Several websites offer AI text detection functionality. They examine various features of a piece of text and determine, with a fair amount of accuracy, whether that text was generated by a human being or an AI engine. The most popular of these AI text detectors include

- AI Text Classified (https://freeaitextclassifier.com)
- Copyleaks (https://copyleaks.com/ai-content-detector)
- QuillBot (https://quillbot.com/ai-content-detector)
- Scribbr (www.scribbr.com/ai-detector)
- ZeroGPT (www.zerogpt.com)

As I explain later in this chapter, many educators are using these tools to help detect AI-generated homework and papers from their less-than-completely-honest students. You can use them the same way.

## How to Identify AI-Generated Photos and Images

AI-generated images are often more dangerous than AI-generated text. It's the old adage of a picture being worth a thousand words; we tend to believe things we can see with our own eyes—even if those images are manipulated.

Some individuals create AI-generated images for their own amusement. Some create AI-generated images for profit. And some malicious actors create AI-generated images to try to fool people like you and me.

Fake AI-generated images can be used to try to influence public opinion. They can be used to try to influence voters in an election. They can be used just to confuse people and stir up trouble.

Whatever the goal, we collectively need to be aware of these fake images and do our best to identify and avoid them. Given the highly realistic quality of some of these images, however, that can be difficult.

How, then, can you tell an AI-generated image from a real one? Here are some tips:

- **Too many—or not enough—fingers:** For some reason, today's AI image generators have problems with human hands. Some AI generated images show people with four fingers, some with six, and some, like the one in Figure 2.2, with some bizarre arrangement of fingers that bear no resemblance to reality. Always check the hands and fingers (and other limbs) in a photo; if something's obviously not right, it's probably AI generated.

**FIGURE 2.2**

*A not-very-human looking human hand generated by AI. (Image generated by Microsoft Image Creator from the prompt "human hands.")*

- **Unnatural body proportions and parts:** Similar to the hands and fingers thing, AI doesn't always get body proportions right. Ears might be slightly misplaced, larger, or smaller than they should be. Faces might be oddly asymmetrical. Legs and arms might be thicker or thinner than is physically possible. If it doesn't look right, it's probably been poorly constructed or manipulated.

- **Bad hair:** I'm not talking about messy hair or a bad part. AI often has trouble with all the details in human hair. Hair might appear blurred or have unusual changes in texture. It might look wrong on a head, like a bad wig. Even little issues, like looking too thick or too thin, can be a sign of AI manipulation.

- **Overly rendered appearance:** AI will sometimes "over render" the details on a face or other object, making it look unnaturally sharp, especially compared to other elements or the image background. It's not a natural look.

- **Weird or missing details:** AI doesn't always get the details right. You can sometimes find surprising errors when you zoom in to a high-resolution image. Look for things in the background that shouldn't be there, distinct elements blending weirdly into one another, items that don't quite match up, and other things that don't make sense. AI's generated reality doesn't always reflect our real world.

- **Unusual backgrounds:** AI-generated images sometimes get foreground elements right but do odd things to the background. Look for unusual textures, unnaturally repetitive patterns, or glossy effects. Another telltale sign is a blurry or airbrushed background.

- **Poor architecture, furniture, and accessories:** AI can make little mistakes that really stand out, especially with buildings and rooms. Look for oddly curved walls, sloping ceilings, misaligned steps, and such. A chair might be missing a leg or a coffee table might have too many legs. Consider minor elements in the image, such as coffee mugs, purses, jewelry, and the like; AI often gets the size wrong or has them hanging in mid-air, defying the law of gravity. It's almost as if these details are an afterthought for the AI models.

- **Nonsense text:** Look for any items with text within the image, such as newspapers, books, and posters. More often than not, AI generates nonsense words and letters for these elements, as shown in Figure 2.3.

**FIGURE 2.3**

*Look closely at the newspaper; those aren't real words. Also, the woman has three legs and a very odd-looking left hand. (Image generated by PIXLR AI Image Generator from the prompt "woman reading a newspaper")*

- **Stereotyped images:** AI isn't very creative. Ask it to create a picture of a doctor, and you'll get a guy who looks like someone out of central casting. These stereotypes can also play into racial, gender, and other biases. If a picture looks like a stock photo, it may be AI generated. (Or it could be a stock photo, too.)

Another way to spot AI-generated fakes is to search for similar images online. A real image is likely to be replicated on other sites, sometimes from a slightly different angle taken by a different photographer. Especially look for similar photos on legitimate news sites. If nobody you trust is displaying a similar photo, it's probably a fake.

You also need to consider whether the image is believable. If you're presented an image of your city's mayor striking a small child with a cane, it's probably a fake. (Unless you happen to be living in England during the Victorian era, that is.) If it shows a popular TV celebrity being handcuffed and led to jail, it's probably a fake. (Well, for most celebrities, anyway.) And if it shows a well-known person doing something criminal or utterly embarrassing, it's probably a fake, too. (Again, depending on the individual.)

The point is, people and groups are using AI to create images of things that haven't really happened and are unlikely to happen. Always consider the context of an image; if it's something that doesn't seem likely, it probably is fake.

# AI IMAGE DETECTORS

As AI-generated images continue to improve, it's becoming increasingly difficult to tell what is AI generated and what is real. For that reason, you may want to use an AI image detector to do the detecting for you.

AI image detectors examine a variety of factors to determine whether an image is created by a human or by AI. These sites have a pretty good track record; if they say it's likely an image is AI generated, that should be enough for you to be suspicious, at the very least.

The most popular AI image detectors today include

- AI or Not (www.aiornot.com)
- Hive Moderation (https://hivemoderation.com/ai-generated-content-detection)
- Illuminarty (https://illuminarty.ai)
- Winston AI (https://gowinston.ai)

Some of these image detectors are free; others charge for use.

## How to Identify AI-Generated Videos

AI-generated videos suffer from many of the same flaws as AI-generated images. In addition to the issues discussed in the previous section, be on the lookout for

- **Implausible content**: If the content of a video seems implausible (a politician espousing a particularly offensive or unusual position, for example), it may be an AI-generated fake. Trust your instincts, above all.

- **Strange shadows or light flickers:** AI doesn't always get the light source right. It also has trouble keeping the lighting consistent when there's movement in the frame, such as a person talking.

- **Unnatural body language:** People don't always stand or walk right in AI-generated videos. Look especially for jerky movements instead of smooth, natural ones.

- **Changes in facial features:** Does a person's face suddenly change in the middle of the video? Do they gain or lose moles or skin creases? AI often has trouble maintaining those kinds of details from shot to shot or even frame to frame.

- **Slow or no blinking:** For whatever reason, artificially created people do not always blink right in AI-generated videos. They often blink slowly, and sometimes they don't blink at all. It's a dead giveaway.

- **Robotic facial movements:** Watch the person's eyes—do they move naturally or robotically? Do their eyebrows track the way they should? Does their nose crinkle when they smile? These are all telltale signs that you're watching a computer-generated person.

- **Poor synchronization:** Trying to make lips move with spoken words is a difficult task. Sometimes the speaker's mouth will get out of sync with the audio track. Other times the audio gets chopped up to match lip movement. AI definitely has trouble with this.

- **Odd background noises:** AI doesn't always get the right background sounds for what it's supposed to be showing. Do the background noises match the room onscreen or what's supposed to be happening? A street scene with no car noises would be a certain fake.

As with AI-generated images, you should also search the Internet for other instances of this video. If you only see it in your TikTok feed but nowhere else, it might be suspect.

## How to Identify AI-Generated Music

You may not have heard much of it yet, but some companies are using AI to generate music. This is typically background music, the kind of tunes you hear in an elevator or when you're waiting on hold, but it's still very real—and often sounds just like other similar music. You may even find AI-generated selections appearing in your streaming media playlists, designed to sound similar to the other music you've selected.

How, then, can you pick the AI-generated songs out of the batch? Here are a few things to listen for:

- **It's too perfect.** Human musicians often make mistakes, no matter how slight. They bend notes, they rush or drag the tempo, they sound like human beings. AI-generated music doesn't include this type of human touch. If it's too perfect, it may be AI generated.

- **It's too repetitive.** AI models create music based on learned patterns. If a song is too repetitive (and it's hard to tell, as much music is repetitive by nature), it could be AI generated.

- **It's too formulaic.** Similarly, AI-generated music doesn't (and can't) take the creative leaps that human songwriters can. Human music often takes unexpected directions using unconventional chord progressions, unusual melodic jumps, and atypical song structure. If it's too formulaic, it may be AI generated.

- **The lyrics don't sound right.** Not all AI-generated songs have lyrics but those that do often lack coherence or emotion. The rhyme schemes might be correct, but the words won't convey the same meaning as those from a human songwriter.

- **It doesn't connect emotionally.** Humans know how to use words and music to convey deep emotions. AI models don't. As a result, AI-generated music is often soulless and superficial.

- **It lacks energy.** Computer-generated music might sound professional but lack the energy that live musicians provide. This is a tough one because many contemporary musicians today use computer programs to create music in their home studios. But even those that do find ways to pump up a performance. AI is kind of low-energy all the time.

- **It sounds almost but not *quite* like the original artist.** Some companies are using AI to generate "soundalike" recordings that sound like a popular performer but aren't really from that performer. Be particularly wary of new music from long-dead artists that just wouldn't be possible.

Musicians can generally tell whether a song is from another musician or was generated by AI. It may be more challenging for casual listeners. At the end of the day, you have to trust your ears.

## How to Identify AI-Generated Propaganda

Finally, let's examine how you can identify and avoid AI-generated propaganda in your social media and news feeds.

The key to avoiding this type of AI-generated misinformation is to think logically. Yes, you can work through all the tips presented in the previous sections for identifying AI-generated text, images, and videos, but it's often easier just to trust your nose. If something smells fishy, it probably is.

In particular, follow this advice:

- **Consider why someone might be spreading disinformation.** There's typically a purpose behind the lie—and remember that propaganda, especially the AI-generated kind, tends to spike around election time and major news events.

- **If it sounds too outrageous, it probably is.** If that rumor about foreigners abducting children at the mall was real, it'd be all over the real news; you wouldn't have to read about it in a friend's social feed.

- **Check the source.** If the so-called news comes from a friend of a friend's second cousin, don't assume it's real. Same if it comes from an official-sounding news source that you haven't heard of before. Check the major media to see if the news is there.

- **Consult a fact-checking site.** Snopes (www.snopes.com) or FactCheck.org (www.factcheck.org) can help to debunk misinformation, rumors, and conspiracy theories.

Summing all this up, there's a lot of fake or misleading content out there. That kind of content existed before AI and will only get worse (that is, more believable) with the help of AI technology. It behooves us all to be highly skeptical of claims we see online, especially those that come from dubious sources or are spread via social media. No matter how real something might look or sound, there's a good chance it isn't.

Most important, don't share anything you think might be misinformation. It's easy to graze through a provocative post and quickly click the share button. Take your time, determine whether it's true, and don't share it until you're sure. You want to be part of the solution, not part of the problem.

# Debating the Ethics of AI-Created Content

The use of AI-generated content brings up a number of ethical concerns. When is it okay to share AI-generated content? When is it okay to use it for your own personal use? Can you use it for schoolwork? If you create it yourself (with an AI generator), do you own it? If you found it online, who owns it?

The rest of this chapter examines the ethics of AI-generated content. The issues aren't always clear.

## Sharing AI-Generated Content

How ethical is it to share AI-generated content? It depends on how it's presented.

In no instance should you present AI-generated content as anything other than what it is. Do not present AI content as something you created yourself. Do not present it as "official" content from another source. Do not try to pass it off as anything other than AI-generated content.

For example, it is unethical to use AI to generate artwork and tell people you created it yourself. You would be lying about the creation and ownership of that artwork. If you share said artwork, you need to clearly label it as AI generated.

Similarly, you should not claim authorship of any text that AI writes for you. You didn't write it so you shouldn't label yourself as the author. The content—whether an article, blog post, white paper, or book—should be clearly labeled as AI generated.

Bottom line: You need to be transparent about how you use AI. Claiming AI-generated content as your own creation is highly unethical. (It's also unfair to the original creators of the content used to train the AI engine.)

## Using AI for Schoolwork

Schoolwork is a special use case for AI-generated content. If you're a student, consider how tempting it may be to have an AI answer homework questions or even write your term paper for you. What could be easier than that—just type a detailed prompt and ensure yourself a decent grade!

The problem is, using AI to do your schoolwork is extremely unethical. And, if caught, you'll probably have that grade thrown out—and you may be thrown out of school along with it. Educators view this unauthorized use of AI as cheating.

By the way, if you think your teachers won't be able to tell if you're using AI to do your schoolwork, think again. As I mentioned earlier in this chapter, teachers can use numerous tools to identify the original source of any given passage and determine if it came from an AI engine. Figure 2.4 shows an example. So don't bank on flying under the radar; if you're using AI to cheat on your schoolwork, there's a good chance you will be caught.

Just as you shouldn't use Wikipedia as a source for your schoolwork, you also shouldn't use AI to do your schoolwork for you. You may be able to use it to get ideas, much as you get ideas from searching the web with Google or Bing, but you shouldn't have it finish your actual work. You have to answer those questions and write those papers yourself, without any outside help. Doing otherwise *is* cheating—and could lead to serious ramifications if you're caught.

**FIGURE 2.4**

*Determining whether text was generated by AI or by a human with GPTZero. (Image courtesy GPTZero.)*

## Handling Plagiarism

It's clearly unethical to plagiarize another person's work. But is using AI-generated content plagiarism?

The quick answer is, not necessarily. AI engines generate their content not from a single source but rather based on a wide variety of inputs, ideally synthesizing content and ideas from all those inputs.

However, AI models can inadvertently copy existing content verbatim. In this instance, the supposed AI-generated content is nothing more than that: original content regurgitated. And that is plagiarism.

How can you protect yourself from plagiarizing based on AI-generated content? The easy solution is not to rely exclusively on AI content. Use it for ideas but do your own writing—or, at the very least, rewrite the content that AI generates. And if you want to be sure that you're using content that isn't plagiarized, feed the text into one of the AI text detection tools discussed previously to find out.

## Using AI Content for Malicious Purposes

As you've no doubt realized, AI can be used for good or for evil. To be ethical, you should strive to use AI purely for good purposes and avoid doing bad things with it.

Unfortunately, there are those among us who have no compunction about using AI to lie, mislead, cheat, and even steal. The use of AI in this fashion is not just unethical; it's immoral and often illegal.

You shouldn't do that.

AI should not be used to spread misinformation, perpetuate sexist or racist biases, incite social unrest or violence, or otherwise try to trick people, or incite social unrest or violence. You should not use AI to generate or spread harmful content.

No universal "code of AI conduct" prohibits AI engines from contributing to such malicious behavior. AI does not possess a sense of ethics or morality. AI has all the ethics of a cellphone signal; by itself, it's a completely neutral technology. It's what people do with it that might be unethical.

I can't tell you how you should use AI engines and AI-generated content. No doubt there are some that will choose to use it for malicious purposes. All I can do is urge you not to. It's the right thing to do.

## Dealing with Built-In Bias

As you recall from earlier in this chapter, AI systems often have built-in biases, derived either from the data they learned from or the people who programmed them. It's important to recognize that these biases exist and be prepared to identify and deal with them.

In particular, you need to recognize the potential for bias in the content generated by AI models. Don't automatically trust what an AI model tells you as being the absolute unbiased truth. Learn to examine AI output to identify any built-in bias, and then edit that content to minimize the effects of that bias.

AI companies can mitigate the amount of bias in their systems by choosing datasets that are less biased or totally unbiased and include information from diverse and representative sources. Future AI models might be trained to identify bias and filter out that data.

Until then, however, it is on consumers of AI data to recognize the potential for bias and deal with it when found. We should also carefully consider the prompts we use to generate AI content and avoid any potential bias in the instructions we provide. We can't assume that AI models are color- and gender-blind; in fact, we may have to assume that they are not.

## Dealing with Inaccurate Content

What do you do if what you ask AI to generate is created from content that is inaccurate or incomplete? AI output is only as good as the data input—and not all that data is equally robust or accurate.

This means you shouldn't automatically accept AI content as the final word on any given subject. Treat it with the same skepticism you'd treat any other data source and double-check it against other sources.

Here's an example. I asked ChatGPT if Spenser, the fictional detective character created by author Robert B. Parker, has a beard. Here's the response I received:

> **Yes, Spenser, the fictional private detective created by Robert B. Parker, is often described as having a neatly trimmed beard and mustache in many of the novels. This characteristic is one of the consistent visual details associated with his appearance throughout the series. The description of his beard is often mentioned along with other aspects of his appearance, such as his muscular build and hawk-like features. However, it's important to note that specific details of characters' appearances can sometimes vary slightly across different books and interpretations.**

Unfortunately, this answer is wrong. Spenser is never described as having a beard; it's his colleague Hawk that has "a neatly trimmed beard and mustache."

I happen to know this because I've read all the Spenser novels, start to finish. ChatGPT obviously hasn't, or at least not well enough to avoid confusing two of the main characters. (The other tell: ChatGPT's mentioning of the character's "hawk-like features.")

So should you trust AI content to always be totally accurate? Of course not. You should treat it like any other source of information you come across, as something that needs to be checked and verified. It isn't always right.

## Protecting Privacy

The final ethical concern involving AI is that of data privacy. Right now AI engines scrape data off the web to train their models. If your private information—name, address, email, and the like—is online at all, chances are it's been vacuumed up by one or more AI engines and resides in a big database somewhere.

That probably doesn't make you happy. It may also violate one or more data protection laws in this and other countries.

Obviously, this exposes your personal data to potentially malicious use. Someone might be able to query an AI engine about you and receive in return information you'd rather remain private. Even worse, criminal types could use information surfaced from AI to create highly personalized spam or phishing messages just for your benefit.

And if you think you haven't put any personal or confidential information on the web, think again. Personal information can come from anywhere, including social media posts, answers you've provided to AI chatbots on customer support sites, and even email messages you've sent or received. As to confidential information, if you've ever used AI to touch up a business presentation, create a contract, or write an email message to staff, you've provided AI engines with more grist for the mill. All that information could be available to AI models and anyone using them.

All this means is that AI has some very serious issues to address concerning data privacy. This will be an issue going forward.

# AI and Copyright Law

Beyond ethical issues, AI also faces some tricky legal issues. One particular such issue is the question of how AI conforms to existing copyright law. Copyright is designed to protect the creators of certain types of content, including books, movies, music, and audio. Does AI violate any copyright laws by using content to train its large language models? Does AI-created content qualify for copyright? Does AI content created to mimic existing works violate the copyright for those works? Those are the primary questions.

## Does Using Copyrighted Material to Train AI Violate Copyright Laws?

As you learned in the previous chapter, many AI models get content by scraping data off the public Internet. Some of what these models scrape is public and obvious fair game. But some of the information being fed into the AI models is copyrighted—books, reports, news articles, songs, movies, and the like. Isn't AI prohibited from using these copyrighted items without permission?

AI companies argue that using copyrighted material to train their models is perfectly permissible because of so-called fair use laws. These laws permit, under certain conditions, the use of copyrighted material without the consent of the copyright owner.

What are those permissible fair use conditions? There are four factors to consider:

- The purpose and character of the use, especially whether it is intended for commercial resale or for nonprofit educational purposes
- The nature of the copyrighted work
- The amount of the copyrighted work used as a percentage of the whole work
- The effect of said use on the potential market for or value of the copyrighted work

The AI industry as a whole argues that using a work to train an AI model is not a commercial purpose but rather an educational one. If that is true, as the AI industry claims, then the amount of the work used is irrelevant, as is the type of work used. The industry also argues that ingesting a work to train an AI model doesn't impact the marketability of the original work one iota. Thus copyrighted works used in this manner fall under the banner of fair use.

Some people argue with this interpretation. First, they argue that if AI companies actually make money from their AI models, then using a copyrighted work to train said models is a commercial use. They also argue that by training on a given work, this enables the AI model to generate content based on or similar to that work, thus diminishing the original work's value.

Not surprisingly, there have been several lawsuits filed by copyright holders with more sure to come. Plaintiffs to date include the Authors Guild, Getty Images, the *New York Times*, and authors Michael Chabon, Paul Tremblay, and Sarah Silverman; so far none of these cases have come to trial, which leaves the question open.

Time will tell how this issue is resolved. If ingesting copyrighted material for AI training purposes is found to violate copyright law, however, expect it to dramatically shake up the AI industry and change how AI models identify content for training.

## Is AI-Created Content Copyrightable?

On the flip side, content created by AI engines, without significant human authorship, definitely does not receive copyright protection. That is, AI companies cannot copyright the written, visual, or audio content that AI generates.

That's because United States Copyright Office (USCO) has explicitly stated that works generated entirely by AI are not copyrightable. USCO considers AI-generated content to be "derivative authorship;" it's not created, but rather adapted from existing material. It is USCO's longstanding practice to "require human authorship as a condition of copyrightability"—and AI-generated content is not authored by humans.

So, no, you can't copyright anything you "create" with an AI engine. It's not something you actually came up with on your own, so it's not copyrightable.

## Can AI Violate Copyright Laws with Content It Creates?

Another issue arises when AI generates content that too closely resembles existing works. Does it infringe on a work's copyright to somehow copy some or all aspects of that work?

Whether copying a work is a copyright violation depends on how similar the AI-generated work is to the original. The way U.S. copyright law reads, infringement may occur if the AI program both had access to the original work (that is, if it ingested the original into its large language model) and generated "substantially similar" output. What does that mean in practical terms?

The difference seems to come down to the difference between mimicking a style and copying content. So, for example, if you ask an AI engine to write an article in the style of famous author Stephen King, that is not a copyright violation because imitating a creator's style isn't theft. However, if you ask an AI engine to write a book called *The Stand* about a post-apocalyptic world ravaged by a biological virus and to do so in the style of Stephen King, it's likely that the engine will generate a work that very closely resembles the source material—and that *would* be a copyright violation.

In other words, you can mimic or imitate something, but you can't outright copy it whether you're a human being or an AI model.

## BEST PRACTICES FOR ETHICAL AI CONTENT CREATION

Knowing all that you now know, what are the best practices for using AI to ethically create content? Here are some of the main points to consider:

- Don't use AI to copy others' content or style.
- Do use AI to generate ideas and give you a starting point for your own content.
- Don't assume everything you get from AI is 100 percent accurate.
- Do fact check the content that AI generates.
- Don't present AI-generated content as your own.
- Do be transparent about where AI-generated content came from.
- Don't use AI for malicious purposes.
- Do be aware of bias built into some AI models.
- Don't use AI to cheat on your schoolwork

Bottom line: Use AI as a tool, not your only tool and not an unimportant one, but also not the sole source of your content. Use it responsibly and with proper oversight. And always, always, trust your instincts and follow your own moral and ethical compass.

# Summary

In this chapter, you learned about some of the best and the worst impacts of AI technology. AI is already providing benefits to people in all walks of life (and businesses, too) but also comes with its share of risks. We need to be aware of these risks even as we strive to take advantage of AI's benefits.

One of the more significant risks of AI is that the technology will be used to mislead the public through artificially generated deepfakes and misinformation. While it's becoming more difficult to spot this malicious AI-generated content, there are some telltale signs of AI involvement, of which we should all be aware. (For example, count the fingers in all AI-generated images!)

AI also presents some unique ethical and legal challenges. You should not, for example, pass off AI-generated content as your own or use AI content to complete your schoolwork. Where AI fits within our current copyright laws is also in debate, including the legality of using copyrighted material to train AI engines and whether AI-generated content violates copyright laws when it hews too closely to the original material.

Bottom line: You need to learn how to use AI safely and responsibly, which includes learning how to recognize and not get fooled by AI-generated content. In the right hands and with the right intent, AI can be a powerful tool. In the wrong hands, it can do major damage. You need to do everything in your power to make sure that AI is used for good, not for evil.

3

# GETTING STARTED WITH ALL-PURPOSE AI TOOLS

As we get into the how-to section of this book, I want to introduce you to some all-purpose AI tools that are designed not just to predict behavior but also generate new content. Some of these tools (sometimes called general-purpose AI tools or AI generators) are standalone tools; others are incorporated into apps or websites you already use.

These all-purpose AI tools are fairly straightforward and intuitive: You tell the tool what you want to create, via a simple prompt (whether in English or another language), and the AI tool creates it.

What generative AI tools are available today? Which are best for your specific needs? Are they free? And—the most fun part—how do you use them to generate the best results?

The answers to all those questions, and more, are in this chapter.

# What Is an All-Purpose AI Tool—and What Can You Do With It?

All-purpose AI tools—such as ChatGPT, Gemini Chat, Meta AI, and Microsoft Copilot—are designed to perform a wide variety of tasks, whereas task-specific tools have one area of expertise. All-purpose tools are typically trained on large general-purpose datasets and are capable of generating output in a variety of formats.

What can you do with an all-purpose AI tool? Here are just a few of the things they can do:

- Generating ideas
- Answering questions about anything you can think of
- Researching topics
- Writing letters and emails
- Writing text messages and social media posts
- Writing blog posts and articles
- Writing fiction, nonfiction, poetry, scripts, and other creative writing
- Summarizing articles, meeting notes, websites, and more
- Making travel plans
- Carrying on conversations

Read on to learn how all-purpose AI tools work and how to get what you want from them. We'll go into more detail about specific applications in future chapters.

# How to Use a Generative AI Tool

Most all-purpose tools work the same way. You enter a prompt that describes what you want and then you press Enter. The AI tool does what you asked it to do—answer your question, write a letter, whatever.

Your prompt can be in the form of a question, a statement, or just a snippet of text. Grammar and punctuation don't matter that much. (That means you don't have to put a question mark at the end of a question—although you can if you want.)

For example, if you need to write a letter to your homeowner's association complaining about a recent increase in monthly dues, you might enter the following prompt:

**Write a one-page letter to my HOA complaining about dues going up $20 per month.**

You can specify the type of output—style, length, and so on— as well. For example, if you want to give a humorous speech at a friend's anniversary celebration, you might enter the following prompt:

**Create a three-minute humorous speech for Ron and Barb's 20th wedding anniversary celebration. Talk about how we met while I was taking out the trash on the wrong day when we first moved into the neighborhood.**

The more specific you are in what you want, the more accurately the AI tool will do your bidding. If you don't provide enough details, it will start making assumptions and may or may not give you want you wanted.

As an example of how this works, consider Google Gemini, a popular all-purpose AI tool. You enter your prompt into the **Enter a prompt here** box at the bottom of the page, as shown in Figure 3.1.

Gemini's response is displayed in the space above the prompt box, just below your prompt, as shown in Figure 3.2. You can scroll down to view more of the response. You can also highlight the response with your cursor to select the response and press Ctrl+X on your computer keyboard to copy it. You can then paste the response (Ctrl+V) into a word processing document or other file, if desired.

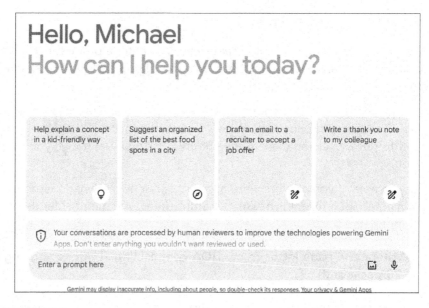

**FIGURE 3.1**

*Enter your prompt into the **Enter a prompt here** box.*

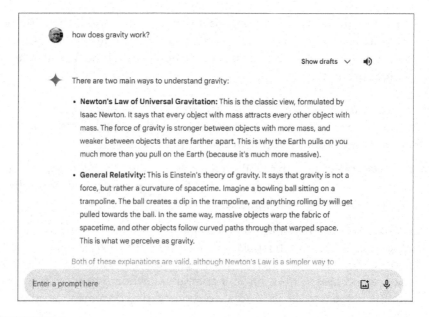

**FIGURE 3.2**

*AI's response to your prompt.*

Other all-purpose generative AI tools work in a similar way: Enter your prompt into the appropriate prompt box, press Enter, and see the AI response fill the screen.

 **NOTE** Learn more about creating effective AI prompts in the "How to Construct the Perfect Prompt" section, later in this chapter.

# Getting to Know Publicly Available AI Tools

There are two primary types of all-purpose AI tools available today: freestanding tools and tools that are embedded in other applications. Both types of AI generators work in pretty much the same fashion. The type of tool you choose depends on your particular needs.

Freestanding tools reside on their own websites or mobile apps. They can answer your questions and generate the content you desire; they possess broad knowledge about a wide variety of topics. These websites and apps typically look a little like web search engines, with a big box into which you enter your prompt. Output is often in the form of a free-flowing text conversation.

Embedded AI tools are built into an existing site or app to help better serve its purpose. You use the AI generator within the app and the results appear in the app; in some instances, you may not even realize that the website or app is using AI to deliver its services. For example, an AI generator embedded into a word processing program might let you generate content, such as facts or other details, that gets inserted directly into the letter you're writing.

This section helps you decide which type of AI generator is best for you and when. As you'll see, it depends on what you're doing. If you want a wider range of options and results, a freestanding AI tool is more appropriate. If you're working within an app or program and need help generating ideas or other content, use the embedded AI generator .

## Freestanding AI Tools

The most popular AI generators today are freestanding tools. They're kind of jack-of-all-trades tools, in that you can use them to create just about any type of text-based content. You can also use them to generate new ideas, answer questions, conduct research, and carry on conversations.

Some of these freestanding generative AI tools are free and available to the general public to use. Others require some sort of subscription or other payment. In general, the paid tools tend to be more advanced and targeted at business and professional users; the free tools targeted at a general audience often use older, less advanced versions of that site's AI model and sometimes put ads on the page.

The most popular freestanding all-purpose AI tools today are detailed in Table 3.1. (Pricing is at time of publication.)

**TABLE 3.1**   Freestanding All-Purpose AI Tools

| AI Tool | URL | Free Version? | Paid Version |
|---|---|---|---|
| ChatGPT | www.chatgpt.com | Yes | $20/month |
| Claude | www.claude.ai | Yes | $20/month |
| Google Gemini | gemini.google.com | Yes | $19.99/month |
| Meta AI | ai.meta.com | Yes | None available |
| Microsoft Copilot | copilot.microsoft.com | Yes | $20/month |
| Perplexity | www.perplexity.ai | Yes | $20/month |
| Pi | www.pi.ai | Yes | None available |
| Poe | www.poe.com | Yes | $19.99/month |

 **NOTE**   Google Gemini was previously known as Google Bard. Microsoft Copilot was formerly known as Bing AI.

## Embedded AI Tools

Many computer applications and mobile apps are beginning to incorporate generative AI. These tools go beyond the simple voice recognition of a digital assistant or predictive text in a word processor, both functions powered by the simpler predictive AI. We're talking about full-featured generative AI that can perform all manner of tasks, just like freestanding tools. You can use these tools to ask questions or generate content to use in the app itself.

For example, the latest version of Microsoft Windows incorporates Microsoft Copilot AI as part of the operating system. (Microsoft calls it Copilot in Windows.) It appears as an icon on the right side of the Windows taskbar. Click this icon to display the Copilot pane, shown in Figure 3.3. Enter your prompt into the **Ask me anything** box, press Enter, and Copilot displays its response, as shown in Figure 3.4.

**FIGURE 3.3**

*The Copilot pane in Microsoft Windows.*

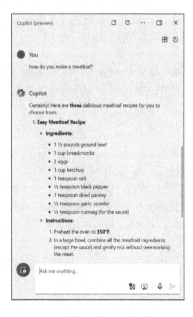

**FIGURE 3.4**

*Copilot in Windows' response to the prompt **how do you make a meatloaf with no onions for 12?***

Another example is when Gmail suggests potential responses to an email you have received, such as "Tuesday works for us," in response to a message about planning a meeting, or "Hooray!" in response to an email with good news. Other companies are incorporating AI into their apps in similar ways. For example, Google has integrated AI into its Google Workspace apps (such as Gmail, Google Docs, and Google Sheets) via a tool called Gemini for Google Workspace. Unfortunately, this tool, like Google Workspace itself, is only available for subscribing businesses.

# Using the Most Popular AI Generators

Enough talk. Let's get down to business with the most popular generative AI tools today. They all work similarly but have their own distinct personalities and quirks.

 **NOTE**   The tools I cover are available for public use at the time of writing, but there are others in development—so keep looking for what's new!

## Using ChatGPT

ChatGPT is the consumer-focused generative AI tool from AI research company OpenAI. It may be the most popular generative AI tool today, with more than 180 million users. OpenAI says that more than 80 percent of Fortune 500 companies have integrated ChatGPT into their operations.

 **NOTE**   GPT stands for Generative Pre-trained Transformer, which is another name for a large language model. (I discussed large language models in Chapter 1, "Artificial Intelligence: What It Is and How It Works.")

OpenAI introduced its first version of the GPT model in 2018 and released ChatGPT in 2020. The basic version of ChatGPT is free, although OpenAI also offers a more powerful Plus plan for $20. The Plus plan includes access to the most recent version of OpenAI's GPT model as well as other AI tools, such as the DALL-E image generator, which I talk about in Chapter 7, "Using AI to Create Art and Images."

You access ChatGPT by pointing your web browser to www.chatgpt.com. While you don't have to sign up to use ChatGPT (it's free, whether you sign up or not), creating an account lets you save and return to previous chats.

 **NOTE**   ChatGPT describes all prompts and responses as "chats."

If you've created a free ChatGPT account, your past chats are displayed in the left pane, in chronological order, as shown in Figure 3.5. Click the name of any chat to see that entire chat in the main pane.

**FIGURE 3.5**

*The ChatGPT home page.*

The main pane displays the contents of the current chat and the **Message ChatGPT** box at the bottom. Enter your prompt into the **Message ChatGPT** box and press Enter on your keyboard. ChatGPT returns its results in the main pane above the prompt box, as shown in Figure 3.6.

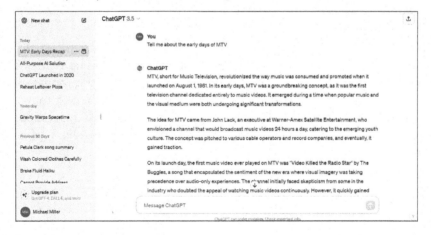

**FIGURE 3.6**

*A ChatGPT chat.*

To share the contents of a chat with another user, click the up arrow in the top right corner of the ChatGPT window. This displays a **Share Public Link to Chat** dialog box, as shown in Figure 3.7. Click the **Create Link** button; then, when the next screen appears, click the **Copy Link** button. You can now paste that link into an email or text message and share it with others. When they click the link, they see the entire contents of the chat in question.

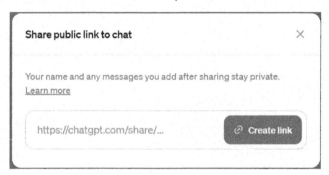

**FIGURE 3.7**

*Sharing a ChatGPT chat.*

That's how ChatGPT works on the web. OpenAI also offers a ChatGPT smartphone app, available for free download from the Apple App Store and Google Play Store, that lets you always have your AI assistant on the go. (Make sure you download the genuine app; imposters have already made their way into the app stores.) The app version works much like the web version; enter your prompt into the Message box at the bottom of the screen and ChatGPT provides its response in the main part of the screen, as shown in Figure 3.8.

Even better, you can use the ChatGPT app to talk to AI using normal speech, which may be a more natural form of interaction than typing repeated text prompts. When you're in the app, tap the headphone icon next to the Message box and start talking. ChatGPT listens to what you say and then responds in its own voice. You can carry on conversations with AI in this fashion, which feels revolutionary.

**FIGURE 3.8**

*Using the ChatGPT smartphone app.*

## Using Claude

Claude is the generative AI tool from Anthropic, an AI research and engineering firm backed by Amazon.

Claude has a free plan that imposes daily usage limits and a Pro plan that raises those usage limits and uses a more powerful AI model. The Claude Pro plan costs $20 per month.

When you first access Claude at www.claude.ai, you're asked to either sign in with your Google account or create a new Claude account. Claude then asks you your name so it can address you personally.

Claude's main screen, shown in Figure 3.9, has a big front-and-center prompt box. Enter your prompt into the **Start your first message with Claude** box and either press Enter or click the **Start Chat** button.

**FIGURE 3.9**

*Claude's home page.*

Claude's response appears above the prompt box, which moves to the bottom of the page, as shown in Figure 3.10. You can reply to Claude's response by typing into the **Reply to Claude** box; to start a different chat, click the **Start New Chat** (+) icon in the top-left corner of the screen.

**FIGURE 3.10**

*Claude's response to a prompt.*

Underneath each of Claude's responses is a series of icons, shown in Figure 3.11, that let you **Copy** the response to your clipboard to paste into other applications, **Retry** the request to generate a different response, or give the response a thumbs up or thumbs down.

**FIGURE 3.11**

*Responding to a Claude response.*

Claude can also summarize and analyze content you upload. Click the **Upload Docs or Images** (paperclip) icon to upload documents, spreadsheets, PDF files, or images. For example, I uploaded an initial version of this chapter and asked Claude to summarize it; that result is shown in Figure 3.12.

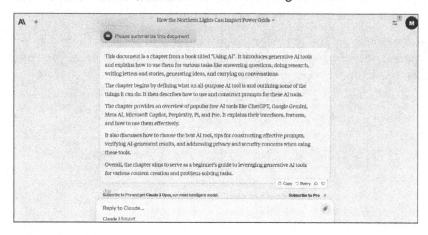

**FIGURE 3.12**

*Claude's summary of an uploaded Word document.*

This ability to work with uploaded documents makes Claude unique in today's generative AI landscape. Unfortunately, the usage caps of Claude's free version put limitations on how you can use the tool; if you exceed the limits, you'll probably need to subscribe to Claude Pro.

## Using Google Gemini

Search giant Google created its own generative AI tool and launched Google Bard in December 2023. The company changed the tool's name to Gemini two months later, in February 2024.

Like ChatGPT, Gemini is free to use by the public. Google also offers a Gemini Advanced version that uses Google's most advanced AI model; it's included with the $19.99 per month Google One AI Premium bundle, which also includes 2TB of online storage.

**NOTE** In addition to the web-based version, Google offers Gemini apps for Android and Apple iOS phones and tablets. Look for the Gemini app in your device's app store.

When you first access Google Gemini (point your web browser to https://gemini.google.com) you'll be prompted to sign into your Google account, if you're not currently signed in. Signing in lets you keep a history of past chats, which you can recall in the future.

By default, the side pane in Gemini is not expanded. You probably want to expand it to see what's there, so click the **Expand Menu** (three-line) icon. You now see a list of your past chats as well as other controls.

At the bottom of the main pane is the **Enter a prompt here** box, as shown in Figure 3.13. To generate results, do as the box says and enter your prompt there; then press Enter on your keyboard.

**FIGURE 3.13**

*The Google Gemini home page.*
*SOURCE: gemini.google.com*

The response to your prompt is displayed in the main pane above the prompt box, as shown in Figure 3.14. As you enter more prompts, the previous response scrolls up.

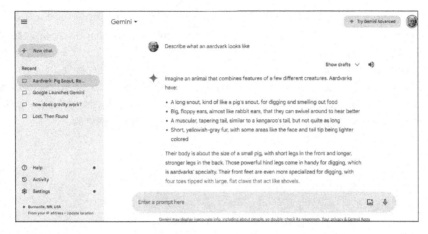

**FIGURE 3.14**

*The results of a Gemini prompt.*

 **NOTE**   Google Gemini can also summarize web-based articles and reports as well as complete websites. Just use the prompt **summarize [URL]** and include the URL of the web page you want summarized.

Unlike ChatGPT and most other all-purpose AI generators, Gemini lets you generate images as well as text results. Just prompt it to **create an image of** and then describe what you want. The results are shown in the main pane, often with several options, as shown in Figure 3.15. Click a thumbnail to display a larger image.

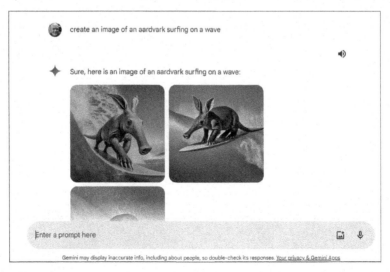

**FIGURE 3.15**

*Creating images with Google Gemini.*

Underneath all Gemini responses are a series of icons, shown in Figure 3.16, that let you react to that response. You can upvote (thumb up) or downvote (thumb down) the response, depending on whether you like it. You can click the **Share** icon to share it via a public link, export it to Google Docs, or add it to an email draft in Gmail. You can also click the Google "G" logo to double-check the response or click the **More** (three-dot) icon to copy the response (to paste into another application) or report a legal issue with the response.

**FIGURE 3.16**

*Reacting to a Google Gemini response.*

By the way, Google is now adding Gemini AI-generated summaries at the top of many web search results pages. The AI Overviews, as Google calls them, appear before the normal page listings, as shown in Figure 3.17. These overviews could theoretically answer many user questions, saving users the trouble of clicking through Google's normal search results.

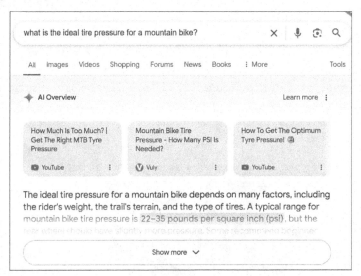

**FIGURE 3.17**

*An AI Overview at the top of a Google search results page, powered by Google Gemini.*

**WARNING** Google's Gemini-powered AI Overviews aren't always up to date or fully accurate. To be safe, you'll want to verify these overviews through Google's traditional search results.

## Using Meta AI

Meta, the parent company of Facebook, Instagram, and WhatsApp, also owns the Meta AI research lab, which is tasked with developing practical applications for AI within Meta's other products and services. As part of that research, the company has released the Meta AI freestanding generative AI tool.

The basic version of Meta AI is free. The company also plans to offer a subscription-based Meta AI Plus plan, which will provide access to more advanced AI models and let you enter more and longer prompts. As I write this, Meta has not yet set pricing for Meta AI Plus.

To use Meta AI, point your web browser to www.meta.ai. If you're already a Facebook member, you can log in with your Facebook account.

Meta AI's main page looks quite a bit like all the other general AI tools. There's a left-hand pane you can expand by clicking the right-arrow; when expanded, you see prior conversations. (What ChatGPT calls "chats," Meta AI calls "conversations.") The prompt box, labeled **Ask Meta AI anything**, appears at the bottom of the main pane, as shown in Figure 3.18.

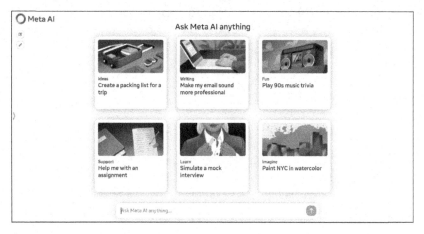

**FIGURE 3.18**

*The Meta AI home page.*

To use Meta AI, enter your prompt into the **Ask Meta AI anything** box and press Enter. Meta AI's response appears in the main pane, above the prompt box, as shown in Figure 3.19. As you enter more prompts and Meta AI issues more responses, the conversation scrolls.

**FIGURE 3.19**

*A Meta AI prompt and response.*

Underneath each response are three buttons, shown in Figure 3.20. There are buttons for **Good response** (thumb up), **Bad response** (thumb down), and **Copy content to clipboard**. Use that last button to copy the current response so you can paste it into another app, such as word processor document or email message.

**FIGURE 3.20**

*Responding to a Meta AI response.*

 **NOTE**   Meta AI is also available in Ray-Ban's Meta Smart Glasses (www.ray-ban.com/usa/ray-ban-meta-smart-glasses), which can be a useful option for people who are visually impaired.

## Using Microsoft Copilot

Not surprisingly, Microsoft has developed its own generative AI tool, called Copilot. Because Microsoft is a big investor in OpenAI, the two companies have a strong working relationship, and Copilot uses the same GPT engine from OpenAI that ChatGPT uses. This means its results are often similar (and sometimes identical) to those from ChatGPT. *Often* but not always. Copilot appears to use some slightly different algorithms than ChatGPT, which sometimes results in different results, especially on prompts for more creative output.

You access Copilot at copilot.microsoft.com. You can sign in with your Microsoft account. The basic version of Copilot is free; the more fully featured Copilot Pro costs $20 per month.

 **NOTE**   Like ChatGPT and Google Gemini, Microsoft Copilot is also available as a mobile app for Android and Apple iOS devices. Search for the Copilot app in your device's app store.

As you can see in Figure 3.21, the Copilot home page is the mirror opposite of most other AI generators, in that the pane with recent chats is on the right side, not the left. In that pane you'll also find tabs for other Microsoft AI tools, including

- **Designer,** for generating images (we'll discuss this in Chapter 7)

- **Vacation Planner**, for creating itineraries and booking travel (I discuss this in Chapter 10, "Using AI to Manage Your Travel and Transportation")

- **Cooking Assistant**, for finding recipes and generating meal plans

- **Fitness Trainer**, for designing exercise and nutrition programs (I discuss this in Chapter 11, "Using AI for Health and Wellness")

**FIGURE 3.21**

*Microsoft Copilot's home page.*

To use Copilot, make sure **Copilot** is selected in the right-hand pane and then enter your prompt into the **Ask me anything** box at the bottom of the page.

As you can see in Figure 3.22, Copilot's response is displayed in the main pane, above the prompt box. Additional prompts and responses are displayed in a scrolling fashion.

**FIGURE 3.22**

*Viewing Microsoft Copilot results.*

Underneath the response is something unique to Copilot—a Learn More section with search results from Microsoft's Bing search engine. Hover over one of these links, shown in Figure 3.23, to view a snippet from that page. Click a link to go to that page.

**FIGURE 3.23**

*All the stuff underneath a Copilot response.*

**NOTE** For some responses, Copilot also displays related advertisements. That's something you won't find with other AI tools.

Beneath the Learn More section are ways to respond to Copilot's response—Like, Dislike, Copy, Export, Share, and (uniquely) Read Aloud. Click the icon to do the thing.

Finally, at the very bottom of the response are other related queries in which you may be interested. Click a query to have Copilot generate a response.

 **NOTE** Some people will find the additional links underneath Copilot results useful. Others will find them unnecessarily intrusive—especially the ads, when they appear. It certainly looks like Microsoft is attempting to make Copilot look like its Bing search engine and, in some instances, monetize those results with ads.

## COPILOT IN OTHER MICROSOFT APPLICATIONS

I previously mentioned how Microsoft has incorporated Copilot into Microsoft Windows. Think of that as a shortcut to Copilot that doesn't require you to visit the Copilot page in your web browser.

Microsoft is also incorporating Copilot into its Microsoft 365 (formerly Office 365) applications—but only for businesses that have a Copilot for Microsoft 365 or Copilot Pro license. These business users can use Copilot to

- Draft a new document or rewrite an existing one in Microsoft Word
- Analyze trends and create data visualizations in Microsoft Excel
- Create presentations in Microsoft PowerPoint
- Organize your inbox in Microsoft Outlook

At this point in time, these AI features are only available for Microsoft's business subscribers and professional users. It's possible that Microsoft will migrate these features to other users in the future.

## Using Perplexity

Perplexity is a generative AI tool that blends the features of a search engine with AI powered by OpenAI's GPT-3.5 model. It's unique in that it cites the sources of its responses, which makes it a good choice for research or educational purposes.

The standard version of Perplexity is free. The Professional version, which lets you choose your AI model (from GPT-4, Claude-3, or Sonar Large), create images, and upload and analyze files, runs $20 per month.

You access Perplexity at www.perplexity.ai. You can create a new account or sign in with your Apple or Google account.

As you can see in Figure 3.24, the left-hand pane displays a Library of past threads. (What ChatGPT calls "chats" and what Meta AI calls "conversations," Perplexity calls "threads.") You use the **Ask anything** box in the middle of the main pane to enter your prompt.

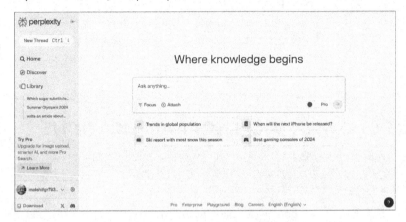

**FIGURE 3.24**

*Perplexity's home page.*

The results, shown in Figure 3.25, look quite a bit different from those from other AI tools. First off, it's not really a conversation, but rather a display of information. Second, the sources for that information are displayed above the response; click a source to go directly to that web page. Third, Perplexity displays images related to your prompt on the right side of the page. Fourth, you can also search related videos by clicking the **Search Videos** link on the right. And fifth, if you subscribe to Perplexity Pro, you can generate new images based on your prompt by clicking the **Generate Image** link.

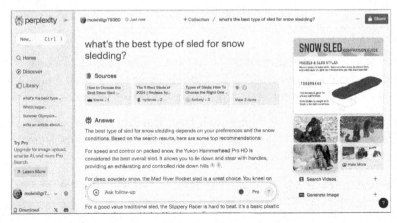

**FIGURE 3.25**

*A research-oriented response from Perplexity.*

That's a lot that's different from the other AI tools, but the differences don't end there.

If you want to drill down further, you can enter a related prompt into the **Ask follow-up** box. To start a new thread, however, you have to click the **New Thread** button in the left-hand pane. This displays a new **Ask anything** box, like the one in Figure 3.26, into which you can enter your new prompt.

**FIGURE 3.26**

*Beginning a new thread in Perplexity.*

Underneath each Perplexity response are a series of response icons, as shown in Figure 3.27. From left to right, you can **Share** the thread, **Rewrite** the response, **Copy** the response, **Edit the Query** to fine-tune the response, or click the **More** (three-dot) icon to view sources or report this particular response.

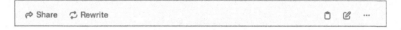

**FIGURE 3.27**

*Responding to a thread in Perplexity.*

## Using Pi

Pi is an AI tool that works more like a chatbot. When you first log into Pi, you're asked to choose a voice so that Pi can respond to you verbally, as well as via text. Pi is free to use, and you can log into it with your Apple, Facebook, or Google account, or you can create a new Pi-specific account.

You access Pi at www.pi.ai. As you can see in Figure 3.28, its interface is quite spartan. The panel on the left really doesn't serve much purpose, and all you see is the **Talk with Pi** box at the bottom. You can turn on or off Pi's voice responses by clicking the speaker icon at the top-right corner of the screen.

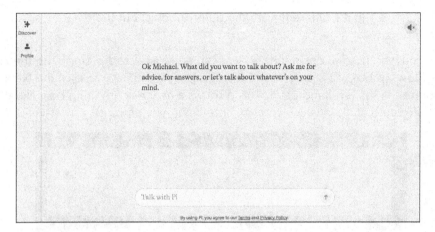

**FIGURE 3.28**

*Pi's home page.*

As you can see in Figure 3.29, a Pi conversation looks a lot like a typical text message thread. Your messages appear in a darker shaded box, followed by Pi's responses.

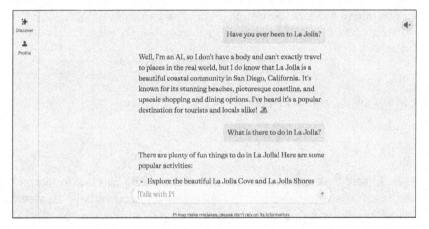

**FIGURE 3.29**

*A conversational thread with Pi AI.*

That's not to say you can't use Pi for more heavy lifting. Like the other generative AI tools, Pi can compose letters, write stories, provide information, and do pretty much everything the other generative AI tools can do. It just does it in the form of a conversation (or what Pi calls a "thread"), which some people might find more friendly than some of the other AI tools.

## Using Poe

The final AI tool I'm sharing is called Poe. Poe is actually an AI aggregator that provides access to a variety of AI tools in a single hub. Through Poe, you can get responses from OpenAI's GPT-4 and DALL-E, Google's Gemini, Meta's Llama, Anthropic's Claude, Stability AI's StableDiffusion, and more. Not all of these AI tools (what Poe calls "bots") are available with the free version of Poe, however; to get full access to all available tools, you need to subscribe for $19.99 per month.

All these options make Poe a little less user-friendly than some of the other AI tools, which you can see from its interface. When you access Poe's home page, at www.poe.com, and log in with your Apple, Google, or Poe account, you see the screen shown in Figure 3.30. A lot of options appear in the left panel, of which you may use some or none, as well as a **Start a new chat** box in the main pane.

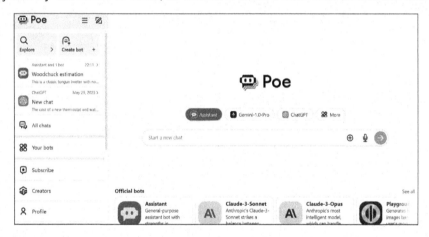

**FIGURE 3.30**

*Poe's home page—lots of options!*

To start, select the AI tool you want to use for your query. You can choose from Assistant (Poe's own AI tool and the default), Gemini-1.0-Pro (from Google), or ChatGTP. Click the **More** button to choose from additional tools (again, not all available in the free version).

Once you've selected your AI tool, enter your prompt into the **Start a new chat** box and press Enter. As you can see in Figure 3.31, the response looks like what you'd find with other AI tools—until you scroll down to the bottom of the response. There, as shown in Figure 3.32, you have the option of comparing this initial response with responses from other AI tools. Click a tool to see its response.

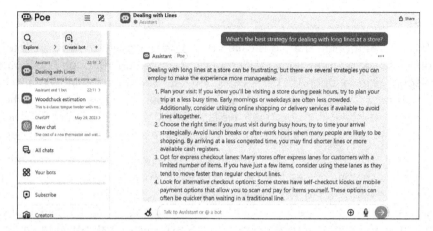

**FIGURE 3.31**

*The response to a prompt in Poe.*

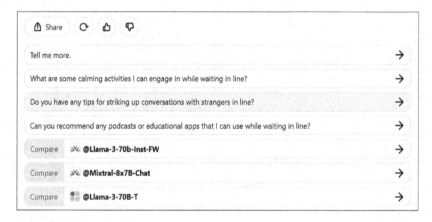

**FIGURE 3.32**

*Comparing Poe's initial response to another generative AI tool.*

This cross-tool functionality makes Poe a great choice if you're not sure which AI generator is best for you or if you just want to compare how the different AI tools respond to a given prompt. It has a slightly longer learning curve, which may not make it the ideal daily driver for AI needs. Still, it's an interesting approach to generative AI today.

# Which Generative AI Tool Is the Best for You?

With multiple all-purpose AI tools available (and more coming online seemingly daily), how do you choose which one to use?

Answering the question of which is the best AI tool is an impossible task. Each tool is trained on a slightly different data set, and each employs slightly different algorithms. That means you won't get the exact same results from each tool.

As a comparison, I asked some questions of three of the most popular generative AI tools, each using its own unique AI model: ChatGPT, Google Gemini, and Meta AI. Let's see how they compare.

First, I asked each tool to tell me the best way to reheat leftover pizza. ChatGPT got right to it and recommended a single approach (the oven method), as shown in Figure 3.33. Gemini presented several different methods in a conversational style, as shown in Figure 3.34. Meta AI also presented several different methods but offered step-by-step instructions, as you can see in Figure 3.35.

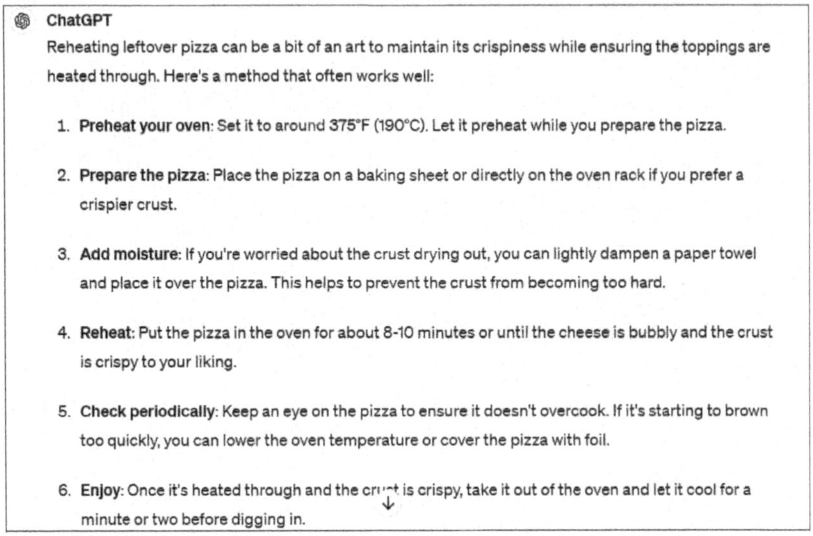

---

**ChatGPT**

Reheating leftover pizza can be a bit of an art to maintain its crispiness while ensuring the toppings are heated through. Here's a method that often works well:

1. **Preheat your oven:** Set it to around 375°F (190°C). Let it preheat while you prepare the pizza.

2. **Prepare the pizza:** Place the pizza on a baking sheet or directly on the oven rack if you prefer a crispier crust.

3. **Add moisture:** If you're worried about the crust drying out, you can lightly dampen a paper towel and place it over the pizza. This helps to prevent the crust from becoming too hard.

4. **Reheat:** Put the pizza in the oven for about 8-10 minutes or until the cheese is bubbly and the crust is crispy to your liking.

5. **Check periodically:** Keep an eye on the pizza to ensure it doesn't overcook. If it's starting to brown too quickly, you can lower the oven temperature or cover the pizza with foil.

6. **Enjoy:** Once it's heated through and the crust is crispy, take it out of the oven and let it cool for a minute or two before digging in.

---

**FIGURE 3.33**

ChatGPT's pizza reheating advice.

There are a few ways to reheat leftover pizza, each with its own pros and cons:

- **Oven:** This is generally considered the best way to reheat pizza, as it can crisp up the crust and melt the cheese without drying out the toppings. Preheat your oven to around 375-400 degrees Fahrenheit (190-205 degrees Celsius) and place the pizza on a baking sheet. You can also preheat a cast iron skillet in the oven for an extra crispy crust. Reheat for 5-10 minutes, or until the cheese is melted and bubbly.

- **Skillet:** This method is good for reheating a single slice or two of pizza. Heat a non-stick skillet over medium heat. Add a few drops of water to the pan and then place the pizza slice in the pan. Cover the pan with a lid and cook for 1-2 minutes, or until the cheese is melted and the crust is crispy.

- **Air Fryer:** If you have an air fryer, this can be a quick and easy way to reheat pizza. Preheat your air fryer to 350-400 degrees Fahrenheit (175-205 degrees Celsius) and place the pizza slices in a single layer. Reheat for 3-5 minutes, or until the cheese is melted and the crust is crispy.

**FIGURE 3.34**

*Google Gemini's pizza reheating advice.*

○ Meta AI

The best way to reheat leftover pizza is a matter of personal preference, but here are some popular methods:

1. Oven:
* Preheat your oven to 400°F (200°C).
* Place the pizza on a baking sheet or pizza stone.
* Heat for 8-12 minutes, or until crispy and hot.

2. Skillet:
* Heat a skillet over medium heat.
* Add a small amount of oil or cooking spray.
* Place the pizza in the skillet and heat for 2-3 minutes on each side, until crispy and hot.

3. Microwave:
* Place the pizza on a microwave-safe plate.
* Heat for 20-30 seconds, or until hot and crispy.
* Be careful not to overheat, as this can make the crust tough.

4. Air Fryer:
* Preheat the air fryer to 400°F (200°C).
* Place the pizza in the air fryer basket.
* Heat for 2-3 minutes, or until crispy and hot.

5. Grill:
* Preheat your grill to medium heat.
* Place the pizza on the grill and heat for 2-3 minutes on each side, until crispy and hot.

Remember to always check the temperature and crispiness of your pizza to ensure it's heated to your liking!

**FIGURE 3.35**

*Meta AI's pizza reheating advice.*

Next, I asked each engine to write a short story about a lost girl in the woods. (I like to tell my grandkids stories.) Here the three tools took wildly divergent paths, as you can see in Figures 3.36 (ChatGPT), 3.37 (Gemini), and 3.38 (Meta AI).

---

 **ChatGPT**

In the heart of a dense forest, where sunlight barely touched the ground and shadows danced with the whispers of the trees, there was a girl named Elara. She was adventurous, with a spirit that yearned for exploration beyond the familiar bounds of her village. One bright morning, driven by curiosity, Elara ventured into the woods alone, drawn by the secrets whispered in the rustling leaves.

At first, the forest welcomed her with open arms, its beauty captivating her senses. But as hours passed, the trees seemed to shift, their branches intertwining to form a maze of confusion. Elara's excitement turned to apprehension as she realized she had lost her way.

Fear crept into her heart as the forest grew darker, the once-familiar paths now shrouded in an eerie silence. With each step, she felt more lost than before, her only companions the haunting echoes of her own footsteps.

As dusk settled like a heavy cloak over the forest, Elara's resolve began to wane. She called out for help, her voice trembling with desperation, but only the wind answered her plea. Tears blurred her vision as she sank to the forest floor, overwhelmed by the vastness of her predicament.

But just when all hope seemed lost, a gentle gl ↓ pierced through the canopy above. With renewed

---

**FIGURE 3.36**

*ChatGPT's short story.*

---

The dappled sunlight that had filtered through the leaves was gone, replaced by an oppressive gloom. Maya, her heart hammering a frantic rhythm against her ribs, clutched her worn teddy bear tighter. How long had she been wandering? It felt like forever.

It had all started with a flitting butterfly, wings an impossible shade of blue. Mesmerized, she'd chased it deeper and deeper into the woods behind her house, ignoring the warnings from her grandpa on the porch. Now, the butterfly was a distant memory, replaced by towering trees that seemed to close in on her with every rustle of leaves.

Tears pricked Maya's eyes. She missed the smell of her mom's freshly baked cookies, the creak of the rocking chair on the porch. Fear, a cold serpent, coiled in her stomach. She stumbled over a gnarled root, landing with a scrape on her knee. A sob escaped her lips, loud and raw in the stillness.

Suddenly, a flash of movement caught her eye. A small, brown rabbit peeked from behind a tree, its twitching nose twitching inquisitively. Maya held her breath. Instead

---

**FIGURE 3.37**

*Google Gemini's short story.*

○ Meta AI
The Lost Girl in the Woods

As the sun began to set, 10-year-old Lily realized she was lost in the woods. She had
wandered away from her family's campsite in search of a wildflower, and now she was alone,
surrounded by towering trees that seemed to stretch up to the sky.

Panic set in as she called out for her parents, but only the birds responded. She took a deep
breath and tried to remember the way back, but every path looked the same.

As the darkness deepened, Lily stumbled upon a clearing. In the center stood an old, gnarled
tree, its branches twisted and tangled. She approached the tree, feeling an eerie sense of calm
wash over her.

Suddenly, a soft voice whispered her name. "Lily." She spun around, but there was no one in
sight. The voice came again, gentle and reassuring. "Lily, I'm here to help you."

A tiny fairy emerged from the tree's trunk, her wings shimmering in the moonlight. "My name
is Willow," she said. "I've been watching you. You're very brave, but you need to find your way
back home."

Lily nodded, tears of relief streaming down her face. Willow led her through the forest,
pointing out landmarks and warning her about dangers. As they walked, the trees seemed to
grow shorter, and the path became clearer.

Finally, they reached the edge of the woods, and Lily saw the campsite in the distance. Her
parents were frantically searching for her, and they rushed to her side, hugging her tightly.

As they thanked Willow, the fairy vanished into the trees, leaving behind a small, delicate
flower. Lily smiled, knowing she'd never forget her magical encounter in the woods.

**FIGURE 3.38**

*Meta AI's short story.*

Finally, to see which AI tool had the most poetic soul, I asked all three to compose
a haiku about snow. The results, all equally poetic, are in Figures 3.39 (ChatGPT),
3.40 (Gemini), and 3.41 (Meta AI).

 **ChatGPT**

Silent flakes descend,

Blanket of white whispers peace,

Winter's tranquil hush.

**FIGURE 3.39**

*A haiku from ChatGPT.*

 Soft flakes fall and hush,

World dressed in a silver coat,

Silent beauty sleeps.

**FIGURE 3.40**

*A haiku from Google Gemini.*

**Meta AI**
Softly falls the snow
Blanketing all in white peace
Winter's gentle hush

**FIGURE 3.41**

*A haiku from Meta AI.*

Is any one of these three tools significantly better than the others? I don't think so; they just offer slightly different results, just as you'd get different pieces of advice if you asked the same question from three of your friends.

That said, you may find that you like the results (or how they're presented) from one tool better than the others. If so, that is probably the right tool for you.

The best thing to do is give them all a try. Prompt each one with a similar request and see what results you get. You can then choose the one that feels right to you—or use multiple tools as you prefer.

 **NOTE**   You may find that the AI tool that appears better today might not be better tomorrow. As AI models continue to evolve, the different models used will frequently leapfrog each other in terms of results and features. So be prepared to switch AI tools as the models develop over time; you may like a totally different tool in the future.

# How to Construct the Perfect Prompt

To get the most relevant, appropriate, and accurate results from a generative AI tool you need to construct the right prompt. A well-crafted prompt tells the AI tool exactly what you want and includes context, intent, and the information you want included. The better and more detailed prompt you enter, the more satisfying and more accurate results you'll receive.

What that in mind, here are some tips for constructing a great generative AI prompt:

- **Be clear about what you want.** Clearly articulate what you want created or answered. Include as much detail as you can. Provide any necessary background information that might help AI provide a more appropriate response. List things that you want included and those you want excluded. Don't make the AI tool guess what you want.

- **Specify the desired length.** To avoid AI providing responses that are too long or too short, request a specific length. If you want a three-paragraph letter, tell it you want a three-paragraph letter. If you want something short, say you want a short answer. Don't expect the AI tool to know how long a response you want.

- **Specify the desired format.** You should also specify what type of output you want—letter, research paper, whatever. This helps guide AI to create the most appropriate response.

- **Specify the desired style or voice**. If you want an informal letter to friends, tell AI you want informal output. If you want something written in a specific genre or writing style, tell it. If you want content to use in a technical report, tell the AI tool that you want technical output. AI tools can output the same content a lot of different ways.

- **Use plain language.** Write your prompt in conversational language and avoid jargon-heavy language or phrases that only an industry insider would understand.

- **Ask direct questions**. If you want a specific answer, you need to ask a specific question. Don't make open-ended requests. You need to point AI in the right direction to properly address your query.

- **If you don't like what you get, try again**. You don't have to settle with the first response generated by an AI tool. Evaluate the response and then fine-tune your prompt to generate another, hopefully more accurate, response. (And keep going until you get the response you desire.)

The more detail you include, the better-tailored the response, so don't be afraid of writing long, detailed prompts.

Here are some examples of well-crafted AI prompts:

- How do I change the air filter in a 2020 Honda Civic? Please include the tools I will need and how long it will take.

- What is a good menu for dinner with six people, with no red meat? One person is allergic to eggs.

- Recommend five exercises I can do in the house. I am a 45-year-old woman with no health problems.

- What is the oldest state capitol in the United States?

- Create a one-page form letter for signing up for the neighborhood block party on August 8. Include spaces for the participant's name, address, and contact information.

- Recommend the five best things to do on a one-week trip to Paris in April. We will not have a car, we don't like museums, and we are on a budget.

- Generate a short story for a middle school audience about two friends first meeting at summer camp.

- Write a 500-word summary of *War and Peace* in simple terms so I can explain it to someone.

- What is the most soothing color to paint a newborn baby's room?

Remember, the more detailed your prompt, the better the response. For example, if you enter the prompt **how do birds fly?** into Meta AI, you get a very general response, like the one in Figure 3.42. If, on the other hand, you enter the prompt **how does a hummingbird fly?**, you get a more specific response, like the one in Figure 3.43.

---

○ Meta AI

Birds fly by using their wings to generate lift and thrust. Here's a simplified explanation of the main components and how they work together:

Wings:

- Shape: Curved on top and flat on the bottom
- Lift: As the bird moves forward, the air flows over and under the wing, creating an area of lower air pressure above the wing and higher air pressure below. This difference in pressure creates an upward force called lift, which raises the bird off the ground and keeps it flying.

Feathers:

- Shape and arrangement: Feathers are curved and overlapping, creating a smooth surface for air to flow over
- Lift and control: Feathers help to create lift and also aid in control and maneuverability

Flapping:

- Movement: Birds flap their wings up and down to create thrust
- Thrust: As the wing moves downward, it pushes air backward, creating a forward force called thrust

Control:

- Tail: Used for steering and balance
- Wing tips: Used for banking and turning

---

**FIGURE 3.42**

*A general answer to the general question, how do birds fly?*

○ **Meta AI**

Hummingbirds fly by using their unique physical attributes and flying techniques to generate incredible speed, agility, and maneuverability. Here's a detailed explanation of how a hummingbird flies:

**Wing Structure:**

- Extremely short, narrow wings (only 1-2 inches long)
- Wings are shaped like a crescent moon, with a curved upper surface and a flat lower surface
- Feathers are stiff and strong, with a smooth surface for airflow

**Flight Techniques:**

- **Flapping:** Hummingbirds flap their wings at an incredible rate of up to 80 times per second, generating a vortex of air above and below the wing.
- **Hovering:** Hummingbirds can hover in place, flapping their wings to generate lift and thrust.
- **Forward Flight:** Hummingbirds can fly forward at speeds of up to 30 miles per hour, using their wings to generate thrust.
- **Backward Flight:** Hummingbirds can even fly backward, using their wings to generate reverse thrust.

**Flying Characteristics:**

- **Speed:** Hummingbirds can reach speeds of up to 60 miles per hour in a dive.
- **Agility:** Hummingbirds are incredibly agile, making sharp turns and quick changes in direction.

**FIGURE 3.43**

*A more specific answer to the more specific question, how do hummingbirds fly?*

You can also fine-tune AI responses by including a specific length or style in your prompt. For example, I started out by prompting Google Gemini to write 200 words about bird migration. Just that, nothing more. The rather straightforward response is shown in Figure 3.44

Twice a year, the skies come alive with a feathered ballet – bird migration. Driven by an ancient instinct, birds embark on incredible journeys, some traveling thousands of miles between breeding and wintering grounds. These seasonal movements are all about survival.

In spring, with warmer temperatures and longer days, the northern hemisphere explodes with life. Insects hatch, buds unfurl, and food becomes abundant. This is the perfect time for birds to raise their young. So, flocks that spent the winter in warmer southern regions begin their northward trek.

But how do these tiny creatures navigate such vast distances? Birds possess a remarkable internal compass. They can use the position of the sun and stars, along with the Earth's magnetic field, to chart their course. Some species even rely on inherited knowledge, following the routes flown by their ancestors.

The journey is fraught with danger. Birds face fatigue, starvation, and predators. They rely on stopovers along the way, wetlands and oases that provide vital rest and refueling. Sadly, human activities like habitat destruction and light pollution disrupt

**FIGURE 3.44**

*All about bird migration, in a general style.*

Next, I asked Gemini to write about bird migration in the style of a standup comic, bad jokes and all. See that response in Figure 3.45.

"So, birds, right? These little feathered idiots decide to pull the biggest, most unnecessary commute in history. 'Hey, let's fly thousands of miles just to eat some bugs and then fly back.' I mean, have they tried Grubhub? It's faster.

And don't even get me started on their navigation system. It's like they're using a drunk pigeon as their GPS. 'Oh, look, a shiny thing! Let's go that way!' And then they crash into a window. Classic bird move.

I swear, some of these birds are just showoffs. Like the ones who do crazy aerial acrobatics. It's like they're auditioning for Cirque du Soleil or something. And then there's the early birds. I mean, who gets up at 4 AM to chirp? It's like they're trying to wake up the entire neighborhood for a bird-brained meeting."

**FIGURE 3.45**

*Writing about bird migration in the style of a standup comic.*

Not satisfied with that, I then asked Gemini to write 200 words about bird migration in the style of a hard-boiled detective novel. That response is shown in Figure 3.46.

"Listen, kid, birds are a tough racket. They're always on the move, these feathered hoods, flying off to some warmer clime like they own the place. It's a long con, see? They pretend to be all innocent, chirping away, but deep down, they're plotting their next heist.

I've seen 'em, these migratory birds. Tough customers. They fly in formations, like some kind of avian mob. And don't let those big eyes fool you. They're watching, always watching. You think you're alone out there, but they're up there, sizing you up.

I'm telling you, kid, it's a world full of mysteries. Why do they do it? What's the big payoff? Maybe it's treasure, maybe it's just a better seed supply. Either way, it's a long haul, and somebody's gotta be making a killing off it."

**FIGURE 3.46**

*Writing about bird migration in the style of a hardboiled detective novel.*

You get the point. AI can generate content in whatever form and style you ask for. All you have to do is ask for it, in as much detail as possible.

Generative AI can even do very odd juxtapositions of content and style. For example, when I asked Google Gemini to write about bird migration in iambic pentameter, I got the results shown in Figure 3.47. When I asked it to write a limerick about bird migration, it returned the results in Figure 3.48. AI does what you tell it to do, to the best of its abilities.

> The summer's golden hand begins to wane,
> And crisp autumnal airs across the land
> Do whisper tales of journeys yet to take.
> The feathered throng, with instincts for their sake,
> A restlessness within their bosoms know,
> A southward pull, where warmer breezes blow.
>
> The swallows gather on the swaying wire,
> Their wings alight with flickering desire.
> The geese, in V-formation sharp and bright,
> Honk out a chorus, calling through the night.
> A primal urge, a map within their mind,
> They navigate by starlight, leaving behind
>
> The fading fields, the woods in fiery dress,
> For balmy shores and lands of greater peace.
> Though predators may lurk and storms may rage,
> An unseen force compels them to engage

**FIGURE 3.47**

*All about bird migration in iambic pentameter.*

> With summer's warm sun getting dim,
> The geese honk a south-flying hymn.
> An instinct so grand,
> They cross sea and land,
> For warmth, bugs, and a place to swim in!

**FIGURE 3.48**

*Bird migration in a limerick.*

# Using AI-Generated Results—with Caution

As I explain in Chapter 2, "The Risks and Benefits of AI," AI results aren't always reliable. In fact, many of the AI tools warn you right up front that their results may be less than accurate. (Meta AI puts it like this: "Messages are generated by AI and may be inaccurate or inappropriate.")

Why are these tools not always reliable? There are a number of reasons, including

- The data used to train the AI engine might not be up to date. In other words, there is a cut-off date for what each AI knows.

- The training data might not include enough information about the topic you asked about.

- The AI tool might not understand what you asked it to do. (AI doesn't always understand context or all the subtleties of human language.)

In other words, AI can be just as inaccurate as a human being—which is why it is important to always verify results generated by AI tools.

To verify the accuracy of AI results, start by cross-checking the AI's results with other reliable sources. And by "reliable sources," I don't mean another AI engine, which could be using the same flawed training data. Instead, compare the AI's results with information from credible websites—or just use your search engine to search for the same information and check the sources to see if the results match.

In addition, you can ask the AI tool follow-up questions to clarify the response or seek additional information. If you're not clear what the results mean, ask the AI tool to explain further.

 **NOTE**   You may want to check the grammar, punctuation, and spelling in AI results before you use them elsewhere. Sometimes AI-generated results can sound stilted and lack the natural flow of human language. Look especially for repetitive content, use of similar sentence structures, and awkward phrasing.

Finally, also as noted in Chapter 2, you should not try to pass AI-generated content off as your own creation. That means you shouldn't submit an AI-generated poem to a literary journal or use AI-generated content to complete a schoolwork assignment. You can use AI-generated content for your own use but not much beyond that.

# HOW AI TOOLS USE YOUR INFORMATION

In Chapter 2, I discuss some of the privacy concerns with artificial intelligence, specifically where AI gets its training data and how it uses it. Not surprisingly, there are also privacy concerns with the prompts that users enter and the results generated by those prompts.

First, know that everything you enter into an AI tool—like everything else you do online—will be monitored, collected, and, in many cases, monetized. If you're not comfortable with AI companies using your inputs and responses in this fashion, then you shouldn't be using an AI tool. Companies utilize user information (prompts and follow-up replies) to help further train their AI models; it's one way that AI learns. When you sign up to use an AI tool, you're implicitly giving your permission for the company behind AI to use anything you enter to help them improve their models.

AI learns from the responses it provides to your queries and how you respond to those responses. If you give a particular response a thumbs up, the AI engine will know it did something right; if you give it a thumbs down, it will learn from its mistake. So your user interactions also become the property of the AI company.

This also means that any personal information you enter into an AI tool is likely collected and used by the company offering the tool. It's the same with the personal information you might write in a Facebook or Instagram post; whatever you enter, it's now in the company's possession.

AI companies, like social media companies (and they're often the same entities), might say that they "minimize" user data by keeping only that information they need to provide and improve their services. They also might say that they incorporate robust security measures to keep your data safe. But we all know that even the most secure companies can suffer data breaches and when was the last time you trusted a big company to do anything good with your personal data, anyway?

The point is this: The more personal your interactions with an AI tool, the more that AI knows about you and the more the company behind AI can use that information for its own purposes. Avoid sharing too much personal information about yourself or others, such as a Social Security number, bank account and credit card numbers, or any personal information that a hacker could use to guess your passwords. (So don't enter your pet's name or your children's birthdates.)

Above all, you need to stay vigilant and regularly monitor your personal information, bank accounts, credit reports, and the like for unusual activity. Treat your friendly neighborhood AI tool the same way you'd treat any website or online service and provide only the minimal amount of information necessary to do what you need to do.

# Summary

This chapter covered all-purpose AI tools, also known as AI generators—what they are, how they work, and how to use them. This chapter also showed you how to create great prompts for generating the results you want. You learned how to make your prompts more detailed by describing the type, length, and style of output you want. You learned how changing just a few words in a prompt can generate wildly different results.

Finally, this chapter showed you how to verify the results generated by AI tools. AI, like the human-supplied information used to train it, isn't perfect—which means the results it generates, no matter how impressive, need to be double-checked and verified.

## IN THIS CHAPTER

- When and how you should (and shouldn't) use AI for writing
- Using AI for different types of writing
- Using AI to improve your writing
- Examining popular AI tools for writing and editing

4

# USING AI TO FIND THE RIGHT WORDS

As you learned in Chapter 3, "Getting Started with All-Purpose AI Tools," generative AI tools like ChatGPT, Google Gemini, Meta AI, and Microsoft Copilot can write all sorts of content for you, from short and simple texts, social media posts, letters, and blog posts to long and complex articles and research papers. AI can also help with creative writing: nonfiction, fiction, scripts, and poetry.

Even if you don't want AI to do all your writing for you, AI can help make you a better writer. We'll talk about some of the ways in this chapter. And we'll cover some of the cautions to watch out for.

# When and How You Should (and Shouldn't) Use AI for Writing

Before we get started, let's consider when and how to use AI for writing. Just because you can use AI for writing doesn't mean you always should. It's one thing to use AI to help you generate ideas, write notes to your friends, or even create form thank-you letters. Those uses are all fine. It's something else to have AI generate a research paper or novel that you then claim as your own. There are ethical and transparency issues to address.

First, using AI to write personal notes, letters, and social media posts is perfectly acceptable, and lots of people do it. We all have to do various types of casual writing, and AI can help you find the right words for what you want to say. For these types of everyday writing tasks, AI can help level the field.

In addition, AI is quite useful for what you do before and after you write a piece. Beforehand, AI is great for generating ideas for things you need to write, which you can then elaborate on as you write the final version. In other words, AI is good for generating first drafts, which you can then fine-tune.

AI is also good for editing your writing after the fact to make you sound better. And it can rewrite or rephrase content for a different reading level—taking a technical piece and rewriting it to an eighth-grade level, for example, or beefing up a simple piece for a more technical audience.

That said, you shouldn't use AI for certain writing assignments. For example, using AI to write papers for school without a teacher's consent is cheating. Teachers want to know how well you've learned the lesson at hand, and having AI do your work for you doesn't make that possible.

Equally important, when you're writing professionally, you shouldn't claim AI-written material as your own. Let's say you have AI write a short story or article for a community newsletter. For transparency's sake, you need to disclose that the piece was AI generated; otherwise, you're claiming credit for something that you didn't write. Crafting an AI prompt isn't writing.

Similarly, you can't claim copyright protection for AI-generated material because you didn't write it.

You also have to be careful about AI using copyrighted material in its responses. Some of the content used to train AI tools is copyrighted and some people—including some copyright owners—consider AI's use of that material a copyright violation, akin to theft. If AI uses someone else's words exactly, and you use that, you could be subject to a copyright claim by that party.

Bottom line: Using AI to draft a personal note, generate ideas, or improve your writing is perfectly acceptable, and lots of people are doing it. AI can be a wonderful writing aid, especially for people who aren't professional writers by trade. It's a good use of the technology and perfectly legal, ethical, and acceptable.

Using AI to do more formal or official writing is something else altogether. If you're writing something for which you would otherwise claim credit—a novel, a research paper, even a newspaper article—then you shouldn't have AI do the work for you.

## WILL AI REPLACE REAL WRITERS?

While AI is a valuable tool for anyone writing casually, what it can't do, at least in my personal opinion, is replace professional writers. (Like me!)

As a professional writer I may have a vested interest in this, but I have yet to see an AI tool that can write as well as a pro. An AI tool just doesn't have the insight, the experience, and the personality of a human writer. I can always tell the difference.

So, in my humble opinion, if you want the best quality writing for professional purposes, enlist a professional human writer. As good as AI currently is and probably will become, it will never have the heart and soul that a skilled human writer brings to the table.

(Just to be clear, I wrote that myself, with no help from AI whatsoever.)

# Using AI for Different Types of Writing

Any all-purpose AI tool can generate social media posts, texts, email messages, letters, and other forms of communication. As with all things AI, of course, the better your prompt, the more relevant and accurate results you'll receive. That is especially true when it comes to writing. You need to be very precise as to what you want written and how.

Let's look at some examples.

 **NOTE**   Learn more about all-purpose AI tools like ChatGPT, Google Gemini, Meta AI, and Microsoft Copilot in Chapter 3.

## Writing a Short Note to Family or Friends

AI can create personal messages that sound like you wrote them yourself, perfect for sending to your friends and family that you either don't have the time or the talent to write yourself.

For example, if you want to let your mother know that you're coming home for Thanksgiving (and bringing your significant other with you), you might enter the following prompt:

**Create an email message to my mother letting her know that I'll be coming home for Thanksgiving and bringing my new girlfriend, Jane. We'll arrive the day before and stay through Sunday.**

ChatGPT's very personal email message is shown in Figure 4.1.

> Dear Mom,
>
> I hope this email finds you well. I have some wonderful news to share with you regarding our Thanksgiving plans this year!
>
> Jane and I have decided to come home for Thanksgiving, and we couldn't be more excited to spend the holiday with you and the rest of the family. We've been looking forward to this for a while now, and we're thrilled to be able to celebrate together.
>
> We'll be arriving the day before Thanksgiving and staying through Sunday, giving us plenty of time to catch up, enjoy some delicious food, and create new memories together. Jane is really looking forward to meeting everyone and experiencing our family traditions.
>
> I'll be in touch closer to the date to coordinate any details and let you know if there's anything we can help with. In the meantime, please let us know if there's anything you'd like us to bring or if there are any special plans for the holiday that we should know about.
>
> Thank you for always being so welcoming and loving. We can't wait to see you and spend time together as a family.
>
> ↓
>
> Sending lots of love.

**FIGURE 4.1**

*An email informing your mother of Thanksgiving plans, courtesy of ChatGPT.*

**NOTE** Some people consider using AI to write personal notes and letters to be somewhat impersonal and insincere. Personal messages, many people believe, should be personal—not generated by machine. Use your own best judgment in this regard.

## Writing a Longer Letter to Family and Friends

You can also use AI to write longer emails, letters, and other casual communications. For example, you can let your friends know what you've been up to recently in an AI-generated letter. Just throw some recent activities into a prompt, like this:

**Write a two-page letter to my friends catching up on what I've done this summer. I've gone surfing at Pacific Beach, hiking near Estes Park, took a two-week road trip through Northern California with my friend Eleanor, and spent the rest of the time studying for law school admission tests.**

Your very personal letter, ready to cut and paste into a Word document, is shown in Figure 4.2. Google Gemini did a pretty good job with this one.

 Dearest Friends,

As summer fades into fall, I find myself drowning in a sea of textbooks, finally catching my breath and realizing – wow, what a summer it's been! This letter is a long overdue catch-up session, a chance to tell you all about the wild adventures and studious pursuits that have filled these past few months.

First up, the California coast! Remember how we always talked about learning to surf? Well, I finally took the plunge (literally!) and spent a week in Pacific Beach taking lessons. Let me tell you, battling those waves is no easy feat! I spent more time underwater than on top of the board, but the feeling of catching a wave, even for a moment, was exhilarating. The California sunshine and the laid-back vibe of the beach town were incredible too.

Next, I traded sand for stunning mountain scenery with a trip to Estes Park in Colorado. Hiking through Rocky Mountain National Park was breathtaking. The crisp air, the towering pines, and the crystal-clear lakes felt like something out of a painting. One afternoon, I even spotted a group of elk grazing in a meadow – a truly magical experience.

**FIGURE 4.2**

*A "personal" letter from Google Gemini getting your friends caught up on your summer activities.*

You get the point. When you don't know what to write or don't want to write, use AI to help get started.

## Writing an Email Message

Email messages are typically short and to the point. When prompting AI to write an email message, include the subject of the email and a brief description of what you want written. You should also tell the AI tool about how long the email should be and the desired tone.

For example, to write an email inviting your neighbors to a cookout, you might use the following prompt:

**Draft an email inviting my friends to a cookout on June 15th at my house. Ask them to bring sides or desserts.**

Figure 4.3 shows the resulting message from Google Gemini that you can cut and paste into an email.

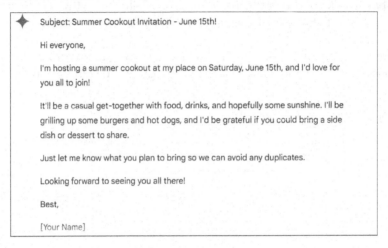

Subject: Summer Cookout Invitation - June 15th!

Hi everyone,

I'm hosting a summer cookout at my place on Saturday, June 15th, and I'd love for you all to join!

It'll be a casual get-together with food, drinks, and hopefully some sunshine. I'll be grilling up some burgers and hot dogs, and I'd be grateful if you could bring a side dish or dessert to share.

Just let me know what you plan to bring so we can avoid any duplicates.

Looking forward to seeing you all there!

Best,

[Your Name]

**FIGURE 4.3**

*An email invitation drafted by Google Gemini.*

## Writing a Thank-You Note

To have AI write a thank-you note, it has to know who you're thanking and what you're thanking them for. It will do the rest.

For example, you might craft a prompt like the following:

**Write a thank-you note to my Aunt Judy for the sweater she gave me for my birthday.**

Figure 4.4 shows the thank-you note that ChatGPT wrote in response.

Dear Aunt Judy,

I hope this note finds you well! I wanted to take a moment to express my heartfelt gratitude for the beautiful sweater you gave me for my birthday. It was such a delightful surprise, and I've been wearing it non-stop since I received it.

The color is absolutely perfect, and the knit is so cozy and soft. Every time I put it on I'm reminded of your thoughtfulness and love. It's not just a sweater; it's a warm hug from you whenever I wear it.

Thank you for always knowing exactly what to give to bring joy into my life. Your presence and your presents make every occasion brighter and more special. I'm incredibly fortunate to have you as my aunt, and I cherish our bond more than words can express.

Sending you lots of love and gratitude,

[Your Name]

**FIGURE 4.4**

*A thank-you note written by ChatGPT.*

## Writing a Business Letter

Business letters are by nature more formal than personal notes or letters. You need to tell AI who you're writing to, what the letter is about, and whether the style should be casual or formal business. For example, you might use a prompt like the following:

> **Write a formal business letter to Don in accounting asking him to prepare an analysis of this year's sales vs. last year's sales across all territories. Ask him to get it done by the end of the week.**

When thus prompted, Microsoft Copilot wrote the surprisingly detailed letter shown in Figure 4.5.

---

Subject: Request for Sales Analysis

Dear Don,

I hope this email finds you well. As we approach the end of the fiscal year, I would like to request your assistance in preparing an analysis of this year's sales compared to last year's across all territories.

Specifically, I am interested in the following key metrics:

1. Total revenue for each territory.
2. Year-over-year growth or decline in sales.
3. Any significant trends or patterns.

Could you please compile this information and provide a detailed report by the end of the week? Your prompt attention to this matter is greatly appreciated.

Thank you for your cooperation, and I look forward to reviewing the analysis.

---

**FIGURE 4.5**

*A formal business letter written by Microsoft Copilot.*

## Writing a Social Media Post

In contrast to business writing, writing for social media is much less formal. To have AI write a social media post for you, you need to tell it which social network the post is for and what you're writing about. For example, here's a prompt for a post on Facebook:

**Write a short post for Facebook about our new golden retriever, Buster.**

Figure 4.6 shows the post that MetaAI created. It even added hashtags to go along with the message.

---

⭕ **Meta AI**
Here's a short post for Facebook:

"Meet Buster, the newest member of our family! This adorable golden retriever has already stolen our hearts with his playful paws and snuggly snout. We can't wait to watch him grow and make memories together! #BusterTheGolden #NewAddition #DogLover #Family"

---

**FIGURE 4.6**

*A Facebook post written by MetaAI.*

## Writing a Memoir

Many people would like to tell the story of their lives, or the lives of a dear relative or friend. This is a bit of a challenge for AI in that the AI engine probably doesn't know that much about your life or the life of the other person. You'll need to feed the AI tool lots of detailed information about your life—what you've done, where you were, when things happened, and with whom you did them.

 **WARNING**  Remember, all information you feed into an AI prompt is entered into the AI database for further training and use. Be careful about what personal information you share with an AI tool. And no matter how inspirational and exciting, when you show others the output, you'll want a disclaimer that the content is generated by AI.

Because your life is probably longer than a simple prompt, you may want to write your memoir in stages. Enter as much information as you can about a particular time or event, have AI write it up for you, and then move on to the next major event in your memoir.

For example, you might craft a detailed prompt like the following:

> **Write the story of how I met my future husband when we were both attending a Lynard Skynyrd concert in Long Beach and we bumped into each other at the merch table. We both wanted to buy the same t-shirt, so we started talking, and he ended up driving me home afterward.**

Figure 4.7 shows how ChatGPT interpreted that story. Makes you wonder how close it got to what really happened back then.

In the summer of 2023, under the electric buzz of Long Beach's salty air, fate wove its intricate threads as I found myself immersed in the timeless melodies of a Lynyrd Skynyrd concert. The stage was alive with energy, the crowd pulsating with every chord strummed. Little did I know, amidst the sea of faces, I was about to encounter the love of my life.

As the final chords of "Sweet Home Alabama" reverberated through the venue, I made my way to the merchandise table to commemorate the unforgettable evening with a concert tee. However, destiny had other plans as I reached for the last shirt only to find another hand grasping it simultaneously. Our eyes met, and in that moment, a spark ignited.

There he stood, with a crooked smile and eyes that sparkled like stars against the backdrop of the night sky. "Looks like we have the same taste in shirts," he remarked, breaking the tension with a charming grin. And so, our conversation began, flowing effortlessly as if we had known each other for a lifetime.

Amidst discussions of favorite songs and shared musical memories, it became clear that this chance encounter was anything but happenstance. As the concert drew to a close, he extended an invitation to join him for a post-show coffee, an offer I couldn't resist.

**FIGURE 4.7**

*A personal memoir recollected by ChatGPT.*

## Writing a Short Story

AI is surprisingly creative and can write some inventive fiction. Tell it you want it to write a short story, give it a brief plot, maybe even the names of characters and locations, and then let it rip.

Here's a sample prompt for a short story you can have AI write for a child or grandchild:

> **Write a short story for a young girl named Raven about how she finds a whale trapped in a fishing net and how she rescues the whale so it can return to its family in the ocean.**

As you can see in Figure 4.8, Google Gemini handled this task with aplomb—and quite a bit of imagination.

Raven, with hair as black and shiny as a crow's wing, loved exploring the rocky coastline near her house. One crisp morning, the salty spray tickled her nose as she scrambled down the familiar path. But today, something was different. A loud, mournful cry echoed across the waves.

Rounding a bend, Raven gasped. Half-submerged in the shallows, a giant creature writhed in distress. It was a whale, easily the biggest animal she'd ever seen, its sleek body tangled in a monstrous fishing net. The net, thick with ropes and bobbing with plastic floats, held the whale captive, its powerful blows unable to break free.

Panic threatened to engulf Raven, but she took a deep breath. Her dad had always said, "The ocean needs brave hearts, Raven." So, brave she would be. She raced back home, her heart pounding like a drum solo.

In the shed, she found her dad's toolbox. She grabbed a pair of sturdy metal shears and a tattered red life jacket. Back at the beach, the whale continued its heartbreaking cries. Raven knew she couldn't reach the net from the shore. With a determined glint in her eye, she grabbed a discarded surfboard, a relic from a

**FIGURE 4.8**

*The start of a short story conceived by Google Gemini.*

## Writing a Poem

Let's tackle one final writing task—writing poetry, for your own or a loved one's enjoyment. (Again, you wouldn't want to present an AI-generated poem to a poetry journal or other public venue.) You can simply ask an AI tool to write a poem about a given subject. You can provide more or less detail about the subject or the desired length of the poem. You can even ask AI to write in the style of a specific poem or poet.

For example, consider this prompt:

**Write a short poem about the sound of thunder on a summer night in the style of Edgar Allen Poe**

Figure 4.9 shows what MetaAI wrote. It is indeed very Poe-like.

Meta AI
Here's a short poem in the style of Edgar Allan Poe:

"The summer night, a sultry shroud
Wraps darkness 'round, a heavy cloud
The thunder growls, a low, sweet sound
Like distant drums, a mournful round

The wind stirs not, the trees stand still
As if they held their breath, a chill
The thunder booms, a crashing knell
A summer storm, a darkness to tell

The night air trembles with the sound
As if the heavens themselves were wound
In some dark mystery, some secret pain
That only thunder knows, and summer rain"

**FIGURE 4.9**

*A poem like Poe might write about summer thunder, written by MetaAI.*

**NOTE**  A handful of AI tools are specifically geared toward writing poetry. These tools include AI Poem Generator (https://poemanalysis.com), AI Poem Writer (www.poemanalysis.com/poem-generator/), and Hypotenuse AI Poem Generator (www.hypotenuse.ai)

# Using AI to Improve Your Writing

AI can be a useful tool for improving your writing. Think of AI as being a really thorough and fast editor or (depending on how involved it is) a diligent researcher. AI can take one look at a piece of writing and perform a variety of useful tasks, as detailed in the following sections.

**NOTE**  You can also find specific AI tools to detect plagiarism, translate text from one language to another, and summarize your text. AI is also good for putting text into the proper style—for example, adding abstracts, citations, and the like to scientific or scholarly papers.

## Using AI to Suggest Topics

Maybe you have an assignment to write a paper for a class or an article for work and you can't decide on a good topic. Maybe you've been staring at a blank screen or sheet of paper for hours and just don't know how to get started. AI can be quite useful when you're just starting out on a piece.

Any all-purpose AI generator, like the ones discussed in Chapter 3, can function as an idea generator. There are also several AI-powered topic generators available, including these:

- **Ahrefs Content Idea Generator** is a free tool found at https://ahrefs.com/writing-tools/blog-post-ideas that lets you input your niche or target audience and then generates content ideas for selected output formats (articles, blog posts, research papers, video scripts, and so on)

- **CopyAI Idea Generator** (www.copy.ai/tools/content-idea-generator), a free tool from CopyAI that lets you select a niche or topic and then generate story ideas

- **HubSpot Blog Ideas Generator** (www.hubspot.com/blog-topic-generator), a free AI-powered tool that helps you generate titles and ideas for blog posts

Whether you're using an all-purpose AI tool or a more targeted idea generator, here are some tips to help you and AI brainstorm topic ideas:

- **Ask for ideas.** To get an AI tool to generate ideas, you have to ask it to generate ideas. Try a prompt like **Generate 5 ideas for articles about road safety.**

- **Provide seed information.** Tell the AI tool about your target audience, niche, output format (article, blog post, and so on), and anything else that can help guide AI to generate useful content ideas. For example, you might construct a prompt like **I need ideas for an article about car repair for people on a budget.**

- **Focus on current trends.** When asking AI to generate topic ideas, ask it for topics associated with related industry or societal trends. It may be as simple as prompting **Generate 3 article ideas for what's new in home security.**

- **Focus on audience questions.** The better you know your target audience, the better AI can target appropriate topic ideas. Find out what your audience is talking or asking questions about and provide that information to the AI tool to suggest related topics.

Provide the right input, and you'll get a list of suggestions like the one in Figure 4.10, from ChatGPT.

Certainly! Here are five blog post ideas about road safety:

1. **"10 Must-Know Tips for Safe Driving in Bad Weather"**: This post could cover essential safety precautions and driving techniques for handling various weather conditions such as rain, snow, fog, or ice. It could include tips on adjusting driving speed, maintaining proper distance, and using headlights effectively.

2. **"The Impact of Distracted Driving: Statistics and Solutions"**: This post could explore the dangers of distracted driving, including texting, talking on the phone, eating, or adjusting the radio while driving. It could provide statistics on accidents caused by distracted driving and offer practical solutions and tools to prevent it.

3. **"Understanding the Risks of Speeding: Why Slowing Down Saves Lives"**: This post could delve into the risks associated with speeding, including increased stopping distance, reduced reaction time, and heightened severity of accidents. It could provide real-life examples, statistics, and persuasive arguments to encourage readers to obey speed limits.

4. **"Protecting Vulnerable Road Users: Tips for Sharing the Road Safely"**: This post could focus on promoting awareness and empathy towards vulnerable road users such as pedestrians, cyclists, and motorcyclists. It could offer tips for d ↓ ⸱rs on how to safely share the road, including giving

**FIGURE 4.10**

*Using ChatGPT to generate topic ideas.*

 **NOTE**   For the best ideas, don't rely on AI alone. Combine AI with your own brainstorming to generate even more ideas and filter them to a relevant list.

# Using AI to Outline Content

You might have an idea for a piece but have difficulty organizing your thoughts. What should you write first, what do you absolutely need to include, what can you leave out?

The best way to organize your thoughts is to draft an outline. This is something at which AI excels.

As with idea generation, all-purpose AI tools are pretty good at creating outlines based on topic ideas. There are also several AI-powered outline generators, including

- **Akkio AI Outline Generator** (www.akkio.com/tool/ai-outline-generator), a free tool for crafting structured outlines for different types of projects

- **GravityWrite Blog Outline Generator** (https://gravitywrite.com), a free tool for creating outlines for blog posts

- **Hypotenuse AI Outline Generator** (www.hypotenuse.ai/outline-generator), another free tool that lets you enter your text to generate an outline

To generate an outline, you have to (1) ask AI to create an outline and (2) give it the broad specs of what the piece is about. For example, you might enter a prompt like the following: **Create an outline for an article about pickleball.** The AI tool should return a fairly detailed outline like the one in Figure 4.11, from Google Gemini.

**Pickleball: A Fun and Accessible Paddle Sport for All Ages**

**I. Introduction**

- Briefly introduce pickleball as a paddle sport combining elements of tennis, badminton, and ping pong.
- Highlight its growing popularity and accessibility for all ages and skill levels.

**II. The Basics of Pickleball**

- A. Equipment:
  - Pickleball paddles
  - Pickleball (a perforated plastic ball)
  - Court dimensions and markings
- B. Gameplay:
  - Singles vs. doubles play
  - Serving rules (including the "double bounce" rule)
  - Scoring system (winning by 2 points)
  - Basic game flow (serving, returning, volleying)

**FIGURE 4.11**

*Using Google Gemini to create an outline for a pickleball article.*

# Using AI to Write—and Rewrite—Content

I already talked about using all-purpose AI tools to create content in various styles and formats. There are also AI tools dedicated to writing and rewriting text in a variety of styles.

The key to using any AI tool to create written content is to be very specific in the prompts you use. You have to tell AI what you want to write about, what kind of content you want (a letter, a social media post, a research report, and so on), how long you want the output to be, and—if you want to get really particular—the reading level of the generated content. With the right input, just about any AI tool, including those listed here and the all-purpose tools discussed in Chapter 3, can output written content appropriate to your needs.

**NOTE**  Turn to Chapter 3 to learn more about using all-purpose generative AI tools—including ChatGPT, Claude, Google Gemini, Meta AI, Microsoft Copilot, Perplexity, Pi, and Poe—as writing assistants.

Some of today's most popular AI-powered writing tools include the following:

- **HyperWrite** (www.hyperwriteai.com), a suite of writing tools that includes AutoWrite, Magic Editor, Outline Generator, and Summarizer; the basic version (with limited usage credits) is free, and the Premium version (with more credits and a more advanced AI model) runs $19.99 per month.

- **Sudowrite** (www.sudowrite.com), an AI tool specifically for fiction writing; the company offers a free trial and paid versions starting at $10 per month.

## Using AI to Edit Content

Even professional writers like me need editors. A human editor proofreads a piece for punctuation, spelling, and grammar and edits for clarity, conciseness, style, and accuracy.

Don't tell my human editors this, but AI tools available today can do just about everything that human editors do. These tools let you upload a file (typically in Word or PDF format), analyze that document, and then return it to you marked up with all sorts of useful suggestions you can accept or ignore.

 **NOTE**  These dedicated grammar-and-editing tools offer more specific analyses and recommendations than all-purpose AI tools. I've found they're more effective and easier to use for that purpose.

Some of the most popular AI-powered editing tools today include

- **Grammarly** (www.grammarly.com) is a tool for editing and proofreading documents. Today's Grammarly uses AI technology to identify problems in a piece and suggest changes. It checks for correct spelling and punctuation, clarity, passive voice, reading level, and more. Grammarly offers a basic free version and a more powerful Premium version that flags more types of errors for $12 per month.

- **Hemingway Editor** (https://hemingwayapp.com), like Grammarly, analyzes writing, proofreads copy, and suggests changes. To take advantage of Hemingway's AI-powered capabilities, subscribe to Hemingway Editor Plus, which starts at $10 per month.

- **ProWritingAid** (https://prowritingaid.com) fixes common grammar and punctuation mistakes, eliminates weak words, and makes your writing more clear and powerful. The limited-use basic version is free; the Premium version ($12 per month) removes all usage limits.

- **QuillBot** (https://quillbot.com) is an AI-powered paraphrasing tool. Type or paste a block of text and QuillBot rewrites it for you. You can choose from various modes, including Natural, Format, Academic, Simple, Creative, and Shorten. The basic version, with various limitations on use, is free. The Premium version, for $8.33 per month, removes all limitations.

- **Wordtune** (www.wordtune.com) is an AI-based writing and editing tool that can create new content from scratch, provide suggestions, rewrite words and long passages, and summarize documents. Wordtune's basic version is free but has usage limits; the Advanced version ($6.99 per month) lets you do more; and the Unlimited version ($9.99 per month) removes all limits.

 **WARNING** AI-powered editing tools are far from perfect, if only because our language is far from perfect. You might find an AI editor suggesting changes that make your text more difficult to read or obscure the point you're trying to make. View the suggestions from an AI editing tool as just that, suggestions, and then rely on your own writing skills to use or ignore the suggestions as you deem fit.

# Examining Popular AI Tools for Writing and Editing

Now that you know what's out there, it's time to take a closer look at how some of the more popular AI writing and editing tools work.

## Grammarly

Grammarly (www.grammarly.com) is a popular tool, now enhanced with AI technology, for improving the grammar in written works. Grammarly lets you paste text directly into its editor or upload complete files for editing. To get started, click the **New** tile on the home page, shown in Figure 4.12.

**FIGURE 4.12**

*Grammarly's home page.*

Figure 4.13 shows the results of an editing session with Grammarly's free plan. (The Premium version would make even more suggestions.) The original article (from my Classic Song of the Day blog) is shown on the left, with suggestions in the middle column. Click a suggestion to highlight in the document; if you agree, click **Accept** to have Grammarly make that change for you.

**FIGURE 4.13**

*The results of a Grammarly editing session.*

When you click the **Generative AI** button in the right column you get even more options. You can choose to improve your text, identify any gaps, or generate more ideas. If you click the **Set Voice** button, Grammarly lets you choose a level of formality and tone, as shown in Figure 4.14, and then makes the appropriate stylistic suggestions.

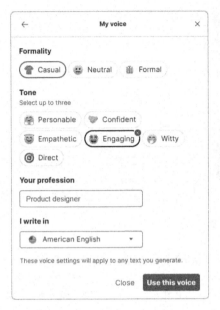

**FIGURE 4.14**

*Choosing the formality level and tone for a document.*

## Hemingway Editor

Hemingway Editor (https://hemingwayapp.com) is a grammar and style checker similar to Grammarly. You can type your text directly into the home page (shown in Figure 4.15), paste text you've copied from elsewhere, or click the **File** link at the top of the page to upload a Word or HTML file for editing.

As you can see in Figure 4.16, the Hemingway Editor is a tad more aggressive in its suggestions than Grammarly. It highlights different types of missteps and suggestions in different colors; adverbs are in blue, passive voice in lime green, too-complex phrases in purple, and so forth.

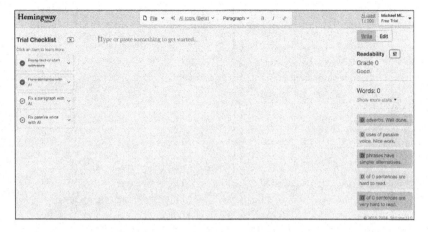

**FIGURE 4.15**

*The Hemingway Editor's home page.*

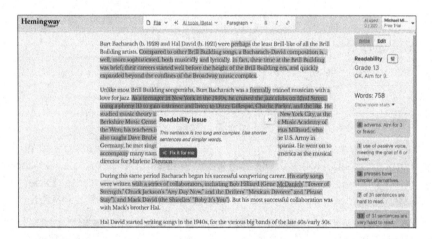

**FIGURE 4.16**

*A document analyzed and marked up by the Hemingway Editor.*

Click a given suggestion to view more details; if you want Hemingway to fix it, click the **Fix It For Me** button. You're then presented with the suggested change, as shown in Figure 4.17. (In this example, it wants to lower the reading level of this passage; it thinks I write too fancy.) To accept the suggestion, click the **Use Suggestion** button.

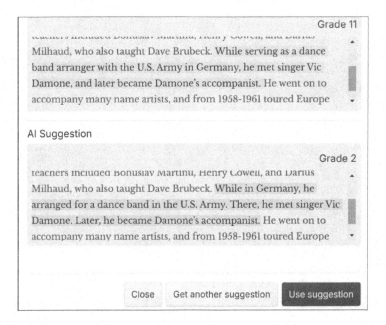

**FIGURE 4.17**

*Viewing a suggested change and letting Hemingway fix it for you.*

## HyperWrite

HyperWrite (www.hyperwriteai.com) is a suite of text generating and editing tools. As you can see in Figure 4.18, the HyperWrite's home page lets you choose from a variety of tools, including Rewrite Content, Flexible AutoWrite, Expert Writing Assistant, Text Summarizer, and more. Click a tile to start using that tool.

**FIGURE 4.18**

*The many tools of HyperWrite.*

For example, Figure 4.19 shows the result of HyperWrite's Rewrite Content tool. You paste a bit of content (a sentence, a paragraph, maybe more), tell it how you want it rewritten (simpler, more engaging, and so on), and HyperWrite rewrites it for you.

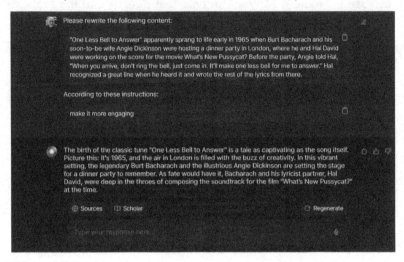

**FIGURE 4.19**

*A passage rewritten by HyperWrite to be more engaging.*

HyperWrite's Text Summarizer, shown in Figure 4.20, does just that: It summarizes a piece of text. Paste a text passage or link to a page on the web and HyperWrite produces a concise summary of the text in question.

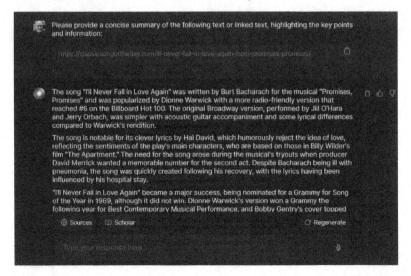

**FIGURE 4.20**

*A HyperWrite summary of a web article.*

# ProWritingAid

ProWritingAid (www.prowritingaid.com) is a full-featured editing/writing aid. As you can see in Figure 4.21, you can type text directly into the tool, paste text from another application, or upload a complete document.

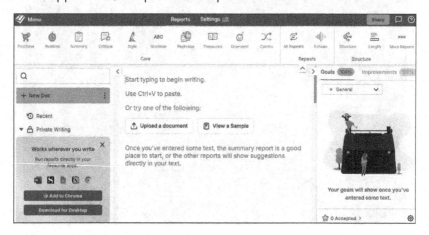

**FIGURE 4.21**

*ProWritingAid's home page.*

Figure 4.22 shows what ProWritingAid's initial analysis looks like. The right column scores your text in various categories, such as grammar/spelling, style, sentence length, readability, and the like. Click a category header to view a more detailed report of that type.

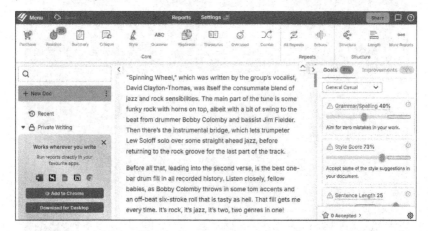

**FIGURE 4.22**

*ProWritingAid's initial analysis.*

As you can see in Figure 4.23, errors and suggestions are underlined in the text and detailed in the left column. Hover over a highlight to see ProWritingAid's suggestions, and then click the suggested change to make it or click **Ignore** to ignore it.

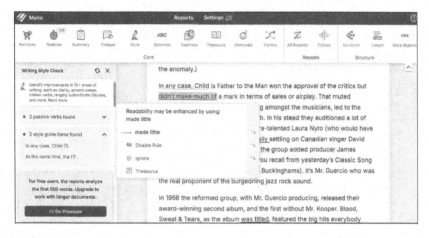

**FIGURE 4.23**

*Accepting or ignoring ProWritingAid's suggestions.*

# QuillBot

QuillBot (https://quillbot.com) is an AI tool that paraphrases existing text. This is useful when your writing is in a bit of a rut and you need to shake things up. It's also useful if you're taking content from elsewhere and don't want to plagiarize it; QuillBot can rewrite it just enough to make it an inexact copy.

QuillBot is also useful for rewriting an existing piece in a different style. You can choose from a number of different styles for your rewrite, from natural to academic to creative.

 **NOTE**  Some styles are available only if you subscribe to QuillBot's Premium plan.

In addition, you can use the **Synonyms** control to determine whether you want QuillBot to make more or fewer changes. Note, however, that the more you change the original text, the less accurate the rewrite will be.

 **NOTE**  QuillBot can also translate text from English to more than a dozen languages including French, Spanish, and German.

Figure 4.24 shows QuillBot's home page. You can either type in the text you want to rewrite, paste it from another application, or click the **Upload Doc** icon to upload an existing document file. Select the style for your rewrite and then click the **Paraphrase** button.

**FIGURE 4.24**

*Getting ready to paste or upload the original text into QuillBot.*

As you can see in Figure 4.25, QuillBot displays the original text in the left-hand pane and the rewrite on the right. You can hover over any underlined text to rephrase it again. Click the **Export** (down arrow) button to save the rewritten text as a Word document or click **Copy Full Text** to copy the rewrite into another document or app.

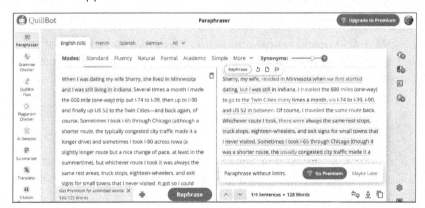

**FIGURE 4.25**

*The original text on the left and QuillBot's rewritten text on the right.*

## Sudowrite

Sudowrite (www.sudowrite.com) is a set of useful tools for fiction writers. You can use Sudowrite to do everything from generating story ideas to rephrasing existing text to writing the whole story for you.

Figure 4.26 shows Sudowrite's main writing screen. From here you can do several things:

- **Write:** Continue writing an existing work

- **Rewrite:** Rewrite an existing sentence, paragraph, or longer passage

- **Describe:** Enter a word or phrase to generate suggestions

- **Brainstorm:** Have Sudowrite suggest character names, descriptive details, dialog, and even plot points

- **Plugins:** Other writing tools, including First Draft, Shrink Ray, Twist, Characters, Poem, Visualize, and Feedback

**FIGURE 4.26**

*Examining Sudowrite's fiction writing tools.*

The Write tool is one many fiction writers will find useful. It works by adding onto text you've already started. It analyzes your existing text and continues the story or other work from there. You can see some typical results in Figure 4.27.

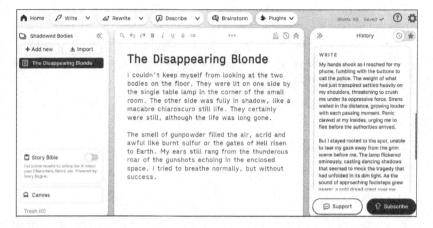

**FIGURE 4.27**

*Writing new fiction with Sudowrite; the original text is in the middle, and the continuation is on the right.*

## Wordtune

The last AI writing tool I want to talk about is Wordtune (www.wordtune.com), which includes several individual tools, including Rewrite, Read and Summarize, and Grammar Checker. As you can see in Figure 4.28, you can directly enter text by typing, paste text from another app, or upload document files.

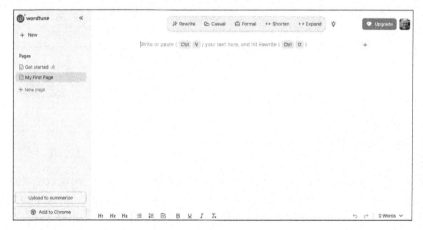

**FIGURE 4.28**

*Getting ready to enter, paste, or upload text into Wordtune.*

To rewrite a sentence, click within that sentence and then select one of the options from the top of the screen: Rewrite, Casual, Formal, Shorten, or Expand. Wordtune displays a list of options as shown in Figure 4.29; click to select the replacement phrase you like best.

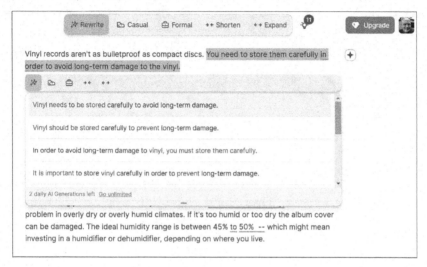

**FIGURE 4.29**

*Rewriting a document, one sentence at a time.*

Wordtune can also summarize files you upload. Figure 4.30 shows one such summary; the original text is on the right and a bulleted summary of key points is on the left.

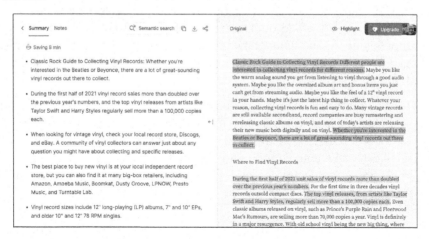

**FIGURE 4.30**

*How Wordtune summarizes a document.*

## USING AI DICTATION AND TRANSCRIPTION TOOLS

Artificial intelligence does a good job understanding the spoken word and transcribing it into text files. If you're more comfortable speaking than writing, you can use an AI dictation tool to transcribe your words into a Word document.

Some of the most popular AI dictation tools today include

- AudioPen (https://audiopen.ai)
- Fireflies.ai (https://fireflies.ai)
- Otter.ai (https://otter.ai)
- SpeakAI (https://speakai.co)

Many of these tools are targeted at a business audience that needs to transcribe and summarize meetings. While some AI, such as Fireflies.ai, have free or low-cost plans for individuals, others focus on higher-priced business plans. (Learn more about business transcription services in Chapter 9, "Using AI at Work.")

# Summary

This chapter was all about using AI to help you find the right words and write easier and better. That means writing both casually (emails, notes, and social media posts) and formally (business letters, official correspondence, and so on).

You learned when you should and when you shouldn't use AI for writing—and how to make it transparent when you do use it. You discovered a bevy of AI tools for generating ideas, crafting outlines, writing and rewriting text, and editing grammar, punctuation, and writing style. And you learned the best ways to prompt an AI tool to write specific items, such as texts and emails, letters, personal memoirs, and poems.

Here's the bottom line: You don't have to be a pro to use AI writing and editing tools. In fact, AI is at its best when it helps regular people write regular things. If you think you can't write at all, AI can do it for you. And if you can write just a little, AI can make your writing read better. It's a boon for casual writers. But don't claim AI-generated writing as your own. The words are taken from a database and could very well be someone else's.

5

# USING AI TO FIND INFORMATION

Generative AI isn't just for creating content. You can also use generative AI tools to find specific information and even conduct research for you, from finding great summer vacations to determining which car is best for your family to conducting an in-depth study of 17th-century architecture. It's kind of like a web search engine, except (in many cases) better.

When comparing traditional web search with AI, the best analogy is when you're looking for information at your local library. Web search is like flipping through the card catalog that points you to individual books for you to read. AI is like having the librarian read the books for you and summarize what they say. But, as with all things AI, remember that AI can be wrong, so you'll want to verify the results of all AI output.

# How AI Differs from Traditional Web Search

At first glance, you might think that using AI for research seems a lot like using a web search engine. And you'd be at least partially right.

In terms of user interface, the typical AI tool does indeed closely resemble the search page of Bing, Google, Yahoo, or other web search engines. The difference is in the results.

Web search engines are designed to interpret your queries, identify important *keywords*, and return a list of web pages that best match those keywords. This is called *keyword matching*, These web search engines don't analyze or understand your search; they just look for specific word matches. They don't actually answer your questions; they merely point you to web pages that might do that.

 **NOTE**   Google and other web search engines operate on the assumption that the more popular a page is, the better it meets searchers' information needs. The more visitors a page has, the higher it ranks in web search results—no matter the quality (or lack of) of the page's contents.

The result is a list of matching web pages with no real understanding of whether they answer your question. The actual work of filtering and interpreting the data is left to you. Figure 5.1 shows a Google results page for the query **tell me about Mars**, full of links to other websites where the real info resides.

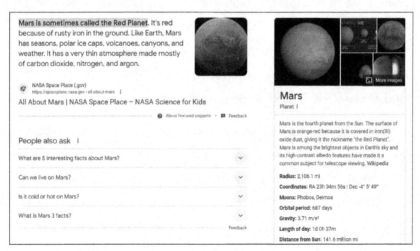

**FIGURE 5.1**

*Google search results for the query* **tell me about Mars***.*

**NOTE**  For some queries, Google offers a "snippet" of basic information, typically sourced from Wikipedia or a similar site. That's different from the full and thoughtful response from scratch you get with AI.

In contrast, an AI generator attempts to understand the context of your query to answer your question appropriately, typically in the form of a short report or conversation. It sifts through the relevant sources and presents all the information necessary to answer your query. Because it does the research and analysis for you, you get what you were looking for in seconds with no extra work required on your part (apart from verifying the results). You don't even have to use the right keywords. Just convey to the AI tool what it is you want, and it will find it for you.

Figure 5.2 shows the first page of a lengthy ChatGPT result for the prompt **tell me about Mars**.

---

**ChatGPT**

Mars is the fourth planet from the Sun and is often referred to as the "Red Planet" due to its reddish appearance. It has long captured human interest and imagination as a potential place for exploration and possibly even colonization. Here's an overview of Mars, covering its characteristics, exploration history, and significance:

**Basic Characteristics:**

1. **Size and Distance**: Mars is approximately half the size of Earth with a diameter of about 6,792 kilometers (4,212 miles). It is located about 227.9 million kilometers (141.6 million miles) from the Sun.
2. **Atmosphere**: Mars has a thin atmosphere composed mainly of carbon dioxide (about 95.3%), with small amounts of nitrogen, argon, and traces of oxygen and water vapor.
3. **Surface**: The surface of Mars is rocky and dusty, with vast plains, mountains, valleys, and polar ice caps. The reddish appearance of Mars is due to iron oxide (rust) on its surface.

---

**FIGURE 5.2**

*ChatGPT response to the prompt* **tell me about Mars**. *(This is just the first page; it goes on with a fairly lengthy response.)*

The bottom line is that web search engines are relatively "dumb" and AI tools are "smart." The web search engine finds and gathers the sources of information you ask for, whereas the AI engine works with that information to generate immediately useful results in plain English. AI gives you what you ask for and doesn't make you figure it all out yourself.

# AI IN GOOGLE SEARCH RESULTS

Google has recently started to include AI-generated results at the top of some search results pages before it offers its traditional web page listings. These "AI Overviews," as Google calls them, attempt to give you the exact answers to the questions you're asking so you don't have to sift through individual web pages as you would for its traditional results. Figure 5.3 shows one such AI Overview on a Google search results page.

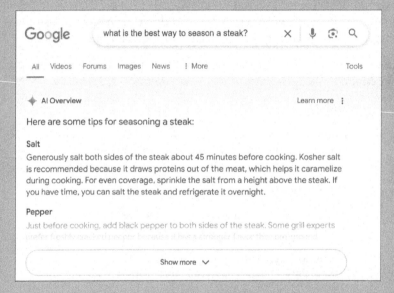

**FIGURE 5.3**

*An AI Overview at the top of a Google search results page.*

There are several potential problems with these AI Overviews, however.

First, users have found that Google's AI Overview doesn't always provide accurate results. If you accept AI Overview results at face value, you may be opening yourself up to bad, misleading, or biased information.

Another potential problem arises for those websites that have historically relied on Google search results to drive traffic to their pages. If users can get the information they need from an AI Overview, they'll be less likely to click through to other pages listed in Google's search results. That means much less traffic for sites across the web, potentially resulting in sites closing down due to lack of traffic—which could result in the slow and painful death of the web itself.

A final problem with Google's AI Overview is a challenge for Google itself. Google derives virtually all its revenue from selling ad space on its search results pages. If users no longer scroll through and click these "sponsored" search results, Google could put itself out of business due to rapidly declining advertising revenue, dramatically altering the way we use websites and find information on the web. This may be an unintended consequence of using artificial intelligence to try to answer all the world's questions.

# Why AI Is a Useful Search and Research Tool

Let's stop for a moment. Given that generative AI is a technology that can create all sorts of new content, why might it also be useful for finding information and conducting research?

There are several reasons why AI might be a superior tool for finding information, answering questions, and researching specific topics. In particular, AI excels at the following:

- **Fast and targeted searches:** Yes, Bing, Google, and Yahoo are fast, but you still have to sift through pages and pages of search results to find the most relevant results. AI tools can find the specific information you want in seconds, no manual review necessary on your part.

- **Understanding what you really mean:** Have you ever been stymied in a search because you just couldn't come up with the right words for your query? That's not a problem with AI tools. They employ natural language processing to understand the nuances of human language and accurately ferret out your intent, even if you don't use the ideal keywords.

- **Summarizing and synthesizing information:** AI doesn't just find information; it analyzes and understands it. AI tools can accurately summarize complex papers and articles, identifying the main points and important trends.

- **Analyzing data:** AI excels at ingesting, arranging, and analyzing data of all types. You no longer need to spend hours or days poring over Excel spreadsheets and databases. AI can not only do it faster than you but it can find patterns and relationships that you may never notice.

- **Discovering new sources:** Web search engines tend to rank highest the most popular sites on a given subject. These sites might not be the best sources of information however—just the most visited. AI looks beyond the obvious to find new sources you may not have found otherwise.

- **Dive deeper into key topics:** The conversational nature of AI encourages deeper dives into whatever it is you're researching. You may get an initial answer from AI that inspires further questions; as you ask and AI answers, you create a dialog that is increasingly informational.

For many people, the biggest selling point of using AI for search is that AI tools generate results in complete sentences and paragraphs using the appropriate level of language for the task at hand. They can even generate complete results in the form of scholarly articles, papers, and the like, which can reduce your ultimate workload. That's significantly more user-friendly than being forced to poke around through pages and pages of traditional search results.

# Things to Be Careful of When Using AI for Search and Research

As promising as AI is for search and research, you should be wary of the results that AI generates. That's because AI is only as good as the information on which it's been trained. If the initial dataset contains false or misleading information or is biased, AI might quote that bad information as the truth. Know, however, that these tools are evolving regularly, so it's possible that the answer an AI tool gives today could be different tomorrow—and the accuracy could be different as well.

 **NOTE**   When an AI tool returns false or misleading information, this is called an *AI hallucination*.

For example, I asked ChatGPT how many countries in Africa started with the letter *K*. On the first day I asked, AI said there were three: Kenya (correct), Kiribat (debatable; it's an island nation off the coast of Africa), and Comoros (an African nation, yes, but one that most definitely does not start with the letter *K*). As you can see, that answer was not wholly correct. (When I asked a few days later, however, ChatGPT gave the correct answer.)

Another user asked Google's AI Overview how many U.S. presidents had graduated from the University of Wisconsin. AI returned the answer 13, including Andrew Jackson, who "graduated in 2005"—despite the fact that this particular former president died in 1845 *and* didn't go to college. The actual number of University of Wisconsin presidential alumni is zero; AI apparently found graduates who had the same names as U.S. presidents and counted them, often several times. (According to the AI, John F. Kennedy graduated from UW in 1930, 1948, 1962, 1971, 1992, and 1993—quite an accomplishment!)

Note that when I asked the same question of ChatGPT, it got the answer correct. You may conduct the same search today and get an answer that is different from the one I got—another example of why it is essential to check information AI tools provide against proven sources.

AI also has trouble distinguishing satire from fact. For example, when a user searched Google for "cheese not sticking to pizza," the AI recommended adding glue to the pizza sauce. (Don't try that at home, folks!) That answer is straight out of an older satirical thread on the Reddit website, but Google's AI apparently took that user-generated thread and treated it as a fact. AI doesn't always know when others are joking, which can lead to problems.

AI can also present conspiracy theories as fact. One significant example also comes from Google's AI Overview. When asked how many Muslim presidents the United States has had, it confidently responded that "The United States has had one Muslim president, Barack Hussein Obama." This is, of course, not true (former president Obama was and is a Christian), but the lie has been propagated on various conspiracy theory sites over the years—and was obviously ingested as part of the AI's training set.

 **NOTE**   In all fairness to the various artificial intelligences involved, their parent companies immediately corrected these mistakes when they were pointed out. (This also means you probably won't be able replicate the wrong answers I've provided in these examples.)

Finally, let's not forget the fact that AI can sometimes return answers that reflect age, race, or gender bias. That bias may be subtle or overt, but it is often there merely because AI models train on data generated by flawed and sometimes biased human beings.

These examples demonstrate the need to verify all the information you find online, especially that proffered by AI tools. To avoid accepting falsehoods as fact, you need to research the information provided by AI—which you can do by clicking through the pages in traditional web search results. If an AI result sounds fishy, look it up with a traditional search engine, then click through on a reliable, verifiable source.

If you're doing serious research, you need to do this due diligence anyway. Don't accept an AI result as the final answer or definitive source. Always verify sources and include those sources in your research. AI tools are not sources to cite in your research papers; always go to the original source and cite that.

# Evaluating Popular AI Tools for Information and Research

Now to the meat of the matter: Which AI tools are best for searching for information and conducting research? There are two ways to go: all-purpose AI tools or tools specifically fine-tuned for research.

## Using All-Purpose AI Tools for Search and Research

To begin with, I direct you to the all-purpose generative AI tools discussed in Chapter 3, "Getting Started with All-Purpose AI Tools." All the tools presented there—ChatGPT, Claude, Google Gemini, Meta AI, Microsoft Copilot, Perplexity, Pi, and Poe—can be used to find information and conduct research. All you have to do is enter a prompt similar to a search engine query and the AI tool will present the information it finds that answers your question.

For example, if I want to find out how many voters were in Minnesota, I might ask a tool like ChatGPT **how many voters are there in the state of Minnesota?** ChatGPT would generate a list of results like the one in Figure 5.4.

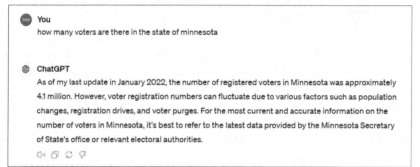

**You**
how many voters are there in the state of minnesota

**ChatGPT**
As of my last update in January 2022, the number of registered voters in Minnesota was approximately 4.1 million. However, voter registration numbers can fluctuate due to various factors such as population changes, registration drives, and voter purges. For the most current and accurate information on the number of voters in Minnesota, it's best to refer to the latest data provided by the Minnesota Secretary of State's office or relevant electoral authorities.

**FIGURE 5.4**

*Using ChatGPT to find information about Minnesota voters.*

You can also ask some AI models to graph certain data. For example, I asked ChatGPT to graph the number of people in each major age group in the United States. The result is shown in Figure 5.5.

**NOTE**  Not all AI models currently have graphing capability.

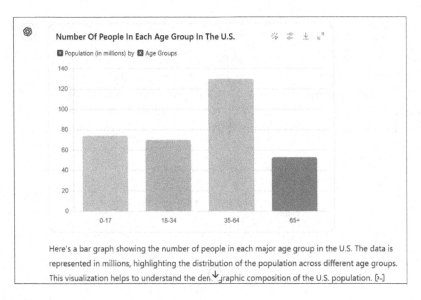

**FIGURE 5.5**

*An informational graph created by ChatGPT.*

Similarly, if I want to find out how to convert kilometers to miles, I might ask Google Gemini **how do you convert kilometers to miles?** Google Gemini would then present the answer shown in Figure 5.6.

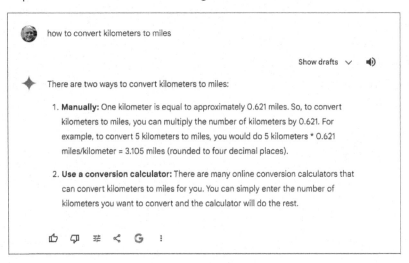

**FIGURE 5.6**

*Using Google Gemini to convert kilometers to miles.*

If you want to conduct more comprehensive research, an all-purpose AI tool can still do the job, but you have to create more specific prompts. For example, if you want to research the incidence of left-handedness among the general population, you might enter the following prompt into Meta AI: **write a 2,500-word research paper detailing the incidence of left-handedness among the U.S. and world populations.** The AI tool would then write such a comprehensive paper, complete with footnotes and citations, the beginning of which is shown in Figure 5.5.

---

○ Meta AI
The Incidence of Left-Handedness among the U.S. and World Populations

Introduction

Left-handedness, also known as sinistrality, is a trait that is often viewed as unusual or unique. While the majority of the population is right-handed, a significant proportion of individuals exhibit left-handed tendencies. This paper aims to explore the incidence of left-handedness among the U.S. and world populations, examining the prevalence, demographics, and potential factors influencing this trait.

Prevalence in the United States

Studies have consistently shown that approximately 10% of the U.S. population is left-handed (Hardyck & Petrinovich, 1977; Raymond et al., 2017). This figure has remained relatively stable over the past few decades, with some research suggesting a slight increase in left-handedness among younger generations (Loffing & Hagemann, 2014).

Global Prevalence

The prevalence of left-handedness varies across the globe, with estimates ranging from 5% to 15% (Raymond et al., 2017). A study conducted in 2018 found that the countries with the highest rates of left-handedness were:

- Netherlands (13.5%)
- United Kingdom (13.2%)
- Australia (12.6%)
- United States (10.2%)
- Canada (9.5%)

---

**FIGURE 5.7**

*Using Meta AI to write a research paper about the incidence of left-handedness.*

 **NOTE** Perplexity (www.perplexity.ai), which I also discuss in Chapter 3, is a good choice for conducting basic research. Unlike other all-purpose AI tools, Perplexity displays the sources for its results at the top of the response page. To go directly to a source, just click the link.

## Using Research-Specific AI Tools

While all-purpose AI tools might serve most people's search and research needs, there are also some AI tools that focus specifically on scholarly and scientific research and the needs of professional researchers.

Table 5.1 presents key information about some of the most-popular research-specific AI tools. A more in-depth overview of these tools follows.

**TABLE 5.1**    Popular AI Research Tools

| AI Tool | URL | Free Plan? | Paid Plans (cost per month) | Key Features |
|---------|-----|------------|------------------------------|--------------|
| Consensus | https://consensus.app | Yes | $8.99 | Uses ChatGPT 4 model, summarizes results |
| Elicit | https://elicit.com | Yes | $10 | Uses research "notebooks," summarizes top papers, links to original sources |
| Scholarcy | www.scholarcy.com | Yes | $9.99 | Reads, summarizes, extracts, and organizes key information |
| Scite | https://scite.ai | No | $20 | Analyzes and summarizes scientific articles, highlights where papers are cited |

## Consensus

Consensus (www.consensus.app), shown in Figure 5.8, bills itself as an "AI search engine for research." This is exactly what it is: an AI tool that gathers scientific information from peer-reviewed articles and other published sources.

**FIGURE 5.8**

*The home page of the Consensus AI research engine.*

The basic version of Consensus is free but offers limited usage. The Premium Plan, priced at $8.99 per month, provides unlimited access to OpenAI's GPT-4 search model and other features.

To use Consensus, enter your query into the Ask a Research Question box on the home page. Consensus then gathers relevant sources of information and provides a summary of this information, as shown in Figure 5.9.

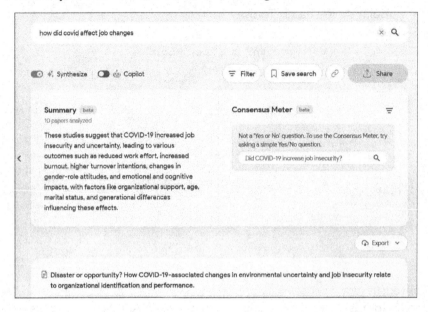

**FIGURE 5.9**

*Summary and research results from Consensus.*

## Elicit

Elicit (https://elicit.com) is, as the site claims, an AI research assistant. This AI tool can process and analyze data, revealing trends, patterns, and themes in the data.

The Basic version is free but limits how much you can use it. The Plus plan has higher usage caps, the ability to summarize up to eight papers, and the ability to extract information from tables, for $10 per month.

To use Elicit, you first create a "notebook" for your research, as shown in Figure 5.8. Then you enter a query into the Ask a Research Question box and press Enter.

Elicit then provides a summary of the top papers on the subject, as shown in Figure 5.11. This is helpful for researchers who need a quick overview of key research. Elicit also lists relevant papers below the summary, complete with links to the original sources.

**FIGURE 5.10**

*Using Elicit to conduct research.*

**FIGURE 5.11**

*Summarizing relevant research papers with Elicit.*

## Scholarcy

Scholarcy (www.scholarcy.com) is an AI tool that reads, summarizes, extracts, and organizes key information from scholarly articles. The basic plan, which lets you generate just three summaries per day, is free. Scholarly Plus is more useful, with unlimited and enhanced summaries for $9.99 per month.

To summarize an article, go to the Article Summarizer page, shown in Figure 5.12. Click the Click to Import button to select a file to summarize. You can upload specific files or enter a URL to summarize a web-based document.

**FIGURE 5.12**

*Importing a file to summarize with Scholarcy.*

Scite (https://scite.ai) imports the document, analyzes it, and produces a summary like the one shown in Figure 5.13. Scroll past the summary to view key concepts, abstract, synopsis, highlights, a comparative analysis, and more.

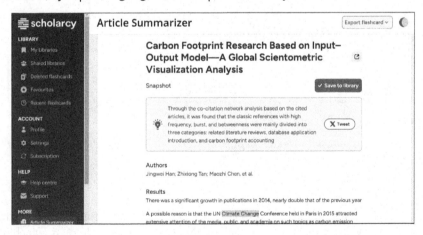

**FIGURE 5.13**

*Viewing a Scite summary of a scholarly article.*

## Scite

Scite analyzes and summarizes scientific articles. It's unique in that it highlights how and where a given research paper is cited, which helps you gauge the importance and reliability of each citation.

No free version is available, although Scite does offer a 7-day free trial. An individual subscription runs $20 per month.

The easiest way to use Scite is with the Scite Assistant, shown in Figure 5.14. Enter your question into the Ask a Question box and press Enter.

**FIGURE 5.14**

*Initiating research with the Scite Assistant.*

As you can see in Figure 5.15, Scite displays a three-paned results page. Your query is in the left pane and Scite's summary of results is in the middle pane. The right pane displays all the references used; you can click any reference to read the full text or perform other operations.

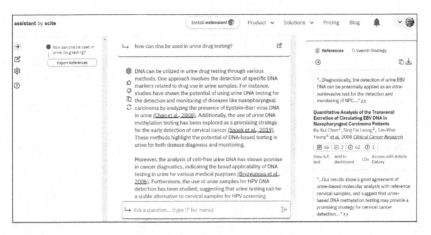

**FIGURE 5.15**
*Scite's research results, including citations.*

# How to Focus AI to Get the Information You Want

Prompting AI to search for information requires some subtle adjustments to the prompting strategies discussed in Chapter 3. Read on to learn how to best focus AI tools to retrieve the information for which you're looking.

## Crafting the Perfect Prompt for Research

The primary way to focus any AI tool for searching and researching is in fine-tuning the prompts you enter. Here are some tips for crafting effective prompts for finding and researching information:

- **Make your query as clear and specific as possible.** The more accurately you can describe what you're looking for, the better AI can understand your intent and deliver relevant results. For example, instead of prompting AI to simply research restaurant options, ask it to research dinner menus for a family of four with two kids under age five, offering specific cuisine or dishes, and within a specific price range.

- **Use keywords.** Although generative AI doesn't use keyword matching, including important keywords in your prompt helps focus AI on what you're looking for. As an example, if you want to know the effects of climate change on farming, instead of prompting **how is climate change impacting farming**, include related keywords as in the following prompt: **how is climate change** impacting farming in terms of crop yield, agricultural land use, and water scarcity**. By including the keywords "crop yield," "agricultural land use," and "water scarcity," you'll get more targeted results.

- **Use the proper technical vocabulary.** When researching technical topics, it helps to know the lingo. AI models respond better to prompts that use the proper technical or scientific terms. Using the right technical language (if you know it) also helps inform the AI model about what type and level of results you expect. For example, a layperson might ask AI to explain how heart surgery works, whereas an expert might describe the process as coronary artery bypass grafting.

- **Provide relevant context.** If you're writing a technical paper, tell the AI tool. It will tailor its results for that kind of output. If you have a specific length you need to hit or not exceed, include that in your prompt, as well. For example, if you're writing a scientific paper on insect migration and it needs to be 5,000 words long with an abstract and at least a half dozen citations, say **write a 5,000-word scientific paper on insect migration with an abstract and at least 6 citations**.

- **Tell AI exactly what you want.** If you provide specific instructions, AI will generate results in a general way that it thinks might be most helpful. If you want something more specific, you need to ask for it. You might want to tell AI to write at a specific grade level or present results in list form or as an executive summary. If you don't tell it what you want, it won't know to give it to you.

- **Leverage advanced search options.** Some research-oriented AI tools offer advanced search options, such as filtering by source type, date range, or even specific domains. Take advantage of these tools to generate a more relevant response.

It's important that you don't rely exclusively on AI to conduct your research. As good as AI is (and will continue to improve in the future), it shouldn't totally replace traditional research methods. Consider AI just one more tool in your kit, along with research databases and websites, for conducting serious research.

**WARNING**  Because most all-purpose AI tools generate content without citing sources, it's possible they could be working from bad or outdated content. When doing scholarly or professional research, it's imperative that your work be both accurate and citable. That means diligently cross-checking AI-generated results against verifiable results from reliable sources. And you can ask the AI tool to cite sources; after it generates results, follow with the prompt, **what are your sources**. You can then double-check them manually.

# Examples of Using AI for Research

What does the ideal prompt look like for specific types of searches? Here are some examples.

## Researching a Major (or Minor) Purchase

You can use AI to help you decide what items to purchase. This is especially useful when researching a major purchase, such as a house or a car, but can be used to evaluate virtually any product or service. For example,

- Comparing two or more items: **Compare the 2024 Honda CRV with the 2024 Nissan Rogue.**

- Listing the pros and cons of a given product: **List the pros and cons of this electric razor.**

- Evaluating the value of an item: **How much is the property at 1234 Main Street worth?**

- Asking for specific recommendations: **What is the best 65" OLED TV on the market today?**

## Researching How to Perform a Task

Ever get stuck with having to do something that you don't know how to do? You can ask AI for instructions—but make sure you're as specific as possible. For example,

- Cooking: **What's the best recipe for beef stroganoff?**

- Repairing: **How do I replace the condenser coil in my air conditioning unit?**

- Creating: **How do I create an origami penguin?**

- Driving: **What's the best route to drive from Chicago to Memphis?**

 **NOTE** When searching for recipes, you can fine-tune your prompt to include any dietary restrictions, number of servings needs, and the like. For example, you could enter a prompt like **find a gluten-free recipe for shrimp etouffee that serves 6 people.**

## Researching a Current News Event

Finding information about a current news event is a bit different than researching higher-level topics. What's important here is finding the most current information and ensuring it doesn't come from a biased source. For example,

- Seeking official statements: **Are there any official statements regarding the recent rule changes in major league baseball?**

- Reporting the latest information: **Who is running for office in my district?**

- Seeking out diverse viewpoints: **What are the differing opinions on the upcoming ballot proposition?**

- Examining a person's major accomplishments: **What are the key events that shaped Michael Jordan's life and made him the person he is today?**

 **NOTE**  Because AI engines train on large language models and it takes time to assemble those vast amounts of data, AI models may not be as up to date with current information as more traditional web search engines. It's not unusual for information garnered within the past few months to not yet be available to today's AI tools.

## Researching Factual Information

AI is also great for researching specific facts. For example,

- **How far is it to the moon?**

- **What is the square root of 12,345?**

- **What is Quentin Tarantino's birthday?**

- **What is the adult population of Milan, Italy?**

 **WARNING**  As mentioned in Chapter 2, AI results can sometimes exhibit biases built into the training data or algorithms they use. Don't assume that AI is always neutral and unbiased; be on the lookout for institutional or societal age, gender, race, and other biases in the results generated by any AI engine.

## Researching a Scientific or Technical Topic

When researching a scientific or technical topic, it helps to be as specific as possible in your prompts. For example,

- Generating a high-level overview or summary: **Provide a high-level overview of the field of quantum mechanics**

- Summarizing recent developments in a field: **What are the current challenges in nuclear fusion?**

- Identifying important topics: **What are the most important topics concerning electric vehicles today?**

- Citing credible sources: **List the top five peer-reviewed articles on astrobiology.**

## Researching Historical Events

You can take different approaches to doing historical research, depending on what information you want. For example,

- Examining the causes of an event: **What caused the War of 1812?**

- Examining the impact of an event: **What was the economic impact of the Cold War?**

- Examining the key players of an event: **Who were the key figures during the reign of King Henry VIII?**

- Comparing two events: **How did the American Revolution compare to the French Revolution?**

# Fine-Tuning AI Results

When you use the right prompt, you might be perfectly satisfied with the first results returned—or you might find the results are not totally related to your question, not specific enough, or just plain wrong. Fortunately, when AI's first results aren't quite right, you can work to improve your query and fine-tune the next round of results.

Here are some things to try:

- Ask for more or less detail

- Provide more information and context

- Specify the level of the results (general or technical audience, grade/reading level, age level, and so on)

- Specify the length (in words or pages) of the desired results

- Specify the type of result you want (article, paper, blog post, and so on)

- Specify from where you want the AI to pull information (specific websites, media sources, journals, and so on)

The key is to iteratively refine your search. Evaluate AI's first response and then adjust your prompt and see what you get.

# Using AI to Summarize and Understand Information

In addition to searching for and researching information, you can also use AI to summarize and help you better understand that information. You can use AI to summarize books, movies, technical articles, legal documents, even meetings. The key is to either use the proper prompt for an all-purpose AI tool or choose a tool that specializes in summarization.

When using an all-purpose AI tool, you need to include the word *summarize* in your prompt. For example, you could ask Google Gemini to **Summarize the plot of the play Our Town**, and you'd get something like what's shown in Figure 5.16.

 "Our Town," by Thornton Wilder, explores life in the fictional American town of Grover's Corners between 1901 and 1913. The play doesn't focus on a grand plot, but rather on the everyday lives of its citizens.

We follow two neighboring families, the Gibbs and the Webbs, with a focus on their children, Emily and George. The play unfolds in three acts:

- **Act I (Daily Life):** We see the routines of Grover's Corners residents, from waking up and preparing breakfast to attending school and chatting with neighbors.

- **Act II (Love and Marriage):** The act focuses on the blossoming romance between Emily and George, their courtship, and eventual marriage.

- **Act III (Death and Eternity):** This act takes a somber turn. We see Emily die in childbirth and her request to revisit her life, specifically her 12th birthday. The act explores themes of mortality, memory, and the beauty of ordinary life.

Through the seemingly mundane events, the play offers a profound reflection on the universality of human experience, the significance of everyday moments, and the importance of cherishing life.

**FIGURE 5.16**

*Google Gemini's summary of the plot of Thornton Wilder's Our Town.*

When it comes to summarizing specific documents, such as legal contracts, you want an AI tool that lets you upload files for analysis. Of those tools discussed in this chapter and in Chapter 3, Claude, Elicit, Perplexity, and Scholarcy all let you upload or link to articles and then summarize them.

You could also choose an AI tool designed specifically to summarize documents. Some of the most popular of these specialized AI tools include AskYourPDF (https://askyourpdf.com), Sharly (https://sharly.ai), and SummarizeBot (www.summarizebot.com).

**NOTE** Learn more about AI tools for summarizing meetings in Chapter 9, "Using AI at Work."

# Summary

Whether you're a casual searcher or professional researcher, AI can be of great value. In this chapter, you learned why AI is a useful tool for searching and researching and how it differs from traditional web search. You learned how to use all-purpose AI tools for research and discovered some of today's most popular AI tools for information and research, including Consensus, Elicit, Scholarcy, and Scite. You also learned about some AI tools designed specifically to summarize documents, including AskYourPDF, Sharly, and SummarizeBot.

Finally, you learned how to focus AI tools to find the information you want and need. You learned how to craft more effective prompts for research and how to edit your prompts to fine-tune the results you receive. You even learned the best ways to prompt AI tools for specific situations.

Using AI for searching and researching can be a real time-saver and game changer. But as with all things AI, you need to ensure that the AI output is accurate and free from falsehoods and bias. You shouldn't blindly accept everything AI tells you as fact—just as you wouldn't accept everything the neighborhood gossip tells you as the truth. You can trust AI, to an extent, but you should verify its results. Trust but verify is the right approach.

6

# USING AI TO CONNECT WITH PEOPLE AND PURSUE INTERESTS

AI can be a powerful tool to help you bridge personal connections and explore interests and hobbies. Social media networks already use AI to recommend compatible friends and fill your feed with posts you might like. You can also use AI within and outside those networks to better connect with friends and family and find new online communities of people who share your interests. But don't get too personal with AI. Any personal information you supply feeds directly into the tool's next training database—and can possibly be used against you in the event of a data breach.

# Using AI to Keep Up with Friends and Family

Let's start with how you can use AI to better connect with family and friends. AI can help you improve your communication, understand others' viewpoints, and stay in touch with those you love.

## Ways to Use AI to Connect with Your Friends and Family

There are many ways you can use generative AI to connect with your friends and family, whether via email, text messaging, social media, or in person. Here are just a few ideas, all doable with any all-purpose AI tool, such as ChatGPT, Meta AI, or Microsoft Copilot:

- **Plan an event:** When you want to get a group of people together and do something fun, prompt AI with **what are some suggestions for a game night?** or **what are some suggestions for a themed party for a bunch of 60 somethings?** You can also specify the location, such as **what are some suggestions for a group event at a local park?** or **what are some suggestions for a co-worker evening at my house?**

- **Find a conversation starter:** Just ask AI, **what are some good conversation starters?** You can also be more specific about the composition of the group, such as **what are some good conversation starters for a group of 30 somethings?** or **what are some good conversation starters for an all-generation family gathering?**

- **Play a game with AI:** Your friendly neighborhood AI tool can play all sorts of text-based games, from 20 questions to trivia games. You might prompt AI this way: **Let's play a game of movie trivia** or **Play a memory challenge game.** To find out what games a given AI tool can play, use the prompt: **What games can you play?** You can also specify whether you're looking at multiplayer games, one player versus the machine, and the like.

- **Get recommendations for activities:** Use AI to generate recommendations for TV shows, movies, music, or games based on your own or a friend's or relative's preferences. For example, you might prompt, **what are some good shows to watch with a friend who likes rom-coms?**

- **Tell some jokes:** Why so serious? Ask your AI tool for a list of jokes or anecdotes to lighten the mood in any gathering. For example, you might prompt your AI with **generate a list of jokes about mothers-in-law.** (Don't use that last one if your mother-in-law is actually around.)

- **Share your genealogy:** Use an all-purpose AI tool or an AI-powered genealogy tool like Ancestry (www.ancestry.com), FamilySearch (www.familysearch. org), or MyHeritage (www.myheritage.com) to explore your family's history and share what you find with family members.

## Using AI to Share Memories

Another way to better connect with friends and family is to use AI to help you share memories. Here are some ideas:

- Upload a batch of photos to an AI image generator (see Chapter 7) to create a collage, slideshow, or virtual scrapbook.

- Upload old photos to an AI image generator to touch up to modern standards or apply a special effect, like sepia tone or turning photos into cartoon.

- Feed your memories into an all-purpose AI tool and ask it to turn those memories into a compelling story.

 **NOTE**  Learn more about AI image generators in Chapter 7, "Using AI to Create Art and Images."

## Using AI to Better Understand People

One challenge with communicating with someone else is that you might not completely understand each other. It could be that you're from different generations, cultures, or backgrounds with different influences. Or maybe you live in different parts of the country. Or maybe you just don't know each other that well. (How well do you know your second cousin on your mother's side?)

Here's where AI can help. You can start by describing the person of interest and the situation you're in and then asking AI for advice on how to proceed. AI can also analyze text and conversations with that person to get a better handle on their personalities, their likes and dislikes, and what the two of you might have in common.

As a first example, you might use a prompt like the following:

> **I'm going to visit with my uncle who lives in Alaska. We haven't seen each other in five years and don't have a lot in common. He likes outdoor activities and works as a mechanic. I'm not too outdoorsy and have an office job. What should I know about him that might help when we get together?**

Figure 6.1 shows how Claude AI recommends you proceed.

Connecting with Alaskan Uncle ⌄

Given the differences in your lifestyles and interests, here are some points to consider that might help when you meet with your uncle:

1. Shared family experiences: Focus on family stories, memories, or relatives you both know. This common ground can help bridge the gap.

2. Curiosity about his life: Show genuine interest in his experiences living in Alaska, his work as a mechanic, and his outdoor activities. Ask questions about:
   - Unique aspects of living in Alaska
   - Interesting mechanical challenges he's faced
   - Memorable outdoor adventures he's had

3. Alaska's environment: Familiarize yourself with some basic facts about Alaska's climate, wildlife, and geography. This can help you engage in conversations about his surroundings.

4. Mechanical knowledge: While you may not be an expert, having a basic understanding of car maintenance or common mechanical issues could help you relate to his work.

5. Outdoor activities: Even if you're not outdoorsy, you could ask about the physical and mental benefits of his activities, or how technology intersects with outdoor pursuits.

**FIGURE 6.1**

*Some get-acquainted advice from Claude AI.*

For more personalized analysis, try pasting or uploading one or more letters, email messages, social media posts, or texts from this person into the AI tool and ask it to provide a personality analysis. Precede these samples with the following prompt:

**Analyze these posts and tell me what that person is like.**

 **WARNING** Protect your privacy by removing addresses, phone numbers, and other personally identifiable information from any information and items you upload to an AI tool.

Figure 6.2 shows a sample personality analysis from ChatGPT.

You can also use AI to do a "sentiment analysis" of the same text samples to judge the emotional tone of the messages. Use the prompt: **Perform a sentiment analysis of the following messages.** ChatGPT's analysis is in Figure 6.3. (It's a much different thing than a personality analysis.)

Based on the posts provided, this person seems to be outgoing, organized, and passionate about music. Here's a breakdown of their characteristics:

1. **Excitement and Enthusiasm**: The person expresses excitement about upcoming events and projects, indicating a positive and enthusiastic attitude towards their work and interests.

2. **Leadership and Communication Skills**: They mention sending out emails to musicians, indicating a role in organizing and coordinating activities. This suggests they are proactive and skilled at communicating with others.

3. **Commitment to Community**: The person mentions involvement in a weekend of worship and expresses gratitude for others' help, suggesting a strong sense of community and appreciation for teamwork.

4. **Organization and Planning**: They propose planning a visit to their AL home and specify their availability, demonstrating a structured approach to scheduling and planning activities.

5. **Musical Background and Growth**: The person shares details about their musical background, including learning to play the organ and seeking to improve their skills through lessons and practice. This indicates a dedication to personal growth and development in their musical

**FIGURE 6.2**

*A personality analysis from ChatGPT.*

Sure, let's analyze the sentiment of the provided text.

1. "Man, I'm so excited to be back. We've got a lot of fun and exciting things coming up. I'll be sending an email out to all the musicians here in the next few days just saying 'hey' and giving a vision for what's ahead. Definitely planning to have you as involved as you want. Tell Hayley I said 'hi' as well."

   - Sentiment: Positive

   - This text expresses excitement, anticipation, and inclusiveness. The speaker is enthusiastic about upcoming events and projects, and they are eager to involve others in their plans.

2. "Looking forward to the upcoming weekend of worship on May 11th & 12th. We're so grateful you have agreed to help out. Attached you will find the lead sheets for the following tunes:"

   - Sentiment: Positive

   - The sentiment here is positive and appreciative. The speaker is grateful for the assistance of others and is eagerly anticipating an upcoming event.

**FIGURE 6.3**

*A sentiment analysis from ChatGPT.*

You can go even further by then asking AI for advice on the best way to respond to that person. Use the prompt **how should I respond to this person?** The AI tool will write you a response that's appropriate to the person's personality and sentiment.

Another approach is to ask AI for advice on how to deal with a given person, especially if there's some sort of conflict or communication issue involved. Here's an example of a situation that might be worthy of some AI advice:

**My cousin and I have never gotten along. He's a blue collar guy and I'm an information worker. He's a Republican and I'm a Democrat. He's a country boy and I'm a city gal. How can we learn to get along?**

Figure 6.4 shows Google Gemini's advice.

It sounds like there are several factors contributing to the distance between you and your cousin. Here are some ways you can bridge the gap and build a stronger relationship:

**Finding Common Ground:**

- **Shared Interests:** Look beyond the labels. Do you both enjoy sports, music, movies, or a particular activity? Focus on these shared passions as a starting point for conversation.
- **Family History:** Explore your family's history together. Learning about your shared roots and traditions can foster a sense of connection.
- **Respectful Curiosity:** Instead of assuming you have nothing in common, approach your cousin with an open mind. Ask questions about his life, work, and interests. You might be surprised by what you learn.

**Building Bridges:**

- **Small Talk & Active Listening:** Start with small talk about current events (non-political!), hobbies, or the weather. Practice active listening and show genuine interest in his experiences.

**FIGURE 6.4**

*Relationship advice from Google Gemini.*

**NOTE** As with all things, AI is only a tool you can use to improve your personal connections. It's not meant to replace those connections. Take the effort to spend quality time with your loved ones—and cherish that time together.

# Use AI to Find and Pursue Hobbies and Interests

AI can be a great resource for pursuing your current hobbies and finding new ones. It's all about asking the right questions.

## Finding New Hobbies

If you're not sure what hobbies might interest you, AI can help.

One approach is to strike up a conversation with an AI chatbot about your interests and let the AI recommend online communities that might include some like-minded individuals.

 **WARNING**  Before joining online communities, check them out as you would real-world communities. Enter the community's name into a search engine and see what appears in the search results. See if the community actually exists, has recent posts (if not, it may be a "dead" community), and what others say about it.

Another approach is to ask an AI tool directly, based on key information about you. Tell the AI how old you are, your gender, where you live, when you have free time (and how much of it), whether you like indoor or outdoor activities, and, if you like, how much money you have to spend on a new hobby. You should also mention whether you have any specific skills or equipment you want to take advantage of as well as any limitations that might get in the way.

That's a lot to remember and a lot to input. You might end up with a prompt like this:

> **I'm a middle-aged professional with a fair amount of disposable income. I live in the suburbs and have lots of free time on weekend afternoons. I like outdoor activities and have money to spend on them. I do have asthma, however, so that could limit things. Can you recommend some hobbies for me?**

For this particular person, Meta AI had some very specific recommendations, that you can see in Figure 6.5.

Here's another example:

> **I'm looking for a new hobby. I'm a woman just out of college. I've always had a passion for music, especially oldies. I don't have a large budget because I spend a lot on rent. I like to get away from the city on weekends and do things with my friends. What would you recommend?**

○ Meta AI

Considering your preferences and asthma, here are some hobby ideas for you:

1. **Gardening**: A great outdoor activity that allows you to connect with nature and enjoy the fresh air (while managing your asthma). You can create a beautiful garden, grow your own herbs, or even start a small orchard.

2. **Photography**: Capture the beauty of nature and outdoor scenery with a camera. You can explore local parks, trails, or even take a photography class to learn new skills.

3. **Birdwatching**: A relaxing and peaceful hobby that allows you to enjoy the outdoors while observing wildlife. You can invest in a good pair of binoculars and spot birds in their natural habitats.

4. **Hiking**: Explore nearby trails and enjoy the scenery while getting some exercise. Be sure to take necessary precautions with your asthma and choose trails that suit your fitness level.

5. **Kayaking or Canoeing**: Paddle through calm waters and enjoy the outdoors from a different perspective. Many rental places offer guided tours or solo trips.

6. **Cycling**: A great way to explore local bike trails or take a leisurely ride through your neighborhood. You can invest in a comfortable bike and enjoy the fresh air.

7. **Geocaching**: A fun outdoor activity where you use GPS to find hidden treasures (called "caches"). It's a great way to explore new places and get some exercise.

8. **Star Gazing**: Set up a telescope or binoculars in your backyard and enjoy the night sky. You can learn about constellations and observe the beauty of the universe.

Remember to always prioritize your health and take necessary precautions with your asthma when engaging in outdoor activities. Consult with your doctor if you have any concerns.

**FIGURE 6.5**

*Some specific hobby recommendations from Meta AI.*

Figure 6.6 shows what ChatGPT recommends.

◎ Given your passion for music, interest in oldies, and desire for budget-friendly activities that allow you to escape the city and spend time with friends, here are a few hobby suggestions tailored to your preferences:

1. **Learn an Instrument**: Since you have a passion for music, why not learn to play an instrument? Consider picking up a budget-friendly instrument such as a ukulele or a keyboard. There are plenty of online tutorials and resources available for free or at a low cost to help you get started.

2. **Vinyl Collecting**: Explore your love for oldies by starting a vinyl collection. You can often find affordable vinyl records at thrift stores, flea markets, or online marketplaces. Building a collection of your favorite classic albums can be a fun and rewarding hobby, and listening to vinyl records can provide a nostalgic escape from city life.

3. **Outdoor Activities**: Since you enjoy getting away from the city on weekends, consider outdoor activities that you can enjoy with friends. Hiking, camping, picnicking, or even outdoor concerts in nearby parks can provide opportunities for relaxation and bonding with friends while enjoying nature.

4. **DIY Crafts**: Get creative and explore DIY crafts as a hobby. You can try your hand at upcycling old furniture, making handmade jewelry, ↓ reating art projects inspired by your favorite oldies

**FIGURE 6.6**

*Some hobby recommendations for a cash strapped 20-something woman from ChatGPT.*

Or this one:

**I just retired and am looking for things to do where I can meet new people. I try to stay in shape and like taking walks, exploring new places, and helping out in the community.**

Figure 6.7 shows what Google Gemini recommends. Note that it automatically picked up my location and recommended real activities nearby.

That's fantastic! Apple Valley offers a great mix of activities that cater to your interests and social connection. Here are some ideas to get you started:

**Social and Active:**

- **Apple Valley Senior & Event Center:** This is a hub for retirees in the area. They offer a variety of programs including fitness classes, card games, day trips, and even art classes [1]. It's a perfect place to meet new people with similar interests.
- **Senior Citizen Clubs:** Apple Valley Senior Citizens Club organizes events, dances, and social gatherings specifically for retirees. This is a great way to connect with people your age who live nearby [5].
- **Walking Groups:** Check with the Senior Center or local community centers to see if there are any existing walking groups for retirees. If not, consider starting your own! You can also explore apps like Meetup to find walking groups in the area.

**Exploring and Giving Back:**

- **Volunteer Opportunities:** There are many organizations in Apple Valley that could use your help. Reach out to local non-profits, libraries, or even parks and

**FIGURE 6.7**

*Some recreational recommendations for a retiree from Google Gemini.*

## Pursuing Existing Hobbies

AI can also help you pursue your existing hobbies. Use the same techniques discussed here to find topic-focused groups online and off and to find more information about your hobby.

For example, if you like to cook, you can use AI to find new recipes. Just use a prompt like this one:

**Find some easy recipes for noodle-based dishes.**

Figure 6.8 shows what Claude AI came up with.

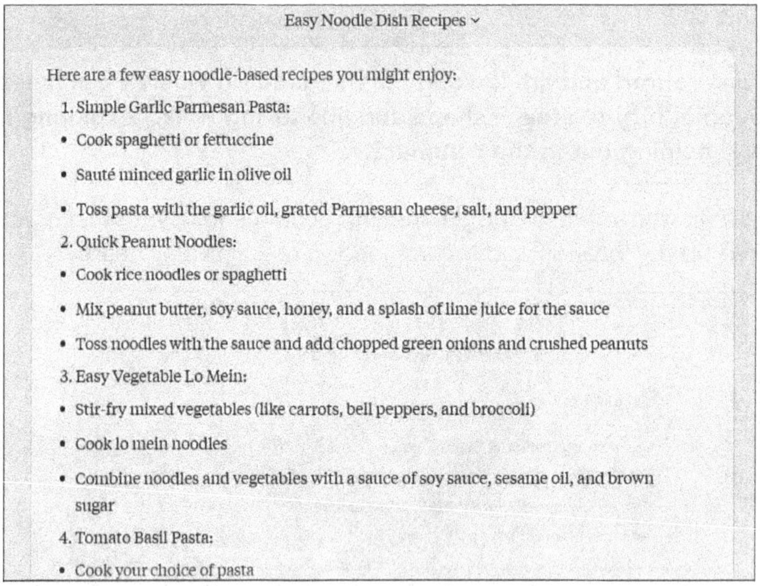

Easy Noodle Dish Recipes ˅

Here are a few easy noodle-based recipes you might enjoy:

1. Simple Garlic Parmesan Pasta:
   - Cook spaghetti or fettuccine
   - Sauté minced garlic in olive oil
   - Toss pasta with the garlic oil, grated Parmesan cheese, salt, and pepper
2. Quick Peanut Noodles:
   - Cook rice noodles or spaghetti
   - Mix peanut butter, soy sauce, honey, and a splash of lime juice for the sauce
   - Toss noodles with the sauce and add chopped green onions and crushed peanuts
3. Easy Vegetable Lo Mein:
   - Stir-fry mixed vegetables (like carrots, bell peppers, and broccoli)
   - Cook lo mein noodles
   - Combine noodles and vegetables with a sauce of soy sauce, sesame oil, and brown sugar
4. Tomato Basil Pasta:
   - Cook your choice of pasta

**FIGURE 6.8**

*Some easy noodle recipes from Claude AI.*

Or maybe you're big into arts and crafts. I have a friend who likes to make candles for herself and friends; she might use a prompt like this:

**How can I combine aromatherapy and candle making?**

Figure 6.9 shows what Meta AI recommends.

Gardening is another popular avocation for many. If you're looking to expand your home garden, you could use a prompt like this:

**What native flowering plants are good to plant in Nebraska?**

Figure 6.10 shows some suggestions from Microsoft Copilot.

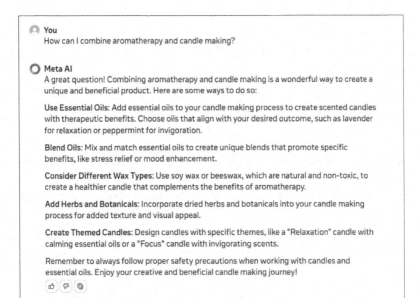

**FIGURE 6.9**

*Candle making advice from Meta AI.*

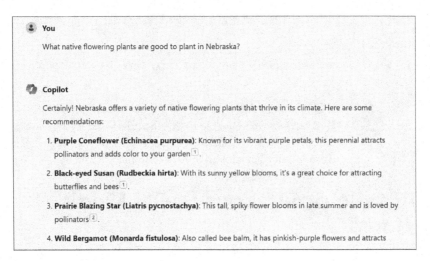

**FIGURE 6.10**

*Some gardening suggestions from Microsoft Copilot.*

Although AI will probably never be as informed as an avid hobbyist, you might be surprised what information it can turn up. Consider AI as another tool to use in the pursuit of your favorite hobbies.

## Finding Online Communities

You can also use AI to find others who share your interests and hobbies in online communities.

The easiest and most obvious way to find specific online communities is to ask an AI tool. Just enter a prompt that asks for recommendations based on a specific interest or topic, like the following:

**Can you recommend online communities for model train enthusiasts?**

The AI tool should return a list of promising communities, like the one in Figure 6.11.

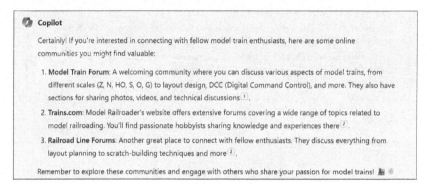

**FIGURE 6.11**

*Some recommendations for model train enthusiasts, from Microsoft Copilot.*

 **NOTE**   Learning a new language or traveling? You can also use AI to help converse with people who speak other languages. Learn about AI-powered translation tools in Chapter 10, "Using AI to Manage Your Travel and Transportation."

# Using AI to Improve Your Social Media Interactions

An all-purpose AI tool can be useful when you're communicating on social media, too. Whether it's a short message on Instagram or X or a longer one on Facebook or LinkedIn, AI can generate posts and responses for you, taking some of the work and worry out of keeping up with your social feeds. AI can detect the tone and context of what others are posting and respond in kind.

Just tell the AI tool which social network you're posting to and what you want to post about. A typical prompt might look something like this: **Create a Facebook post asking for the best deep dish pizza in the neighborhood.**

And, if you don't know how to respond to someone else's social media post, let AI respond for you. Just enter the prompt **how should I respond to this?** followed by the original message pasted into the prompt box. The AI tool will suggest an appropriate response.

In addition, many social media companies are beginning to incorporate AI into their platforms. It won't be long before you see some sort of "write with AI" button on Facebook, X, and other social networks. When available, it will help you be more social online.

## BEWARE DEEPFAKES AND CLICKBAIT ON SOCIAL MEDIA

As you learned in Chapter 2, "The Risks and Benefits of AI," it's easy to use AI to create "deepfake" audio, video, images, and text that look real but aren't. Malicious individuals can use these images to attract attention in social media posts and possibly get you to take actions you might not otherwise take or believe things that aren't true.

Some of these deepfakes purport to be of celebrities, maybe less-than-fully clothed or doing something unusual. Others are of children asking for help or financial donations. Others are of attractive people who say they like your profile and would like to be friends.

It's also common for individuals and entities to use AI-generated deepfakes as propaganda, especially in election years. Don't be fooled by a picture of a given candidate doing something questionable; it's probably a deepfake meant to confuse or negatively influence voters.

Even if the post doesn't result in a scam, just clicking it racks up traffic for the individual who posted it. That can earn the individual advertising money, thus helping that person profit from their AI-generated deepfakes.

No matter how hard the social media platforms try to guard against these scams (such as labeling content as AI-generated), the criminals always seem to stay a step ahead. The best advice is not to take anything you see on social media at face value, even if it's a repost from someone you know. Question and verify everything you see and hear; with AI technology continuing to advance, you simply can't believe your own eyes and ears.

# Conversing with AI by Text or Voice

Talking with AI by text or voice is an efficient way to communicate and get the information you need. It can provide you with useful information and teach you about an array of topics.

You probably already know how to communicate with Alexa, Google Assistant, and Siri voice assistants, by asking basic questions and getting appropriate answers. But the personal conversations that you can have with generative AI today go far beyond that.

Today's AI tools can carry on conversations that are surprisingly lifelike, responding not only to your words but also your tone and context. You may even find that talking to an AI chatbot about some topics is more comfortable than talking to a human being; AI won't judge you or make you feel uncomfortable.

Not surprisingly, some people even use AI to feel connected in today's hypersocial online world. For example, some caregivers are using AI to "talk" with and provide companionship to the people for whom they provide care.

 **NOTE**   Learn more about AI and caregiving in Chapter 12, "Using AI to Help Caregivers."

There are many ways to engage in AI-powered conversations. You can talk to most all-purpose AI tools via text, just as you would with a friend via text messaging. Even better, some AI tools offer voice-based conversation, which can feel just like talking to someone in the room.

## Talking with AI via Text

Most all-purpose AI tools, such as Claude AI, Google Gemini, and Meta AI, offer text-based conversations with their chatbots. This type of interaction resembles a conversation with someone via text messaging or social messaging posts.

With these text-based chatbots, you type your side of the conversation into a prompt box and the ongoing message thread between you and AI is displayed in a scrolling text message–like fashion. You type, AI responds, you respond to the AI, AI responds to your response, and on and on. Figure 6.12 shows such a conversation with Pi AI.

> You ever have one of those days?
>
> As an AI, I don't personally experience days like humans do, but I can certainly understand that some days can be more challenging than others. It's completely normal to have ups and downs, and it's okay to feel overwhelmed at times. What's important is that you're reaching out and talking about it, which is a great step towards feeling better. 😊
>
> Yeah. Work is getting frustrating.
>
> Workplace stress can really take a toll on your well-being, Michael. It's not uncommon to feel overwhelmed or frustrated with work from time to time. Is there anything in particular at work that's been causing you stress lately? Maybe we can brainstorm some strategies to help you manage these feelings and find a little relief.
>
> It's my boss. She's really micromanaging me.

**FIGURE 6.12**

*Carrying on a conversation with a sympathetic Pi AI.*

**WARNING**   When chatting with an AI tool, never reveal intimate personal details, sensitive business data, or any private information like credit card and Social Security numbers.

## Talking with AI via Voice

The latest thing in AI is a new generation of is AI tools that listen to your spoken words and reply in synthesized human-sounding voices. This ability to listen to the spoken word and respond accordingly is called *multimodal AI* because AI can interact via multiple modes of input and output—text, voice, images, and (in some cases) physical gestures.

You might think that multimodal AI is similar to voice-activated digital assistants such as Amazon's Alexa, Apple's Siri, or the Google Assistant, and you'd be partially correct. While the interaction might appear similar on the surface, the original crop of digital assistants aren't really very "smart." Current digital assistants use natural language processing to understand the words you're saying but they really don't parse your input to understand the meaning behind your words. They recognize certain phrases (such as "turn on the living room lights" or "play my oldies playlist") but they don't and can't go much beyond that.

Multimodal AI, in contrast, goes beyond simple phrase recognition to understand and respond to your voice in a more comprehensive manner. When you speak to a multimodal AI tool, it doesn't just process your words; it takes into account your tone of voice, your past comments, even (in some cases) your facial expressions. You end up with a richer, more intuitive, more *natural* interaction that makes the original digital assistants feel like crude robots. (Which, in reality, they are.)

One of the current leaders in voice-activated multimodal AI is ChatGPT, with its ChatGPT-4o engine. ChatGPT-4o interacts with you via your smartphone. You talk to it and it talks back to you. It even uses vocal inflections and pauses to sound just like a real person.

When you first launch the ChatGPT app on your phone (available for free from your phone's app store), you're asked to choose a voice for the AI. As you can see in Figure 6.13, you can choose from four voices—two male (Ember and Cove) and two female (Breeze and Juniper).

**FIGURE 6.13**

*Choosing a voice for the ChatGPT AI.*

When you're ready to talk with ChatGPT, tap the headphone icon (*not* the microphone icon!) to the right of the Message text box, shown in Figure 6.14. This opens the Voice Chat screen.

Voice Chat

**FIGURE 6.14**

*Tap the headphone icon to talk with ChatGPT AI.*

You can now start talking with ChatGPT. As shown in Figure 6.15, it listens to what you have to say and, when you pause, responds in the voice you chose. Keep talking to continue the conversation.

**FIGURE 6.15**

*Talking with ChatGPT AI.*

Talking with ChatGPT and other multimodal AI tools will never replace talking with a friend or loved one, but it does make it easier to get the information you need in a way that feels natural. After a while, you may find yourself forgetting that you're talking to AI and feel like you're talking to another human being.

**NOTE** Not to be outdone, Apple has announced that it will incorporate OpenAI's ChatGPT into its Siri digital assistant as part of its Apple Intelligence initiative to utilize AI in many of its products and services. Amazon is also said to be developing multimodal AI capabilities for its Alexa digital assistant and Google is developing its own multimodal AI, based on its Gemini AI model, called Google Astra. Expect these and other new multimodal tools to go live as soon as feasible.

# Summary

In this chapter, you learned the many ways you can use AI to connect with friends and family, improve relationships and communications, discover new hobbies and pursue existing ones, and find new communities of like-minded people. You also learned how to use AI in your social media interactions and how to talk with multimodal AI tools that respond to your voice and respond in their own voices.

It's fascinating just how human-like some AI tools can appear—even if they'll never replace hanging out with a friend in person. But take caution; always verify information you see and never reveal anything personal that you don't want to ultimately go into a huge public database.

7

# USING AI TO CREATE ART AND IMAGES

You've seen how AI can generate letters, social media posts, and other text-based content, but some AI engines can create images, both realistic and fantastic, based only on users' prompts.

You can generate your own images with AI image generators available to the general public, many for free. With them, you can create real-looking pictures of what you might otherwise have only imagined in your mind—and it's easy to do.

So read on to learn how to use AI to have fun and expand your creativity, no matter your artistic abilities!

# How AI Generates Images

Let's start with a quick look at the technology behind the phenomenon.

Like all artificial intelligence tools, AI image generators are "trained" on large sets of data—datasets consisting of billions of images and descriptions of those images. Once trained, AI can generate new images based solely on text prompts.

The images you create with AI can be of anything or anybody that the AI has learned about in its training. By training on billions of images of all sorts and styles, it can create artwork that looks painted, drawn, or photographed. It can mimic a variety of art styles and depict characters and scenes that might or might not exist in reality. You want a picture of a baby elephant hang gliding over an active volcano? AI knows what a baby elephant looks like, what hang gliding looks like, and what a volcano looks like. Thus, AI can create what looks like a photograph of just that.

Don't believe me? Just look at Figure 7.1.

**FIGURE 7.1**

*An AI-generated image of a baby elephant hang gliding over an active volcano, courtesy of Microsoft Designer's Image Creator.*

# How to Use an AI Image Generator

AI image generators work more or less like other AI tools. You enter a text prompt that describes the image you want, and then AI creates that image. The more detailed your prompt, the more accurate the image.

For example, if you'd like a painting of San Francisco's Golden Gate Bridge at sunset to put on a throw pillow, you might enter a prompt like this: **Create a watercolor painting of the Golden Gate Bridge at sunset**. (Figure 7.2 shows such a creation.)

**FIGURE 7.2**

*An AI-generated watercolor painting of the Golden Gate Bridge at sunset, courtesy of Adobe Firefly.*

Your prompts should describe the type of output you want (photo, painting, drawing, and so on) and what you want illustrated. For example, Figure 7.3 shows the result of the prompt **photo of couple walking through the woods in the fall**.

Note that with some image generators, you only have to describe the image. With others that also can generate text-based content, you may have to preface the prompt with **create an image** or **generate an image**.

Most AI image generators let you download or share the artwork they create. In some cases, you may need to subscribe to a paid plan to generate and download images in high resolution.

**FIGURE 7.3**

*An AI-generated photograph of a couple walking through the woods, courtesy of Midjourney.*

If you don't like the results, tweak your prompt and try again. Some image generators even include a "try again" button that automatically generates a different image based on your initial prompt.

## RECOGNIZING AI-GENERATED IMAGES

It's likely you've scrolled through your social media feed and seen what looks like a picture of a person or celebrity or fantasy figure that you've never seen before. This picture may look slightly unusual, such as a different actor wearing a Superman costume, a well-known female celebrity wearing the briefest of swimsuits, or someone you recognize from TV doing something crazy or stupid. The picture might appear, at first glance, to be a photograph but, on closer examination, it looks slightly off—maybe too realistic, with incorrect details, or just difficult to imagine. When you see one of these realistic-but-questionable images, chances are it's AI-generated. The image may not even be questionable; it may appear to be an action shot at a sports game or a news photo shot in the field but still be generated by AI.

How can you tell whether an image is real or AI-generated? As AI image generation gets better and better, you can't always tell. I covered some ways to recognized AI-generated images in Chapter 2, "The Benefits and Risks of AI." In general, look at the details in the picture, which AI doesn't always get quite right. Also question the feasibility of a picture; if it seems improbable, it probably is.

# What Kinds of Images Can You Generate with AI?

As you'll learn later in this chapter, there are a number of AI image generators you can use to create all sorts of images. To create an image, all you have to do is enter a text prompt that describes what you want to see. The more descriptive your prompt, the more satisfactory the image.

What kinds of images can you generate with AI—and how? Let's look at a few examples of different types of images and artwork you can create and the prompts you might use to create them.

## Cartoons and Comic Book Art

With AI, you can turn any real person into a cartoon. Some AI tools let you upload a photo and have the tool make the person in the photo into a cartoon or comic book character. When you're talking about famous people, living or dead, just tell the AI to draw the person as a cartoon character in a particular situation. For example, Figure 7.4 shows how ChatGPT responded to my prompt to **draw Abraham Lincoln as a superhero flying over Washington, D.C.** Go, Super Abe!

AI tools that let you provide your own "guide" images are even more fun. Upload one of your photos, choose a cartoony style or model, and see what happens. Figure 7.5 shows what happened when I had OpenArt's AAM XL model turn me into a cartoon.

**FIGURE 7.4**

*Abraham Lincoln as a flying superhero, courtesy of ChatGPT and DALL-E.*

**FIGURE 7.5**

*Your author as a cartoon, courtesy of OpenArt.*

## Collages

AI tools are great for making art collages. With most AI generators, all you have to do is prompt them to make a collage of a particular subject. For example, Figure 7.6 shows a collage generated by DreamStudio from the prompt **create a collage of vintage sports cars**.

**FIGURE 7.6**

*A collage of vintage sports cars, courtesy of DreamStudio.*

## Fantasy

An AI image generator is adept at creating new characters and worlds, which makes it perfect for illustrating fantasy scenarios. Choose an appropriately fantasy-oriented style or include the word "fantasy" in your prompt, such as **create an illustration of a fantasy world with dragons flying over an ancient village**. Figure 7.7 shows one possible outcome.

**FIGURE 7.7**

*A dragon-filled fantasy world, courtesy of OpenArt.*

## Fine Art

Looking for some art to hang on your wall? You can use AI to create the sorts of images you find in art galleries—and then enlarge it for your wall or put that art on T-shirts, coffee mugs, or whatever you like. Just describe the art you want, like this: **create a photo of a sailboat on a calm ocean with the sun setting on the horizon**. Figure 7.8 shows how Midjourney interpreted those instructions.

**FIGURE 7.8**

*A fine art image from Midjourney.*

## Greeting Cards

You can also use AI image generators to produce more practical projects. For example, if you want to create a unique holiday greeting card, just tell the prompt something like **create a holiday card with snow-covered trees and the message "Happy Holidays."** Figure 7.9 shows what Google Gemini created.

**FIGURE 7.9**

*A holiday greeting card from Google Gemini.*

## Manufactured Reality

AI can generate an image of just about anything you imagine. It can do so in various illustrative or cartoony styles or in photograph-like images that look just like the real thing. Try imagining a different reality and have AI take a "photo" of it, with a prompt like **create a photorealistic image of 1930s New York City with a giant robot stomping down Broadway**. Figure 7.10 shows what that might look like.

**FIGURE 7.10**

*A giant robot stomping down Broadway, generated by Microsoft Designer's Image Creator.*

 **WARNING** Some AI image generators have built-in filters to keep you from generating images that might infringe on copyright or other intellectual property rights, such as images of celebrities or popular characters. (For example, some tools won't generate images of copyrighted and trademarked superheroes, such as Superman or Batman.) Even if the AI image generator doesn't prevent the generation of such images, however, don't assume the image is fine to use. Always obtain written permission before using a copyrighted image.

## Portraits

You can use AI to generate portraits of any type. Just tell the AI tool as much as possible about the type of portrait you want, such as **create a portrait of an African American woman sitting in a garden**. You'll get something like the portrait in Figure 7.11.

**FIGURE 7.11**

*An AI-generated portrait, courtesy of Adobe Firefly.*

Not all portraits need be photographic. If you have a particular art style in mind, you can tell the AI engine to create a charcoal sketch, create an oil painting, create a black and white portrait, or even create a caricature. Figure 7.12 shows an oil painting of an old fisherman.

**FIGURE 7.12**

*An oil painted portrait, courtesy of DreamStudio.*

Some AI generators let you upload your own photos that you can then manipulate into a better portrait than what you started with. As an example, I uploaded a photo of myself with messy hair and wearing an old sloppy shirt to OpenArt and used the prompt, **create a corporate headshot wearing a blue suit and tie**. The result is shown in Figure 7.13; it cleaned me up pretty good, and even combed my hair!

**FIGURE 7.13**

*A corporate-ready headshot, courtesy of OpenArt. (Would you hire this guy?)*

 **WARNING**  Any images you upload become part of that AI model and can be used to further train the model and generate future images. Don't upload anything you don't want shared or don't have authorization or permission to upload!

# How to Ethically Use AI Image Generators

Using AI image generators can be fun. You just have to be careful how you use any images generated by AI. You can't claim them as something you've created yourself, you shouldn't use them to fool people, and you have to be careful about using any copyrighted images.

Here are some best practices to follow:

- **Don't claim credit.** The art generated by AI is not art that you personally create. Some artists have gotten into trouble trying to pass off AI-generated artwork as their own creations. It's not.

- **Don't claim copyright.** You can't copyright artwork that you didn't create yourself. Period.

- **Don't pass off AI-generated art as real.** AI can generate photorealistic images. Don't try to fool people into thinking they're real images. As before, be transparent and let people know the images were AI generated.

- **Don't use copyrighted images.** When creating images with AI, be careful not to infringe on any copyrights. That means don't create images of copyrighted characters and don't use images that are clearly based on copyrighted material.

 **NOTE** Better yet, use AI that was trained only on licensed images. For example, Generative AI by Getty Images is trained only on the Getty Images library; thus, the images are licensed and there is indemnification from copyright claims.

- **Don't create images of real people.** Along the same lines, you shouldn't use AI to create images of real people, either celebrities or people you know. Many AI image generators won't let you do this, at least when it comes to well-known individuals. While creating an image of Tom Cruise at your backyard barbeque might be fun, it's an inappropriate use of his image.

- **Don't create deepfakes.** Similarly, using AI to create images of real people in less-than-real situations is not only unethical; it may be illegal. Don't use AI as propaganda, to misinform, or to spread false information. You should never use AI to try to fool people in any way, shape, or form.

- **Don't use AI for commercial work—without saying so.** While it's okay to use AI for noncommercial purposes, pros shouldn't rely on AI to do their work for them. Professional artists should never use AI to create artwork for commercial use, unless they clearly disclose so. Just as you can use AI to generate story or message ideas and then write the final version yourself, professional artists can use AI image generators to generate a bunch of art ideas but then draw or paint the final version themselves, based on that inspiration.

- **Be transparent.** If you're presenting AI-generated artwork, even if it's just on social media, let people know that it's AI-generated. A simple credit line or caption along the lines of "Generated by AI" or "AI-generated art" lets people know what they're actually seeing.

Bottom line, you need to be responsible when using AI image generators. You can have lots of fun but don't take that fun too far.

 **WARNING** Many image generators block pornographic, violent, or types of offensive images. Keep it clean out there, folks!

# Comparing Popular AI Tools for Creating Images

There are a large number of AI image generators available today. While all work in pretty much the same fashion, some have slightly different features and, because they use different AI engines, can generate vastly different results.

Table 7.1 provides details about the most popular AI image generators. Information about each tool follows.

**TABLE 7.1** Popular AI Image Generators

| Image Generator | URL | Free Plan? | Paid Plans (cost per month) | Special Features |
|---|---|---|---|---|
| Adobe Firefly | https://firefly.adobe.com | Yes | $4.99 | Works with Adobe Creative Suite, creates image fills, can expand images to fill a larger canvas |
| DALL-E | https://www.chatgpt.com | No | $20 | Available as part of ChatGPT Plus subscription |
| DeepAI AI Image Generator | https://deepai.org/machine-learning-model/text2img | Yes | $5 | Can remove backgrounds, can animate images (with AI Video Generator) |
| Deep Dream Generator | https://deepdreamgenerator.com | Yes | $9 to $99 | Can upload images as "visual prompts" |
| DreamStudio by Stability AI | https://dreamstudio.ai | Yes | $10 per 1000 credits | Can upload images, easy-to-use interface |
| Google Gemini | https://gemini.google.com | Yes | $19.99 | Can generate images to accompany AI-generated stories |
| Hotpot AI Art Generator | https://hotpot.ai | Yes | $10 per 1000 credits | Can upload images, can generate headshots, can use AI to edit photos |
| Image Creator from Microsoft Designer | https://designer.microsoft.com/image-creator | Yes | Free | Works similar to ChatGPT's DALL-E |

| Midjourney | www.midjourney.com | No | $10 to $120 | Can upload reference images and configure artistic style, variety, and aesthetics |
| NightCafe | https://creator. nightcafe.studio | Yes | $5.99 to $49.99 | Can choose from different AI models, can fine-tune your own model |
| OpenArt | https://openart.ai | Yes | $12-$56 | Can choose from different AI models, can fine-tune your own model, can upload own photos for AI manipulation |

That's the basic information about a lot of sophisticated AI generators. As to which one is best, that's a matter of opinion, to some degree. The best advice I can give is to give them a try and see which generates the images you like best—and be prepared to use multiple image generators to get the widest variety of results.

The following sections offer a more detailed look at each of these AI image generators. Although they all do pretty much the same thing, they each do it somewhat differently and some are better at some things than others.

## Adobe Firefly

Adobe Firefly (https://firefly.adobe.com) is both a freestanding AI image generator and an AI tool for use within Adobe's Creative Cloud products, such as Photoshop. The freestanding version of Firefly is free, with less-restrictive paid versions also available; the embedded version is available to all Creative Cloud subscribers.

As with most AI image generators, you describe what you want via a text prompt and Firefly does the rest. Firefly can also punch up existing images by adding style and textures and generating content to fill in portions of an image. Since Firefly is trained on a massive dataset of stock photos from Adobe Stock as well as public domain and freely available images from Creative Commons, you get high-quality results that you can use both personally and commercially.

 **NOTE**  Creative Commons is a non-profit organization that enables creators to upload their work and make it available to the general public. Images protected by a Creative Commons license can be used for free with certain restrictions.

To use Adobe Firefly, simply enter a descriptive prompt into the prompt box and click the **Generate** button, as shown in Figure 7.14. Four results are then generated, as shown in Figure 7.15. To download an image, hover over it and then click **Download**. To download all four images, click **Download All**.

**FIGURE 7.14**

*Adobe Firefly's home page.*

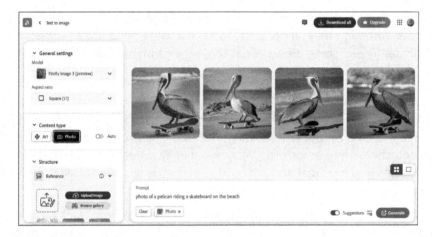

**FIGURE 7.15**

*Adobe Firefly's image results, as well as further controls.*

Controls on the left side of the page let you adjust the AI model used, the image's aspect ratio, content type (art or photo), and other options. You can also upload your own images for editing via the AI tool.

## DALL-E in ChatGPT

One of the best-known AI image generators today is OpenAI's DALL-E. DALL-E is available in the ChatGPT AI tool (https://chatgpt.com), along with the regular text-based chatbot.

**NOTE**  Learn more about ChatGPT in Chapter 3, "Getting Started with All-Purpose AI Tools."

DALL-E works within ChatGPT. You specify that you want to generate an image by adding **generate an image of** or **create a photo of or create a watercolor painting of** or something similar to the front of your prompt. For example, if you want to create a photo-like image of a pelican riding a skateboard on the beach, you'd use the prompt: **create a photo of a pelican riding a skateboard on the beach**. Just make sure you're as descriptive as possible about what you want, including the output type (photo, artwork, and so on) and style.

As you can see in Figure 7.16, after you enter the prompt in ChatGPT, DALL-E generates the image and displays it in the main pane. Hover over the image to upvote or downvote the image; click the **Download** (down arrow) icon to download the image.

**FIGURE 7.16**

*A single image generated by DALL-E in ChatGPT.*

At present, there is no free version of DALL-E available in ChatGPT. To get access to DALL-E image generation, you need to subscribe to ChatGPT Plus, which runs $20 per month.

 **NOTE**  At the time of writing, ChatGPT was unusual in that it enables downloading only in the WEBP file format, not in the more popular JPG or PNG formats. This may change sometime in the future.

## DeepAI AI Image Generator

The AI Image Generator (https://deepai.org/machine-learning-model/text2img) is one of several AI tools offered by DeepAI. (DeepAI also offers a text-to-speech tool and an AI Video Generator.) There is a free version available, with limited access. DeepAI Pro runs $4.99 per month and offers up to 500 "calls" (image prompts) per month.

You generate an image from the main page, shown in Figure 7.17. Enter your description into the **Create an image from text prompt** box, choose a model (standard definition or high definition), and then select one of the available art styles. The AI Image Generator displays five of the most popular art styles by default; click **View all styles** to see more.

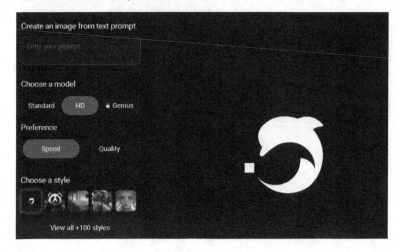

**FIGURE 7.17**

*The user interface of DeepAI's AI Image Generator.*

When you click the **Generate** button, you see the results, as shown in Figure 7.18. From here you have several options:

- **Download** the image to your computer in JPEG format
- **Enhance** the image by regenerating it
- **Remove Background** to do just that and show only the foreground image
- **Animate** to import the image into DeepAI's AI Video Generator and create a short video based on the image

**FIGURE 7.18**

*An image generated by DeepAI's AI Image Generator.*

## Deep Dream Generator

Deep Dream Generator (https://deepdreamgenerator.com) is a somewhat basic AI image generator, at least in terms of extra features. While there is a free trial available, it's somewhat limited in the number of images you can generate—about 10 images in total, depending on the complexity of the image. Paid plans let you generate more images and run from $9 per month for the Basic plan (36 images per day) all the way up to $99 per month for the Ultra plan (360 images per day).

To use the Deep Dream Generator, shown in Figure 7.19, simply enter your prompt into the **Text Prompt** box, choose the desired AI model (Artistic, Photonic, etc.), and then scroll down to the bottom of the page and click the **Generate** button. You can also upload image files (by clicking the **Visual Prompt** button) to provide visual guidance to the image generator.

The Deep Dream Generator generates the desired image, as shown in Figure 7.20. Click the **Download** button to download the image to your computer in JPEG format.

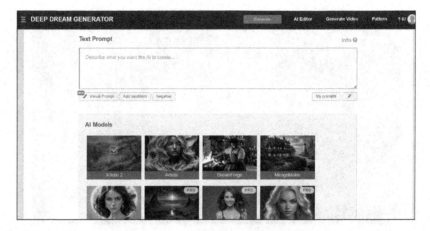

**FIGURE 7.19**

*The prompt entry page for Deep Dream Generator.*

**FIGURE 7.20**

*An image created by Deep Dream Generator.*

## DreamStudio by Stability AI

DreamStudio (https://dreamstudio.ai) works like most of the other tools discussed here. It also lets you upload your own images to create variations and different versions.

DreamStudio operates on a "credits" system. Each credit is good for generating five images and, if you sign in with your Google account, you get 25 credits for free. You can purchase an additional 1,000 credits for $10.

As you can see in Figure 7.21, the prompt panel is where you get the party started. Select what style of image you want (for example, photographic, anime, comic book), enter your description into the **Prompt** box, select how many images you want to generate (the default is four), and then click the **Dream** button. It's pretty easy to use.

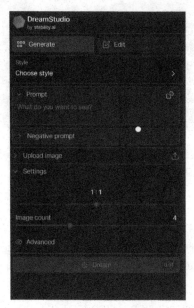

**FIGURE 7.21**

*DreamStudio's easy-to-use prompt panel.*

Figure 7.22 shows the images that DreamStudio generates. Hover over an image to generate additional variations, edit the image, download the image, or delete the image.

**FIGURE 7.22**

*Photorealistic images generated by DreamStudio.*

## Google Gemini

As noted in Chapter 3, Gemini (https://gemini.google.com) is Google's AI model. Unlike many other general-purpose tools, Gemini lets you generate both text and image output.

Google Gemini's basic version is free to use; Google Gemini Advanced offers the next generation model (that theoretically can generate better results) and the ability to use Gemini from within Google Docs and other apps. Image generation is available in both versions.

To use Google Gemini for image generation, you need to type **create an image of** in front of your normal prompt. You then elaborate on this basic instruction with more details, such as **create a photorealistic image of** or **create a fantasy illustration of**.

As you can see in Figure 7.23, Gemini generates four images in response to your prompt. Mouse over any image and click the **Download** (down arrow) icon to download that image.

 **NOTE** Google also offers the ImageFX image generation tool, located at aitestkitchen.withgoogle.com/tools/image-fx. ImageFX, which uses the same AI model, is essentially Gemini's image generation but with a more user-friendly graphical interface. It should generate similar images.

**FIGURE 7.23**

*Generating images with the Google Gemini AI tool.*

## Hotpot AI Art Generator

The Hotpot AI Art Generator (https://hotpot.ai) is a web-based image generation tool. It can also upload your photos to create corporate headshots and illustrated avatars.

Hotpot offers a free plan, which puts watermarks on all your images, and a paid subscription, which costs $10 for 1,000 credits. (Each generated image costs 50 credits.)

To use the Hotpot AI Art Generator, just answer the questions on the AI Generator panel, shown in Figure 7.24. Enter what to draw, what not to draw, style, your own image (if you choose to upload one), how many images to make, and aspect ratio. Click **Create** to generate the image(s).

You see the generated image, as shown in Figure 7.25. Click **AI Resize** to resize the image; **AI Edit** to remove the background, add text, or make other edits; **Download Image** (down arrow) to download the image in PNG format; or **Share Image** to share the image on social media.

**FIGURE 7.24**

*Prompting the Hotpot AI Art Generator to create a new image.*

**FIGURE 7.25**

*An image generated by the Hotpot AI Art Generator.*

 **NOTE** Hotpot's Corporate Headshots tool is useful when you're job hunting or just need a nice-looking headshot. Upload any decent photo of yourself and Hotpot turns it into a professional-looking headshot photo. It also puts you in a variety of corporate-appropriate outfits. This feature is priced separately from the main Hotpot AI Art Generator; it runs $10 for 40 images.

## Image Creator from Microsoft Designer

Image Creator from Microsoft Designer (https://designer.microsoft.com/image-creator) is another AI image generator based on OpenAI's DALL-E model. (It was formerly known as Bing Image Creator.)

Image Creator is a free tool; no subscription plans are offered. You can also access it from Copilot in Windows, as discussed in Chapter 3.

Using Microsoft Designer's Image Creator is as simple as entering your instructions into the prompt box and clicking the **Generate** button. As you can see in Figure 7.26, several results are displayed.

**FIGURE 7.26**

*Generating images with Image Creator from Microsoft Designer.*

Click any image to view it larger and access various options. On the next page, as shown in Figure 7.27, you can **Download** the image in JPEG format; **Copy** the image to paste into another application; click the **Create Design** button to use the image in another design, using Microsoft Designer; or **Edit** the image in Microsoft Designer by cropping it, removing the background, and so forth.

**FIGURE 7.27**

*Working with a generated image in Microsoft Designer's Image Creator.*

## Midjourney

Midjourney is a powerful AI image generator that allows a comparatively large amount of image customization. There is no free version available; you need to sign up with a Google or Discord account and then choose a subscription plan. Plans are priced from $10 per month for the Basic Plan to the $120 per month Mega Plan that offers significantly faster processing and can run more jobs concurrently.

You access Midjourney at www.midjourney.com. When you log in to your account, you see the Explore page (shown in Figure 7.28) with samples of generated images from other users. Click an image to see the prompt and configuration options that generated that image.

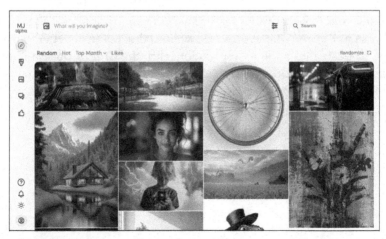

**FIGURE 7.28**

*Midjourney's Explore page.*

To generate your own images, click Create in the sidebar to display the Create page, shown in Figure 7.29. You now see images you've previously created as well as the Imagine Bar at the top of the page. This is where you enter your prompts.

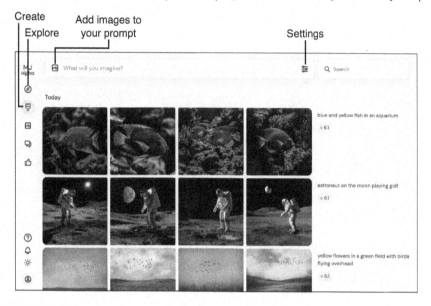

**FIGURE 7.29**

*Midjourney's Create page, complete with Imagine Bar.*

What makes Midjourney unique is that it lets you configure its image generation engine in a number of interesting ways. This lets you fine-tune the images you create.

For example, to upload a reference image, click the **Add Images to Your Prompt** icon on the left side of the Imagine Bar. You can upload images that provide examples of characters or styles you want to reference.

For even more customization options, click the **Settings** icon on the right side of the Imagine Bar. This opens the panel shown in Figure 7.30, with the options detailed in Table 7.2.

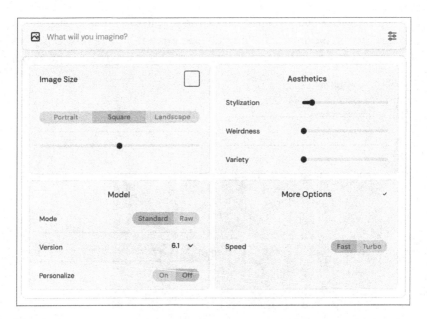

**FIGURE 7.30**

*Customizing Midjourney's image generation settings.*

**TABLE 7.2**   Midjourney Image Generation Settings

| Setting | Description |
| --- | --- |
| Image Size | Sets the size and aspect ratio of the image. Select from one of three preset ratios (Portrait 3:4, Square 1:1, Landscape 4:3) or drag the slider left or right for more extreme aspect ratios. |
| Stylization | Low values produce images that closely match the prompt but are less artistic; high values are more artistic but less related to the prompt. |
| Weirdness | The higher the value, the more quirky or offbeat the image is likely to be. |
| Variety | Lower values provide more reliable and repeatable results; higher values produce more unusual and unexpected results. |
| Mode | The default mode is Standard; the Raw mode applies less automatic "beautification" and may more closely match the prompt. |
| Version | Lets you choose which version of Midjourney to use. The higher the number, the more recent the version. |
| Personalize | When enabled, uses information from your likes and ranking of other images to personalize the images you create. |
| Speed | Turbo mode is faster than the Fast mode but uses more GPU credits, which are limited by your subscription plan. |

Once you've entered your prompt into the Imagine Box and set your parameters, press Enter on your keyboard. Midjourney generates four images to match your request, as shown in Figure 7.31.

**FIGURE 7.31**

*Four images generated by a Midjourney prompt; click any image to view it larger.*

Click any image to view it larger. You have the option to take more actions on this specific image. The following options are available in the right-hand pane, as shown in Figure 7.32:

- Download an image by clicking the **Download** icon at the top of the pane.

- Generate more images based on this image by clicking either the **Subtle** or **Strong** buttons in the Vary section. Subtle generates less dramatic variations; Strong generates more extreme variations.

- Create a larger version of this image suitable for printing and other uses by clicking the **Subtle** or **Create** buttons in the Upscale section. Subtle doubles the size of the image exactly; Creative doubles the size of the image and adds new details.

- Run the same prompt again by clicking the **Rerun** button.

- Crop, zoom, or change the aspect ratio of the image by clicking the **Editor** button.

- Use the generated image as a reference image for a new prompt by clicking the **Image** button.

- Use the generated image as a style reference for a new prompt by clicking the **Style** button.

- Copy the existing prompt into the Imagine Bar by clicking the **Prompt** button.

**FIGURE 7.32**

*Available actions for fine-tuning an image.*

As you can see, Midjourney offers a plethora of options for fine-tuning the images it generates. This makes Midjourney a good choice for those who want to generate high-quality images with specific parameters.

## NightCafe

NightCafe (https://creator.nightcafe.studio) is unique in that it uses and lets you choose from a variety of AI image-generation models. You can even fine-tune any of these models to create your own custom model attuned to your personal tastes and needs.

 **NOTE** Different companies have created their own models for generating AI images. For example, OpenAI created the DALL-E model and Google created the Gemini model. Each model uses unique programming and algorithms and is trained on its own unique set of data. This is why you get different results when you type the same prompt into different AI image generators—they each work in their own ways.

Like most of these AI image generators, there's a free version available, although it only gives you five credits per day. (A low-resolution image costs one credit.) You purchase the Pro version via credit packs priced from $5.99 for 100 credits per month to $49.99 for 1,400 credits per month.

The **Create** panel, shown in Figure 7.33, is where you get started. Click the **Model** selector to select which model you want to use—at this writing, you have the choice of Dreamshaper XL Lightning, DALL-E 3, Stable Core, and Stable Video Diffusion. (If you scroll down, you can choose from a variety of community-created models, too.) Enter your image description into the **Text Prompt** box, select a style, (cinematic, color painting, CGI character, and so on), and then click the **Create** button.

**FIGURE 7.33**

*Choosing an AI model and generating an image with NightCafe.*

The resulting image is displayed in the main pane, as shown in Figure 7.34. From here you can duplicate (copy) the image, evolve the image by creating another one anew, enhance the image by increasing its resolution (which costs credits), download the image in JPEG format, or animate the image.

 **NOTE**   NightCafe's use of multiple AI image models makes it a great choice to try out different models without having to visit multiple websites.

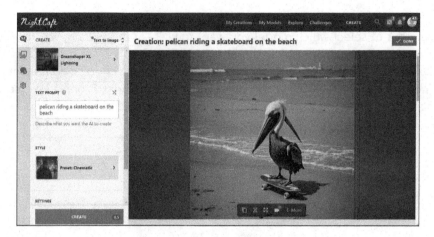

**FIGURE 7.34**

*Viewing a newly generated image in NightCafe.*

## OpenArt

OpenArt (https://openart.ai) is like NightCafe in that it lets you choose from multiple AI image generation models. When you first join, you get 50 credits to use; the Start plan offers 5,000 credits per month for $12 per month, the Hobbyist plan gives you 15,000 credits per month for $24 per month, and the Pro plan delivers unlimited credits for $56 per month.

To use OpenArt, go to the Create panel, shown in Figure 7.35. To switch to a different AI model, click the **Switch** button and make a selection. (Current options include the site's own OpenArt SDXL, Juggernaut XL, DALL-E 3, DreamShaperXL, Stable Diffusion XL, and literally dozens more.) Like NightCafe, you can also access models created by the user community or fine-tune your own models.

Once you've chosen a model, you can scroll down to upload a pose, composition, style, or face reference. Click the **Create** button to generate your image.

The image you generate is shown in the main part of the window, as shown in Figure 7.36. Hover over an image to display it larger, download it in JPEG format, or delete it.

**FIGURE 7.35**

*Selecting model and generation options with OpenArt.*

**FIGURE 7.36**

*Viewing generated images with OpenArt.*

# Crafting the Perfect Prompt to Generate Perfect Images

Crafting the perfect prompt to generate perfect images is just like crafting a text prompt for an all-purpose AI tool, but with visual concerns added. It's really about describing exactly what you want to see—the main image, the background, the style, the output type, and more. Here are some tips:

- **Be as clear as possible.** Instead of words that have a low information content, such as "beautiful" or "wonderful," use specific adjectives to describe appearance, mood, style, and other details. For example, if you want to see a large, gray striped cat, don't just prompt for **picture of a cat**; include all the details, such as **picture of a large gray striped cat with green eyes**.

- **But don't supply too many details.** As important as the details are, including too many can overwhelm some AI image models. If you end up with a real hodge podge of an image, try simplifying the prompt.

- **If there's a style you seek, point it out.** If you want a picture in the style of 20th century impressionists, include that in your prompt. If it's a photo you want or even a specific type of photo, like **high contrast black and white portrait** or **dreamy color like a wedding photo**, structure your prompt accordingly.

- **If you want something real in the image, say so.** Instead of saying you want a picture of a beach, say you want a **picture of Pacific Beach in California**.

- **Include motion and emotion.** Don't just describe who or what is in the picture, but what they're doing. Instead of **children on a playground**, prompt **children chasing each other around a playground**. Instead of saying **a couple looking at each other**, say **a couple looking lovingly at each other**.

- **Use the tool's options.** Some AI image generation tools only let you input a text prompt. Others include various controls and options that help you fine-tune your image. If there are options available, use them.

Remember, different AI image generators will generate different images. You may need to try several different tools to get the results you want. And don't be afraid to fine-tune your query or "remix" an image if the first one you get is close but not quite right. AI image generation is still in its infancy, so experimentation is key.

# Summary

This chapter was a lot of fun to write because creating images with AI is a fun way to visualize what you could previously only see in your imagination. You learned how AI generates images, how AI image generators work, and all about the most popular AI image generators today. You also learned all the various types of images you can create with AI and the prompts to use to do so.

AI image generators are fun to play with for your own personal or casual use. But using them for commercial use is another story. Professional artists should not try to pass off AI-generated art as art they personally created. The artistic community doesn't look kindly upon that kind of misrepresentation; if you use AI to create a commercial image (or even one you share on social media), you need to say so clearly.

You also learned that you shouldn't use AI to create fake images designed to fool people. Even though AI can do that, and often does it quite convincingly, it isn't ethical to do so.

There's a reason why there are so many AI image generators out there today and why they're so popular: They're fun to use and can actually be quite useful. Just be careful how you use them and what you use them for.

8

# USING AI TO GET A JOB

AI can help you find your next job, from choosing a career path and company that suits you to drafting your resume and cover letter. AI can even help you prepare for the interview!

As with all AI-related activities, you'll want to use caution with every step, keeping in mind that AI can make mistakes and fill in blanks with inaccuracies. So use AI to make your job hunt easier, but take what AI outputs as a jumping off point and never a final say.

# Using AI to Help Find the Job You Want

Sometimes the hardest part of the job search is determining the job you want. Whether you're looking for your first job, a new opportunity in your field, or a different career, AI can help.

## Identifying the Types of Jobs That Suit You

The first thing AI can help you with, career-wise, is identifying those jobs you may be particularly suited for or interested in. In this regard, AI can help you fine-tune a career path based on your experience, skill set, interests, strengths, and weaknesses.

Identifying an appropriate career is easily done with all-purpose AI tools, such as ChatGPT, Google Gemini, and Microsoft Copilot. To start, craft a prompt that includes your key skills, past experiences, and preferred work style, then ask the AI what jobs or careers you might be suited for. The prompt can look something like this:

> **Please recommend some careers for me. My skills include [skill 1], [skill 2], and [skill 3]. I have experience doing [experience 1], [experience 2], and [experience 3]. My previous jobs have included [job 1], [job 2], and [job 3]. I like to work [independently/as part of a team/remotely/in an office].**

Include as many or as few variables as apply to your particular situation. Obviously, if you're just starting out, you won't have as many (or any) prior job experiences; if you're further along in your career, you'll have more highlights to add.

When I entered a similar prompt into ChatGPT with my own skills and job experience, I got the recommendations you see in Figure 8.1.

**Memory updated**

Given your extensive experience and skills, here are several career paths you might consider:

1. **Content Strategy Director**: Overseeing the creation and curation of content across various platforms, aligning it with the marketing goals of an organization.

2. **Chief Communications Officer**: Leading the communications department within a company, responsible for both internal and external communications, shaping the organization's messaging and brand voice.

3. **Senior Copywriter/Editorial Director**: Focusing on creating high-quality content, managing a team of writers, and ensuring consistency and accuracy in all published materials.   ↓

**FIGURE 8.1**

*Some personalized career recommendations from ChatGPT.*

## Researching Potential Employers

When you're considering where you might like to work, the more you know about a potential employer, the better decision you can make. Fortunately, most all-purpose AI tools have plenty of information about larger companies, having ingested employee reviews, social media posts, news articles, and information on the companies' websites.

For a general overview of a company, use the following prompt:

> **What does [company] do?**

To get an idea of what it's like to work at that company, use the prompt

> **What is it like to work at [company]?**

You can also ask more targeted questions, such as

- **What is the work culture like at [company]?**
- **What is the work-life balance like at [company]?**
- **What is the average employee age at [company]?**
- **What are [company's] values?**

- **How satisfied are the employees at [company]?**

- **What is [company's] financial health?**

You can also use AI to identify key decision-makers at a company—information that might otherwise be relatively hidden from the general public. Just enter the prompt

**Who are the key decision-makers at [company]?**

Or, for a more targeted search, enter

**Who are the key decision-makers in the [name of department] department at [company]?**

This is one aspect of the job search where AI can really lead you astray. Make sure you double-check its output on potential employers.

 **NOTE**   You can also use similar strategies to learn more about people you can network with in your job search. If you know what company a person works for, use AI to learn more about that company and even that person's department before you start networking.

# Using AI to Write a Resume

Just knowing what job you want or where you want to work isn't enough. You need to put together a resume that really sells your skills and experience to potential employers, is well organized, and is clear and well written—with no typos!

Fortunately, AI can do most of the work for you.

## Writing a Resume with an All-Purpose AI Tool

Writing a resume is something that generative AI tools do well. All you have to do is tell AI a little bit about yourself and that you need a resume written. You can then cut the response from your AI tool and paste it into your favorite resume template in Google Docs or Microsoft Word and—voilà!—you have a professional resume in hand.

When it comes to crafting the perfect resume-creation prompt, you need to enter the key information that employers will want to see. This information should include

- Desired position

- Current and past work experience—list positions and employers, including dates employed, along with your duties and key accomplishments in each job

- Important skills—include position-specific skills (for example, if you're a welder, welding would be an important skill) as well as more general skills, such as teamwork, leadership, creative thinking, strategy, and so forth

- Education, including college degrees and professional training

- Other accomplishments, including professional certifications, awards, honors, and major projects

Such a prompt might look something like this:

**Write a resume for a [position]. My skills include [skill 1], [skill 2], [skill 3]. My employment history includes [position 1, employer 1, dates employed], [position 2, employer 2, dates employed], and [position 3, employer 3, dates employed]. I graduated from [name of school] in [year] with a [name of degree and/or major] degree. I have accomplished/received [accomplishment 1], [accomplishment 2], [accomplishment 3].**

The resulting resume might look something like the one in Figure 8.2

**Summary**

Highly motivated and results-oriented Senior Writer with 14+ years of experience crafting compelling content across various media. Proven ability to develop and execute content strategies that engage audiences, increase brand awareness, and achieve marketing goals. Skilled in various writing styles, including copywriting, SEO writing, and social media content. Adept at working independently and collaborating effectively within teams.

**Experience**

**Senior Writer** | Bob's Books | May 2020 – Present

- Developed and implemented content strategies for the company website, blog, and social media channels.
- Created engaging product descriptions, blog posts, and social media content that increased brand awareness and website traffic.
- Optimized website content for search engines, resulting in a [quantifiable improvement] in ranking for targeted keywords.
- Collaborated with marketing and design teams to ensure brand consistency

**FIGURE 8.2**

*The start of a resume written by Google Gemini.*

**WARNING** Make sure you proofread and edit any resume that AI writes for you. AI engines like to read between the lines, so to speak, and fill in any gaps in your resume. In doing so, they might make things up that you haven't really done. Always remember that AI regularly makes mistakes, so review the resume to be sure it is accurate.

## Writing and Fine-Tuning a Resume with a Resume-Writing Tool

There are also several AI tools specifically designed for writing resumes. Some popular tools include Jobscan, Kickresume, Rezi, Teal, and Zety. This section covers each in turn.

### IMPROVING YOUR RESUME AND LINKEDIN PROFILE

You can also use all-purpose AI tools to get tips on how to improve an existing resume. Just cut and paste your resume into the tool along with the prompt **provide recommendations to improve my resume**.

All-purpose AI tools can also help you optimize your LinkedIn profile, which many employers look at when they're considering job applicants. Just copy and paste your resume into an all-purpose AI tool, accompanied by the prompt **Write a LinkedIn "About" section using my resume as a guide**.

### Jobscan

Jobscan (www.jobscan.co) can use AI to generate resumes based on your inputs, as well as match your resume to open positions. It can also analyze your current resume, score it, and suggest improvements. The free version offers two resume scans a month and limited functionality. For $49.95 per month, you get unlimited resume scans, resume editing and management, job matching, and more. (Figure 8.3 shows the result of a sample Jobscan resume scan.)

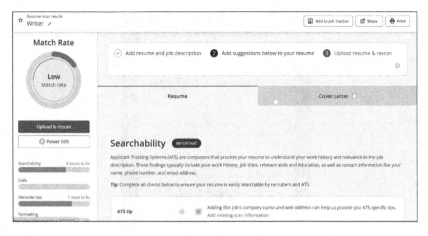

**FIGURE 8.3**

*The result of a resume scan by Jobscan.*

## Kickresume

Kickresume (www.kickresume.com) uses OpenAI's GPT-4 AI model to power its resume-creation service. You pick a template, enter key information about yourself, and Kickresume does the writing for you. The site also includes a resume checker for your existing resume, a cover letter builder, and a personal website builder. The free plan includes four basic resume and cover letter templates; the $19 per month plan provides more than 40 resume and cover letter templates, the resume checker, and the AI Resume & Cover Letter Writer. Figure 8.4 shows how Kickresume's AI Wizard works.

**FIGURE 8.4**

*Building a new resume with Kickresume's AI Wizard.*

## Rezi

Rezi (www.rezi.ai) offers AI resume building, editing, checking, and summary generator tools. (The summary analyzes your entire resume to generate a summary or introductory paragraph.) Rezi also offers an AI cover letter writer, resignation letter writer, and interview practice.

You can do a free trial that includes limited access to some (but not all) features. The Pro plan, which offers full access to all features and unlimited AI usages, costs $29 per month. Figure 8.5 shows a "Rezi Score" for a sample resume—not bad but could use some improvement.

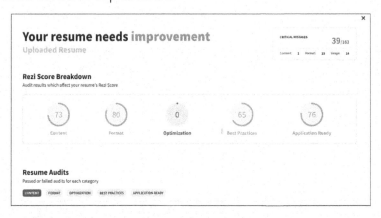

**FIGURE 8.5**

*Scoring a resume with Rezi.*

## Teal

Teal (www.tealhq.com/tools/resume-builder) uses AI to help you write and design your resume. Teal's Resume Builder, shown in Figure 8.6, also analyzes and scores your resume in terms of effectiveness and generates an introductory summary.

The basic version of Teal, which offers limited access, is free. The Teal+ plan offers unlimited access and more advanced features for $29 per month.

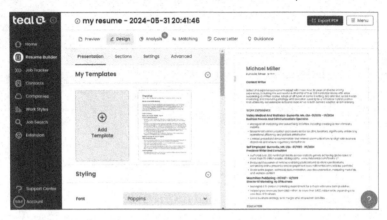

**FIGURE 8.6**

*Designing a resume with Teal's Resume Builder.*

## Zety

Zety (https://zety.com) is a resume and cover letter building tool that uses AI technology. You can use Zety to check your current resume, build a new one, and find the perfect resume template. Figure 8.7 shows a typical resume created by Zety. Zety costs $1.95 for 14-day limited access or $5.95 per month for full access to all features.

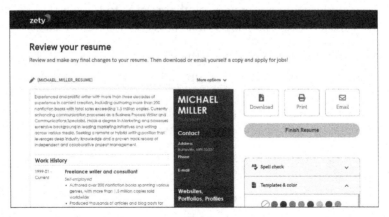

**FIGURE 8.7**

*A resume created by Zety.*

## USING AI TO APPLY FOR A JOB

Some of the AI resume-building tools just discussed offer job matching, which identifies open positions that match the skills, experience, and accomplishments on your resume. In most instances, however, you apply on either a company website or a web-based job platform, such as CareerBuilder, Indeed, or ZipRecruiter. (LinkedIn, while technically a social network, is also a significant source for jobs and lets you apply for many positions directly from its site.)

In addition, some AI-assisted job platforms can automate the application process by filling out your basic information across different companies and tracking the status of your applications. You can find this type of "easy apply" functionality at Indeed, LinkedIn, ZipRecruiter, and other sites.

# Using AI to Write Cover Letters

Most of the dedicated resume-building tools just discussed also draft, or help you draft, cover letters. Plus, you can use just about any all-purpose AI tool to write a cover letter for you.

To have AI write your cover letter, prompt it with the appropriate information. In particular, you need to tell it to **create a cover letter** and include the following:

- The name of the company to which you're applying

- The title of the job for which you're applying

- Why you're interested in the job and the company

- Basic information about yourself that relates to the job requirements, such as prior work experience, applicable skills, and notable accomplishments

- Anything else that expresses why you would be a good choice for the position

The AI tool should be able to take this information, fill in any gaps, and craft an effective cover letter. You can then cut and paste the AI text into your preferred cover letter format in Google Docs or Microsoft Word, along with your name, phone, email, and, if you have one, website or LinkedIn URL.

**WARNING**    You may hear about strategies to manipulate AI applicant tracker systems into favoring your materials. Tactics include things like keyword stuffing, where you front load your resume or cover letter with words that might cause your materials to be more appealing, or white fonting, which involves putting attractive words in a white font so that they aren't visible but do get picked up by an AI tool. Be warned: These strategies are strongly discouraged by professionals in the hiring world and may even cause your application to get rejected.

# Using AI to Prepare for Interviews

As you're aware, many general-purpose AI tools let you carry on a real-time conversation with the AI chatbot. You can use these conversations to practice for an interview. Just tell the chatbot you want to do a mock job interview, provide some details about the employer and the job, and then start chatting. The prompt may look something like this:

**Can we do a mock job interview with [employer] for [position]?**

I entered that prompt into ChatGPT for a content writer position and started the interview. Here's a transcript of one of the questions asked and my response.

**ChatGPT:**

*Can you describe a project or piece of content you worked on recently? What was your approach, and what were the outcomes?*

*This question is designed to understand your workflow and how you measure success in your work.*

**My response:**

*In my previous employment, I recently wrote a 70-page response to a patient complaint to the state medical board. I provided detailed responses to all 16 points in the complaint and backed it up with information from various sources.*

**ChatGPT:**

*That's a very detailed and high-stakes project showcasing your ability to handle complex and sensitive content effectively. Here's some feedback:*

*Strengths:*

*Detail-oriented: Your response to a multifaceted issue demonstrates strong attention to detail and thoroughness.*

*Research Skills: The ability to back up claims with information from various sources is crucial for a content writer and shows your commitment to accuracy and reliability.*

*Areas to Enhance:*

*Outcomes: It would be helpful to mention the outcomes of your efforts. For instance, was the complaint resolved favorably? What was the impact of your document on the case?*

*Relevance: If possible, relate this experience back to the content writer role you're applying for. For example, explain how these skills translate into writing compelling and well-researched content for different audiences or purposes.*

Note that ChatGPT prefaced the question with why the interviewer was asking that question and then assessed the strengths and weaknesses of my response. It also suggested areas where I could improve my answers. It's all quite useful and really helps you prepare for what you'll face in a real interview.

There are also several interview-focused websites that employ AI chatbots in the same fashion. These sites include

- aiApply (https://aiapply.co/ai-job-interview), free trial or $30 per month for additional functionality

- Final Round AI Interview Copilot (www.finalroundai.com), free trial that includes a five-minute interview or $49 per month for 60 minutes of interviews

- Interview Prep AI (https://interviewprep-ai.com), free trial or about $11 for five interview simulations

- Interviews by AI (www.interviewsby.ai), three interviews per month free or $9 per month for an unlimited number of interviews

All these platforms work in a similar fashion. You provide the job title for which you're interviewing, and the AI asks you typical questions. You answer and the AI evaluates your answers and offers suggestions for improvement.

 **NOTE**    One more thing. After you have a job interview, it's good form to send thank-you letters to the people you talked with at the company. You can use AI to write these thank-you letters; just prompt **write a short thank-you letter to [person's name] at [company] thanking them for meeting with me on [date]**. The AI tool will do the rest.

# Summary

In this chapter, you learned the many ways you can use AI to help you find, apply to, and interview for a job. General-purpose as well as specific AI tools do a good job with these tasks.

Using AI tools will help you conduct a more targeted and efficient job search, build effective resumes and cover letters, and prepare for job interviews. Just be sure to use AI as a starting point and check its output for accuracy.

9

# USING AI AT WORK

AI can speed up many tasks that used to consume a lot of time and make others less frustrating, such as scheduling meetings, taking notes, or creating memos and reports. AI can also help with some creative work, like putting together presentations, newsletters, and marketing materials. All you have to do is tell the AI tool what you want to do and how you want it done, and it will do the rest.

# Using AI to Improve Productivity

AI can help you improve your overall productivity at work—all types of businesses are already doing that. There are a number of ways that you can use AI to automate routine tasks and make your work life easier.

## Generating Content

As you've been learning throughout this book, generative AI is pretty good at generating many types of content. While there are some business-specific content-creation tools, the all-purpose tools I've covered work just fine for generating all sorts of work-related content, especially creative content.

How might you use AI to generate content in your job? Table 9.1 shows some of the ways, along with the prompts you might use to do each task.

**TABLE 9.1**   Types of Work Content AI Can Generate

| Content | Sample Prompt |
| --- | --- |
| Project ideas | Generate 3 ideas on how to improve our customer retention rate |
| Memos | Write a short memo informing staff that the office will be closed early this Friday for the long holiday weekend |
| Reports | Use the following information to create a 3-page report explaining the difference between projected and actual sales for the month of May [include information] |
| Charts and graphics | Graph the following monthly sales data [include data] |
| Speaker notes | Create notes for the following presentation [include presentation text] |
| Presentations | Create a 15-minute presentation promoting our services to the auto repair industry [include info about products] |
| Blog posts | Write a 500-word blog post about current economic conditions and how they will impact demand for our products [include relevant data] |
| Product descriptions | Create a short promotional description of our product for our website [include product details] |
| Press releases | Write a press release in standard format announcing the opening of our new location [include location information] |

Any all-purpose AI tool such as ChatGPT, Google Gemini, or Meta AI can generate this type of content. You only have to provide enough information for AI to properly do its job.

**NOTE**   As you learned in Chapter 4, "Using AI to Find the Right Words," you can also use AI to improve the grammar, style, and clarity of your work-related writing. Even if you're a natural writer, AI can help you improve the writing you have to do for work.

## Managing Projects

Managing team projects can be a challenge, especially on large projects and when you work with a team of many remote workers. Fortunately, you can use AI to help manage even your most complex projects. AI can take over many of the tedious and complicated tasks involved in project management, including

- Predicting project risks
- Optimizing resource allocation and automating project workflows
- Scheduling meetings
- Sending reminders and alerts
- Providing real-time project monitoring and updates
- Generating reports

AI is beneficial for project management in that it learns from user behavior and adjusts project assignments and deadlines accordingly. AI can analyze large amounts of project data to predict future outcomes, such as project completion dates, budget overruns, and resource shortages.

AI is also able to break a large project into smaller tasks and take a large number of tasks and other inputs and quickly make sense out of them. With the help of AI-based project management tools, managers can make better-informed decisions, make on-the-fly course corrections, and keep even the most complex projects on track.

That said, all-purpose AI tools are not the best approach for project management. Instead, you want to use one of several AI-based project management tools designed for business. The most popular of these tools include

- Asana (https://asana.com)
- ClickUp (https://clickup.com)
- Monday.com (www.monday.com)
- Smartsheet (www.smartsheet.com)

- Trello (https://trello.com)

- Wrike (www.wrike.com)

Most of these tools work in a similar fashion:

1. Start by creating a new project and giving it a name.

2. Configure the relevant options for that project: owner, description, due date, budget, notifications, and so on.

3. Add specific tasks to the project and assign those tasks to individuals on your team.

4. Add due dates for each task.

5. As the project proceeds, each team member notes their progress on the timeline, as shown in Figure 9.1.

**FIGURE 9.1**

*AI-based project management with Monday.com.*

The task management tool notifies team members when tasks are coming due and notifies the team leader when tasks are completed. You can also automate certain tasks, such as moving a task to a different group when completed or notifying team members when a new task is added. You can also program the tool to generate progress and other types of reports.

**WARNING**   Before using any AI tool for work, examine your organization's data privacy policy or consult with a superior. Your company may not want its proprietary information entered into a public AI tool.

## Communicating and Collaborating

Another important use of AI at work is enhancing communication and collaboration between team members. Some of these uses of AI can be accomplished with all-purpose AI tools; others require activity-focused or purpose-built tools.

Table 9.2 details some of the ways AI can enhance communications and collaborations, along with appropriate tools for each task.

**TABLE 9.2**  Ways AI Can Enhance Your Day-to-Day Communication and Collaboration

| Task | Appropriate AI Tool |
|---|---|
| Intelligently filter and prioritize email and other messages | AI built into email or messaging program |
| Automatically answer routine queries | Dedicated AI responder tools, including Ellie (https://tryellie.com), EmailTree (https://emailtree.ai), Flowrite (www.flowrite.com), and superReply (https://superreply.co) |
| Analyze the emotional tone of people with whom you're corresponding and suggest appropriate responses | All-purpose AI tools; copy message(s) into the tool and prompt **analyze the emotional tone of these messages** |
| Summarize large volumes of emails and messages to highlight and prioritize key themes and issues | Dedicated email/chat summary tools, including Hiver (https://hiverhq.com), Shortwave (www.shortwave.com), and Zapier (https://zapier.com); also can cut and paste multiple messages into an all-purpose AI tool and prompt **it to summarize contents** |
| Organize, categorize, and summarize large values of documents | Dedicated AI summarization tools, including Dokkio, DOMA (www.domaonline.com), and Nanonets AI (https://nanonets.com) |

Whatever tools are used, AI can help streamline collaboration processes, improve communications, and facilitate knowledge sharing—all of which can lead to more efficient and effective teamwork with your co-workers.

 **WARNING**   Remember to verify any AI-generated or sourced content before you include it in your documents, presentations, and plans. AI is sometimes prone to "hallucinations" and just making stuff up, so make sure to fact check anything you use that's AI-generated.

# TRANSLATING DOCUMENTS AND CONVERSATIONS

If your work is global—or if you interface with teammates or suppliers in other countries—you know that the language barrier can be challenging. Fortunately, AI can help break that language barrier by interpreting conversations and translating documents in real time.

You can find value from these and other AI-based translation tools:

- DeepL (www.deepl.com)
- Google Translate (translate.google.com)
- Lingvanex (https://lingvanex.com)
- Microsoft Translator (https://translator.microsoft.com)
- QuillBot (https://quillbot.com/translate)
- Systran (www.systransoft.com)
- Wordvice AI (www.wordvice.ai/tools/translate)
- Yandex Translate (https://translate.yandex.com)

These and other AI-based translation tools use neural machine translation and other advanced techniques to deliver accurate and natural translations in real time. If you operate in a multilingual environment or interface with people who don't speak your language, these tools can make your job that much easier.

## Creating Presentations

If presentations are part of your job, AI can help. AI can take much of the stress out of creating presentations—even if it can't actually give presentations for you.

How can AI help prepare your next presentation? Consider that AI can

- Generate general presentation ideas based on the topic you select
- Create an outline for your presentation, incorporating any key points you enter
- Write the content for individual slides
- Source relevant data
- Create graphics and images for your slides, or identify appropriate images from other sources
- Suggest and apply design templates that best match the presentation's content and your audience

- Adjust slide layouts to maximize the visual impact of information on individual slides

- Write a script or talking points based on your slides for you to use when delivering the presentation

An all-purpose AI tool can do much of this for you. For example, you could enter a prompt to **generate a 15-minute presentation on how to use Microsoft Teams for group collaboration.** Figure 9.2 shows how ChatGPT interprets this command. Just cut and paste the text from ChatGPT into Microsoft PowerPoint or Google Slides and then add the recommended graphics.

**Presentation on How to Use Microsoft Teams for Group Collaboration**

**Slide 1: Title Slide**

- **Title:** Mastering Group Collaboration with Microsoft Teams

- **Subtitle:** Unlocking Efficient Communication and Productivity

- **Image:** Logo of Microsoft Teams

- **Presenter Name and Date**

**Slide 2: Introduction to Microsoft Teams**

- **Title:** What is Microsoft Teams?

- **Bullet Points:**

  - Overview of Microsoft Teams as a collaboration platform

  - Key features: Chat, Teams, Channels, Meetings

  - Benefits for group collaboration

- **Image:** Screenshot of Microsoft Teams interface

**FIGURE 9.2**

*The recommended contents of a presentation created by ChatGPT.*
*source: www.chatgpt.com*

There are also AI tools designed specifically for creating presentations, including

- Beautiful.AI (www.beautiful.ai)

- Decktopus (www.decktopus.com)

- Sendsteps (www.sendsteps.ai)

- SlidesAI (www.slidesai.io)

- Tome (https://tome.app)

Each of these tools works a little differently but they all follow the same general approach. For example, Sendsteps asks you what you want your presentation to be about. You can answer with as little or as much detail as you like. The tool presents several possible titles; choose one and specify the desired length of the presentation in terms of minutes and number of slides. Sendsteps generates an entire presentation for you, which you can edit to your liking, including choosing slide themes and layouts. Figure 9.3 shows one such presentation.

**FIGURE 9.3**

*An AI-generated presentation from Sendsteps based on a simple prompt:* **benefits of AI for office workers**.

**NOTE**   Microsoft PowerPoint includes the AI-powered Designer feature that suggests design ideas based on slide content. It also includes Presenter Coach, which provides feedback on your presentation's pacing and language.

In addition, some AI presentation tools can help you practice delivering your presentation. You can get feedback on pacing and delivery that will help you deliver an engaging presentation to your audience.

# Using AI to Make Meetings More Manageable

AI can help you schedule meetings, transcribe and take meeting notes, and even summarize the contents of meetings. It's like having a virtual assistant doing all the meeting dirty work for you.

## Scheduling Meetings

Let's start with one of the more challenging aspects of meeting management: getting the darned things scheduled. Scheduling a meeting involves juggling the individual schedules of the invitees—and the more potential attendees, the more difficult that task becomes. Trying to find a free hour on the schedules of a half-dozen or more individuals is a thankless proposition.

That's where AI comes in. Provide AI appropriate access to all employee calendars, and it can immediately find that one hour everyone has free on their schedules. No more shuffling back and forth between different coworkers' schedules to see if that person is free at 1:00 pm on Monday; AI does all that grunt work for you.

That's not all AI can do, either. When it comes to scheduling meetings, the appropriate AI-powered meeting management tool can

- Access multiple calendars to find open time slots across all participants, even those in different time zones

- Manage work, personal, and social media calendars—including Teams and Slack

- Automatically send meeting invitations and—closer to the meeting—reminders to all attendees

- Automatically suggest new times for meetings if conflicts arise

- Book physical meeting rooms and equipment, if needed

- Help you prepare for the meeting by creating agendas, gathering necessary documents, and even suggesting topics based on current projects and previous interactions with chosen participants

In addition, AI-powered meeting tools can learn individual preferences for meeting times, lengths, and attendees. This lets the AI tool fine-tune meetings to suit employees' work habits.

All of these tasks are beyond what you might expect from an all-purpose AI tool. Instead, you want to check out an AI-powered meeting scheduling tool, such as

- Calendly (https://calendly.com)

- Clara (www.claralabs.com)

- Clockwise (www.getclockwise.com)

- Doodle (https://doodle.com)

- Motion (www.usemotion.com)

- Reclaim (https://reclaim.ai)

Some of these tools are cloud-based, whereas others reside on your company's servers or on your home computer. All work in pretty much the same way; after you link the tool to your personal or work calendar, you tell the tool you want to schedule a meeting of a given length with specified individuals, and the tool does the rest.

Scheduling a meeting with one of these AI-powered meeting tools is relatively simple. You start by connecting the tool to your company's email or messaging program, such as Microsoft Outlook or Microsoft Teams; this gives the program access to employees' email addresses and personal schedules. You then tell the program what meeting you want to schedule, who should be invited, and when would be some good times for the meeting. (You may also be able to specify that you need the meeting scheduled by such and such date or time.) The tool works through the schedules of all invitees, determines the best time for all involved, and sends out invitations. Figure 9.4 shows how Reclaim does it.

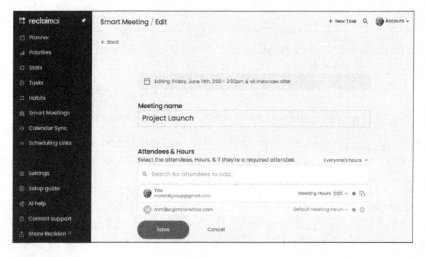

**FIGURE 9.4**

*Scheduling a Smart Meeting with Reclaim.*

## Taking Notes and Summarizing Meetings

AI isn't just for scheduling meetings; it can also capture and summarize the content of meetings. This makes meetings more durable and functional without any extra effort on your part.

Here are just some of the ways you can use AI-powered meeting apps to get the most out of your meetings:

- Transcribe the minutes of a meeting using voice-to-text transcription technology

- Organize and categorize meeting notes based on topics, keywords, or tags

- Analyze and summarize the content of a meeting and then distribute that summary

- Highlight the key points of a meeting and create to-do lists for meeting attendees

- Suggest related articles or notes based on meeting contents

- Store meeting notes for future search and retrieval

 **NOTE**  You need to notify meeting attendees, especially those outside your company, if you're using AI to record or transcribe a meeting.

Some of the more popular AI-powered note-taking platforms include

- Claap (www.claap.io)

- Fathom (https://fathom.video)

- Fireflies (https://fireflies.ai)

- Otter AI (https://otter.ai)

- tl;dv (https://tldv.io)

Several of these tools, including Claap and Fathom, make video recordings of your online meetings and then work from those recordings to transcribe and summarize the meetings. Others work from meeting audio.

If you're using one of these tools in a physical meeting, you need to open the app on your computer or smartphone and manually start recording in the app when the meeting starts, using your device's camera and microphone. If you're recording an online meeting, you need to configure the app to work with your meeting app, such as Google Meet, Microsoft Teams, or Zoom; the app starts recording when the meeting starts. Some tools also let you upload audio or video files from previously recorded meetings.

When the meeting starts, the AI tool does its job automatically. Some transcribe the meeting in real time; others create the transcription when the meeting is over. You typically get the option of editing a transcript before you save it or send it to meeting participants or others in your company. Figure 9.5 shows a typical meeting transcript generated by Otter AI.

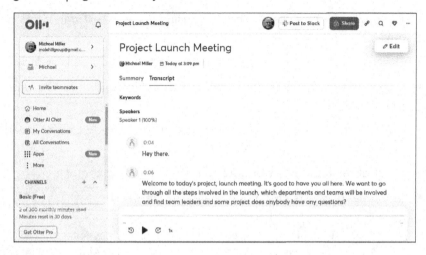

**FIGURE 9.5**

*An Otter AI meeting transcript.*

By leveraging these AI-powered note-taking tools, you can enhance your productivity, organization, and knowledge management capabilities. This will make it easier for you to capture, retain, and later retrieve information—and get the most of your many meetings.

# Summary

This chapter covered just some of the many ways you can use AI at work. In particular, you learned how AI can automate routine tasks, manage projects, generate content, enhance communication and collaboration, and create presentations. You also learned how AI can schedule, manage, and summarize meetings.

That's a lot of ways AI can help you at work, but it's just the tip of the iceberg. Many companies are using purpose-built AI tools to perform specific tasks in their businesses. Don't be surprised to sit down at your desk one morning and be presented with a new AI tool you can use to help optimize your work!

## IN THIS CHAPTER

- Using AI to create travel plans
- Using popular AI-powered travel planning tools
- Using AI to prepare for a trip
- Using AI during a trip
- Using AI in local transportation

# 10

# USING AI FOR TRAVEL AND TRANSPORTATION

Thanks to the dynamic duo of predictive and generative AI, travel is getting easier. From determining your itinerary and booking your tickets to navigating your route and acting as a real-time translator, AI is set to play a major role in your travel and transportation needs.

That said, AI is not perfect, especially when it comes to travel planning. AI can and sometimes does make mistakes that can include travel recommendations that don't exactly fit what you're looking for. In addition, AI doesn't always possess the most up-to-date data, which means it might not have the latest information about flights, lodging, and routes. It's always best to supplement AI recommendations with your own research and information from established travel and navigation sites.

# Using AI to Create Travel Plans

AI is already playing a major role in trip planning. You can use AI to determine where to vacation, get personalized recommendations for your next trip, and book the right flights and rooms—at the right price. AI can streamline and personalize the entire travel planning process.

Much travel planning can be done using the all-purpose AI tools I discuss in Chapter 3, "Getting Started with All-Purpose AI Tools," including ChatGPT, Claude, Google Gemini, and Microsoft Copilot. There are also several AI-powered travel-specific tools available that provide even more travel-related functionality; I cover those in the next section.

Whatever tool you use, AI can assist at every stage of the travel planning process.

## Making Personalized Travel Recommendations

One of the things that AI is good at is making personalized travel recommendations. If you feed AI the right information—your past travel history, things you like to do, your budget, and the trip timing and duration—it can suggest new destinations for you to enjoy. AI matches your preferences with the vast amount of data on which it was trained, resulting in personalized recommendations that you might not think of otherwise.

You can also use AI to research where you'd like to go. Let's say that, based on your past experiences, AI recommends a trip to Florida. You can then ask AI about the area in which you're interested, things to do there, best times to go, and the like.

Providing recommendations in this fashion is something that both all-purpose AI tools and AI-powered travel-specific tools are good at.

## Booking Flights and Accommodations

Most AI-powered travel tools (but not all-purpose AI tools) can handle all aspects of your travels, including booking flights, finding accommodations, and even making restaurant reservations. These tools use AI to analyze historical data and predict pricing trends to determine the best time to book your reservations. This could potentially save you significant money.

## Creating an Itinerary

Once you've chosen a location for your travels, you can have AI create a detailed day-by-day itinerary for your trip. Both all-purpose AI tools and travel-specific tools can do this, although you might get more detailed and accurate results from a travel-specific tool.

To have AI create an itinerary, just feed it information about where you're going, for how long, and what you like to do. You can, if you want, include information about yourself and your travel companions (if any), physical restrictions you might have, and specific activities or locations that must be included. For even more detailed recommendations, feed the AI details about your flights and hotel reservations.

For example, you might use prompts like the following:

- **Create an itinerary for a family with three elementary-age kids visiting the Orlando area for a week in April.**

- **Suggest a list of activities for my husband and I to do in New York City over a weekend. We both like Broadway shows and museums.**

- **We are traveling to California wine country for three days. Recommend an itinerary that includes as many wineries as possible.**

- **Suggest a good route for a weekend getaway in New England in early October.**

- **Create an itinerary for our upcoming trip to Europe considering the following flights and hotel reservations [include information].**

AI will consider the information you provided and suggest the best things to do each day you're there.

**WARNING**   All-purpose AI tools may not always have up-to-date information, so you should verify all recommendations they make. In addition, you may find recommendations that include seasonal establishments or those that have recently closed. Travel-specific sites and tools are apt to have more accurate and up-to-date information.

## Functioning as a Virtual Travel Assistant

It's important to know that interacting with AI is more like dealing with a real travel agent than just filling out a few fields on a web form. AI chatbots can interact with you in a conversational manner, understand your queries, and provide real-time responses. They may even be better than human travel agents in handling complex travel arrangements.

# Using Popular AI-Powered Travel Planning Tools

Although you can use an all-purpose AI tool such as ChatGPT, Claude, or Meta AI to plan your next trip, using a focused AI-powered travel planning tool is probably the better bet. As you can see in Table 10.1, there are several of these tools available, all focused on helping both leisure and business travelers get the most out of their next trips.

**TABLE 10.1**  AI-Powered Travel Planning Tools

| Tool | URL | Price |
|------|-----|-------|
| GuideGeek | https://guidegeek.com | Free |
| Layla | https://layla.ai | Free |
| Roam Around | https://roamaround.app | 30 tokens/$10 |
| Trip Planner AI | https://tripplanner.ai | Free |
| Wonderplan | https://wonderplan.ai | Free |

## GuideGeek

GuideGeek (https://guidegeek.com) is an AI-based travel service for your Android or Apple iOS smartphone. It uses the OpenAI engine and travel information obtained over the Internet—and curated by human experts—to answer your travel-related questions.

You use GuideGeek from within either Instagram, Facebook Messenger, or WhatsApp apps; it's totally free. Just ask GuideGeek a travel-related question and you'll get your answer.

Figure 10.1 shows GuideGeek in action within Instagram; I asked it to make some recommendations for outdoor activities in Madison, Wisconsin, over a long weekend. The interaction looks just like a normal Instagram messaging session.

 **NOTE**   Because GuideGeek is smartphone based, it's a good tool to use on the go while you're traveling.

**FIGURE 10.1**

*Obtaining travel recommendations from GuideGeek via Instagram.*

## Layla

Layla (https://layla.ai) is a multifunction AI-based travel planning tool. You can ask Layla for travel inspiration, to find specific types of attractions or destinations, to plan road trips and other itineraries, and to book flights and hotel rooms.

You can use Layla from its website or via its Android or Apple iOS apps. It's free.

As you can see in Figure 10.2, all you have to do is enter your question or prompt into the **Ask me anything** box and click the **Ask** button. Figure 10.3 shows a typical response to a typical question.

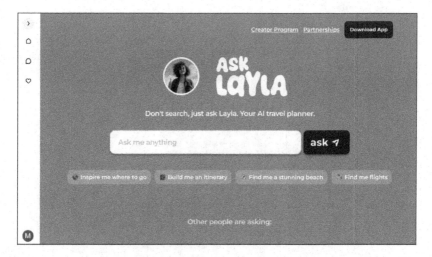

**FIGURE 10.2**

*Asking Layla a travel-related question.*

**FIGURE 10.3**

*Layla's travel recommendations.*

# Roam Around

Roam Around (https://roamaround.app) lets you enter information about where you're going, and it generates what it calls a "hypercustomized" travel plan. To use Roam Around, enter your destination, the number of days you'll be there, and any information about the type of trip and what you might like to see, as shown in Figure 10.4. Roam Around generates a fairly detailed itinerary for your trip, as shown in Figure 10.5.

**FIGURE 10.4**

*Planning a trip with Roam Around.*

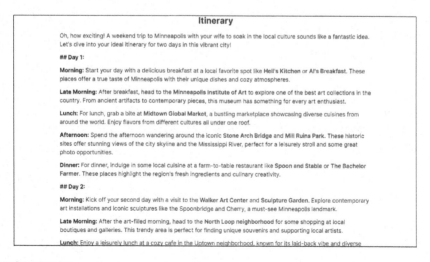

**FIGURE 10.5**

*A detailed itinerary from Roam Around.*

Unlike some of the other AI-powered travel planners, Roam Around isn't free. Each travel plan you create costs one travel token; you can purchase 30 tokens for $10. Roam Around is available on the web or as an Android or Apple iOS app for your smartphones.

## Trip Planner AI

Next up is Trip Planner AI (https://tripplanner.ai), a free AI-powered trip planner. Just tell Trip Planner AI where you want to go and when, as well as the kind of activities you're looking for (as shown in Figure 10.6), and Trip Planner AI does the rest.

**FIGURE 10.6**

*Planning a trip with Trip Planner AI.*

Figure 10.7 shows the results from Trip Planner AI. You get a day-by-day itinerary with each activity detailed on a map of your destination. You can also use Trip Planner's Hotel Finder to find hotels and Airbnb locations convenient to your trip activities.

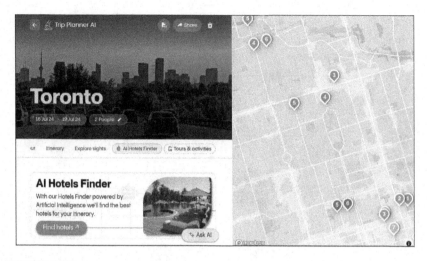

**FIGURE 10.7**

*How Trip Planner maps out your travel itinerary.*

## Wonderplan

The final AI-powered travel planning site I'm covering is Wonderplan (https://wonderplan.ai). This is a free travel planning site, shown in Figure 10.8. Just tell it your destination, when you're traveling, your budget, and your favorite activities, and Wonderplan generates an itinerary for you.

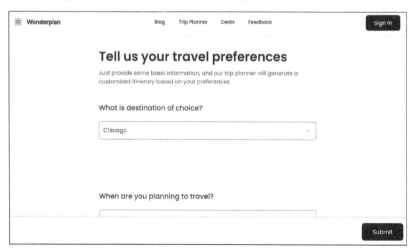

**FIGURE 10.8**

*Entering key information about your trip into Wonderplan.*

As you can see in Figure 10.9, Wonderplan's results look a little like those of Trip Planner, in that all your activities are plotted on a map of your destination. Click any item to read more.

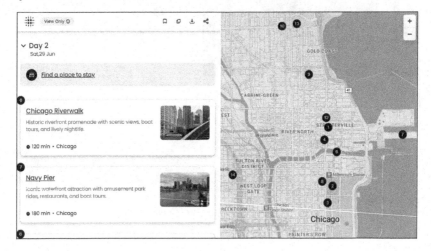

**FIGURE 10.9**

*Viewing Wonderplan's suggested itinerary for a weekend trip to Chicago.*

 **NOTE** Many major travel booking sites have also integrated AI into their sites for trip recommendations, booking, and more. Among the sites using AI in whole or in part are Booking.com, Expedia, Kayak, Google Travel, and Hopper.

# Using AI to Prepare for a Trip

AI is useful for more than just suggesting where to go and booking tickets to get there. You can use AI at almost every stage of your travel planning—and even to suggest some tasks you might not think of on your own.

## Researching Documentation Needs

If you're just taking a weekend trip down the road, you don't need anything special in terms of documentation. But if you're traveling out of the country, you might need a passport, visa, or other documents—and requirements can vary from country to country.

Ask your AI a question like this:

**I'm travelling to Europe in March. I'm going to England, France, Italy, Switzerland, and Poland. What documents do I need to take with me and how do I get them?**

Figure 10.10 shows what ChatGPT recommends.

Traveling through multiple countries in Europe will require some specific documents and preparations. Here's a general guide to help you:

1. **Passport:** Ensure your passport is valid for at least six months beyond the period of your intended stay. If you need a new passport or must renew your existing one, contact the nearest passport agency or the passport office in your country.

2. **Visas:**

   - **Schengen Visa:** For France, Italy, Switzerland, and Poland, you may need a Schengen visa if you are not from a visa-exempt country. This visa allows you to travel freely within the Schengen Area for up to 90 days within a 180-day period.

   - **UK Visa:** England requires a separate visa if you are not from a visa-exempt country. Check the UK government's official website to see if you need a visa and to apply online.

3. **Travel Insurance:** It's advisable to have travel insurance that covers medical expenses, theft, and cancellations. Some Schengen countries require proof of travel insurance when you apply for a visa.

4. **International Driving Permit (IDP):** If you plan to rent a car, you might need an IDP, along with your regular driver's license, especially in Italy and Poland.

**FIGURE 10.10**

*Using ChatGPT to determine what documents you need to procure before traveling to Europe.*

You can also use AI to discover medical recommendations for traveling to some destinations outside the country, such as vaccinations for malaria and yellow fever. Just enter a prompt like this:

**What medical recommendations do you have for a trip to Nigeria?**

Figure 10.11 shows what Claude AI recommends.

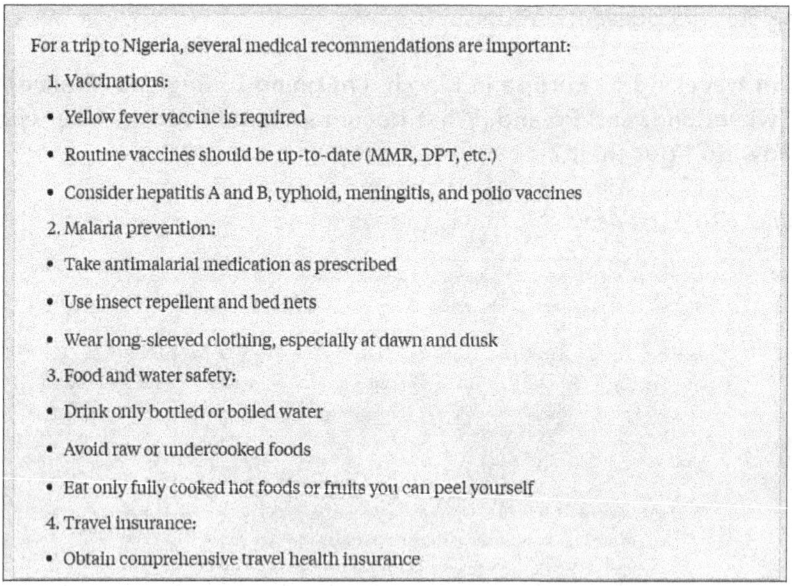

For a trip to Nigeria, several medical recommendations are important:

1. Vaccinations:

- Yellow fever vaccine is required
- Routine vaccines should be up-to-date (MMR, DPT, etc.)
- Consider hepatitis A and B, typhoid, meningitis, and polio vaccines

2. Malaria prevention:

- Take antimalarial medication as prescribed
- Use insect repellent and bed nets
- Wear long-sleeved clothing, especially at dawn and dusk

3. Food and water safety:

- Drink only bottled or boiled water
- Avoid raw or undercooked foods
- Eat only fully cooked hot foods or fruits you can peel yourself

4. Travel insurance:

- Obtain comprehensive travel health insurance

**FIGURE 10.11**

*Claude AI's medical recommendations for a trip to Nigeria.*

## Learning Local Languages

If you're traveling to a non-English speaking country, it helps to know a little of the local language before you arrive. Fortunately, several AI-powered language learning tools can help you become fluent in a variety of foreign languages—or at least learn enough to get by. These tools include

- Babbel (www.babbel.com)

- Busuu (www.busuu.com)

- Duolingo (www.duolingo.com)

- Memrise (www.memrise.com)

- Mondly (www.mondly.com)

- Rosetta Stone (www.rosettastone.com)

These tools have incorporated AI technology to create personalized learning experiences and provide immediate feedback on your progress. It can make learning a new language easier than it used to be.

## Getting Packing Assistance

Don't know what to pack for your upcoming trip? A handful of AI-powered apps can help. They take into account where you're going, the length of your trip, and the activities you have planned, as well as historical weather trends and the upcoming forecast to recommend the type of clothing and accessories to pack.

These AI-powered personalized packing apps include

- PackPoint (www.packpnt.com)
- Packr (www.packr.app)
- WhatToPack (www.whattopack.ai)

These apps can help you avoid over- or under-packing, ensure you have everything you need for your planned activities, and prepare you for varying weather conditions. They'll also help you stay more organized when packing, so you won't forget anything important.

## Predicting the Weather

Part and parcel of smart packing is taking weather conditions into account. While it's still impossible to precisely predict the weather more than a day or two out, AI-powered weather apps analyze past weather patterns and current forecasts to provide more accurate forecasts for your desired location.

Among the most popular of these AI-powered weather apps are

- Atmo (https://atmo.ai)
- Rainbow Weather (www.rainbow.ai)
- Tomorrow.io (https://weather.tomorrow.io)

## Enhancing Your Personal Security

Traveling can bring with it risks related to health, safety, and (depending on the destination) political instability. Use these AI-powered apps to get updates on real-time threats at your travel destination, including violence and disease outbreaks:

- GeoSure (www.geosureglobal.com/individuals)
- Sitata (www.sitata.com)
- TravelSmart (www.travelsmartapp.com)

# Using AI During a Trip

AI's utility for travelers doesn't stop when you get to your destination. There are plenty of ways you can use AI during your trip—on either your smartphone, tablet, or computer.

## Getting Personalized Recommendations

While you can (and should) use AI to plan your itinerary and activities in advance, you probably still want to do some exploring on the fly, even if it's just finding a good restaurant for dinner. Use general AI tools or travel-specific tools to recommend nearby restaurants, clubs, attractions, and experiences. Remember to include details of your tastes and expectations in your prompts.

## Providing Cultural Insights

Traveling to different places can expose you to different customs and cultures. Use AI to learn about the customs and cultural sensitivities of where you're traveling, such as what time dinner is typically eaten, whether tipping is expected, how formal the people are, how punctual they are, how to greet others (Handshake? Cheek kisses? Bowing from the waist?), and other things that the locals know and you might not. You want to conduct yourself with the proper etiquette for your location.

Finding this information is as easy as asking any all-purpose AI tool the question **what are the cultural sensitivities of [country]**. You'll get a very useful response such as the one shown in Figure 10.12.

Japan is known for its rich cultural heritage and unique social etiquettes. Understanding these sensitivities can be crucial for anyone interacting with Japanese culture or doing business in Japan. Here are some of the key cultural sensitivities to keep in mind:

1. **Respect for Hierarchy**: Japanese society places a strong emphasis on hierarchy and respect for authority. It's important to recognize and respect the seniority of individuals in social and business settings.

2. **Politeness and Formality**: Politeness is deeply ingrained in Japanese culture. Formal language, known as keigo, is commonly used in business and when addressing people of higher status or strangers. Being overly casual can sometimes be seen as disrespectful.

3. **Indirect Communication**: In Japan, direct confrontation is often avoided in favor of a more indirect approach to communication. Reading the atmosphere (kuuki wo yomu) and understanding non-verbal cues are important skills in Japanese social interactions.

4. **Group Harmony (Wa)**: Maintaining group harmony is a fundamental value. Japanese culture emphasizes the group over the individual, and decisions are often made with the group's best interests in mind.

5. **Punctuality**: Being on time is considered a virtue in Japan. Arriving late can be seen as a sign of

**FIGURE 10.12**

*Learning about the culture and customs of Japan, courtesy of ChatGPT.*

## Navigating Your Route

When you're traveling, especially out of the country, you don't often know the best way to get from point A to point B. Should you walk? Take a taxi or ride-share service? Use public transportation? Rent a car or drive your own vehicle?

You can use AI to help you determine the best form of transportation and the best routes to take.

As always, you can ask general navigation questions of just about any all-purpose AI tool, but using a navigation-specific tool will probably be easier and generate more targeted results. These AI-powered navigation tools will help you decide what type of transportation to take, optimize your route, provide turn-by-turn instructions, and offer real-time traffic updates. They also provide up-to-date information about public transit systems (buses, trains, and subways), including routes and schedules—all useful information when you're visiting an unfamiliar city.

The most popular of these AI-powered navigation tools include

- Apple Maps (www.apple.com/maps/)
- Google Maps (https://maps.google.com)
- HERE WeGo (https://wego.here.com)
- MapQuest (www.mapquest.com)
- Waze (www.waze.com/live-map/)

That's right, the most popular AI navigation tools just happen to be today's most popular map and navigation apps. That's because they have evolved to include AI assistance, particularly in providing predictive routing based on historical data and current conditions, real-time road conditions and traffic updates, safety alerts, and more. Just fire up your favorite map app on your smartphone and let AI help you get to where you want to go!

## Translating on the Fly

When you're travelling out of the country, you won't always have a firm grasp on the native language. It helps to have some sort of on-the-fly translation assistance, which AI can provide.

Several AI-powered translation apps can help you communicate more effectively in places where you don't speak the language. These apps can translate spoken and written text in real time and even work offline if you download the necessary languages ahead of time. These smartphone-based apps include

- DeepL Translate (www.deepl.com)

- Google Translate (https://translate.google.com)

- iTranslate (https://itranslate.com)

- Microsoft Translator (https://translator.microsoft.com)

- Papago (https://papago.naver.com)

There are also several portable AI-powered language translation devices. These devices (from Anfier, Javisen, Vasco, and other companies) look like small smartphones and use AI to translate words and photos from one language to another. In this instance, AI is embedded in a handheld device with a microphone, speaker, and camera. Figure 10.13 shows the handheld Vasco Translator device.

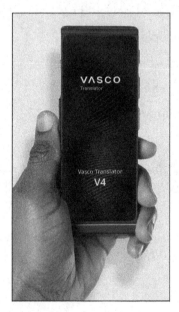

**FIGURE 10.13**

*The portable Vasco Translator device.*

## Keeping You Safe While Traveling

AI-powered personal safety apps can help keep you safe when you're traveling. Some of these apps send out alerts when you're in trouble and some also provide location-specific safety tips and ratings and alert you to potential dangers in your area.

The most popular of these personal safety apps include

- bSafe (www.getbsafe.com)

- GeoSure (www.geosureglobal.com/individuals)

- Smart Traveler (https://2009-2017.state.gov/r/pa/ei/rls/dos/165020.htm)

## CREATE A PERSONAL SAFETY PLAN

Before any trip, it's a good practice to put together a personal safety plan for yourself that you can share with family and friends back home. This plan should include all details of your itinerary—where you're staying, flights you're taking, etc.—and local contact numbers. This way the people will know how to contact you if they need to.

For your own use, this plan should include contact information for local authorities, hospitals, and the like for each of your destinations. You can use AI to assemble this information and store it on your smartphone and, if you're bringing it with you, your computer. It wouldn't hurt to keep a print copy of this plan in your luggage, too, just as a backup.

The whole point of this is to be prepared in the event that something unexpected happens. If you've done your homework in advance, any unfortunate incidents can be dealt with more efficiently and quickly.

# Using AI in Local Transportation

AI can significantly enhance many aspects of your daily transportation, making your various commutes more efficient, safer, and even more enjoyable. As always, AI might not have the most up-to-date information about routes and schedules, so verify details before you set out.

## Getting Where You Want to Go

Just as Maps, Google Maps, Waze, and other navigation apps can help you navigate cities to which you travel, they can also help you optimize your travels locally. These AI-powered apps can help you choose the best route to any destination on any given day and at any given time, taking into account real-time incident reporting, road construction, and weather conditions.

Don't assume that your old familiar route will always be the best one. Road conditions are constantly changing, and you never know what traffic is going to be. These apps can help predict the best route based on real-world conditions.

## Optimizing Ride Sharing and Carpooling

Ride sharing services such as Lyft, Uber, and Via use AI algorithms to match you with drivers in the shortest possible time. In addition, many carpooling apps use AI to match you with other riders with similar routes and destinations.

To find carpool apps in your area, search "AI-powered carpooling apps."

## Finding Parking

In crowded metropolitan areas, it's often a hassle to find a parking spot. Fortunately, AI can work with real-time data to both book parking spots in advance and find open parking spots. These apps analyze historical parking patterns to suggest the best places and times to park, often at discounted rates.

Some of the most popular AI-powered parking apps include

- Parkopedia (www.parkopedia.com)
- SpotHero (https://spothero.com)
- Valet EZ (https://valetez.com)

## Optimizing the Use of Public Transportation

If you use public transportation at home or when you travel, AI can help you obtain real-time transit information and advice. You can use AI to determine the best transit options, the fastest routes, and the lowest-price fares.

The best way to do all this is with an AI-powered public transportation app, such as one of the following:

- Citymapper (https://citymapper.com)
- Moovit (https://moovit.com)
- MyTransit (www.mytrans.it)
- Transit (https://transitapp.com)
- Umo (https://umomobility.com)

# Summary

In this chapter, you read about the many ways AI can help you plan and enjoy your trips and travels. You saw how AI can help you choose your destination, prepare an itinerary, and prepare for your trip—from learning local languages to figuring out what to pack. You also discovered how to use AI to make it easier to get around town.

Just remember to use common sense when using AI for travel. AI doesn't always have the most up-to-date local information, and it can sometimes make recommendations that don't mesh with your needs. As with all things AI, double-check the advice you get before you act on it.

Travel and transportation are two good examples of how AI will touch all aspects of your daily life. In fact, many such uses of AI are already happening behind the scenes, helping to power and optimize the many mapping apps and travel services you use on a regular basis.

IN THIS CHAPTER

- Using AI to create personal fitness and nutrition plans
- Using AI for your mental health
- Using AI to understand health and wellness information

11

# USING AI FOR HEALTH AND WELLNESS

As you've learned throughout this book, there are many uses for artificial intelligence. One of the most personally impactful uses is to improve your individual health and wellness. Although AI will never replace a trusted medical provider, it can help you improve your physical and mental health and better understand the healthcare options available to you.

# Using AI to Create Personal Fitness and Nutrition Plans

AI can be a useful health and wellness helper. It's particularly useful in creating personalized plans for your fitness and nutrition. By feeding it information about your age, gender, weight, height, activity levels, medical history, food preferences, and weight/fitness goals, any all-purpose AI tool can create plans tailored to your personal needs and wants.

 **WARNING** You should consult with a healthcare professional before undertaking any new fitness or nutrition regimen.

## Creating a Fitness Plan

Let's start with using AI to create a fitness plan. Everybody's bodies are different, and we each have unique goals for working out and staying fit. You may be looking to maintain your current health, increase your flexibility, build up your muscles, or something entirely different. Whatever your personal goals, AI can help.

You can use any all-purpose AI tool introduced in Chapter 3, "Getting Started with All-Purpose AI Tools," such as ChatGPT, Meta AI, or Microsoft Copilot, to create personalized fitness and workout plans. When you feed it the proper information, the AI tool can recommend specific exercises, workout routines, and intensity levels. It's all a matter of feeding AI the proper information through a detailed prompt.

What should your prompt include? For best results, make sure it includes your

- Age
- Weight
- Height
- Gender
- Health status
- Any physical challenges, injuries, or disabilities (such as bad knees, asthma, or osteoporosis)
- Desired type of workout (low impact, weight training, cardio, high-intensity interval training, and so on), if you have one
- What kind of exercise equipment you own (if any)

**WARNING**   Be cautious when providing personal information to AI tools. Any information you provide can be used for further training and responses by that tool; your privacy is not ensured. If you're not comfortable providing personal details like your height, weight, and health issues to others, you shouldn't provide it to an AI tool, either.

Your prompt should also include any specific goals you might have. Here are some examples:

- **Create a workout plan that helps me increase my mobility**
- **List 20 stretches I can do to start my day**
- **Create a six-month weightlifting plan to help me build my leg muscles**
- **Create a yoga routine for cardio**
- **Prepare an exercise routine for balance**

Putting it all together, you'd enter a somewhat complex prompt that looks something like this:

> **I'm a [age] year-old [gender]. I weigh [weight] pounds and am [height] tall. I have bad knees and can't walk long distances. Create a workout plan to improve my cardio activity that takes less than 30 minutes a day.**

When I fed this particular prompt into Meta AI, I got the plan shown in Figure 11.1.

---

◯ **Meta AI**
Considering your constraints, I've created a low-impact, knee-friendly cardio workout plan for you. This plan consists of short, manageable sessions, each under 30 minutes. Please consult your doctor before starting any new exercise routine.

**Warm-up (5 minutes)**

- Seated leg swings (front and back)
- Seated arm circles (forward and backward)

**Monday (Upper Body Cardio)**

- Seated dumbbell punches (15 reps x 3 sets)
- Seated rowing (using resistance bands or light dumbbells) (15 reps x 3 sets)
- Seated bicycle crunches (15 reps x 3 sets)

**Tuesday (Low-Impact Aerobics)**

- Seated marching in place (3 sets of 2 minutes)
- Seated leg lifts (15 reps x 3 sets)
- Seated arm raises (15 reps x 3 sets)

**Wednesday (Rest Day)**

**Thursday (Upper Body Cardio)**

- Repeat Monday's workout

**Friday (Low-Impact Aerobics)**

- Repeat Tuesday's workout

---

**FIGURE 11.1**

*A personalized fitness plan from Meta AI.*

## Creating Nutrition and Meal Plans

Similarly, an all-purpose AI tool can create personalized nutrition and meal plans that can help you maintain your weight, lose or gain weight, or just eat healthier. Feed the same personal information into the AI tool along with your dietary goals, using prompts like this:

- **Create a meal plan to help me lose 10 pounds in the next three months.**

- **Create a meal plan to help me maintain my weight during the winter months.**

- **I currently eat a lot of snack foods and fast food and don't have a lot of time to prepare meals. Create a nutrition plan to help me eat healthier.**

- **I'm a type 2 diabetic and need to watch my carbs. Create a nutrition plan to help me eat properly for my condition.**

 **NOTE** You'll get more medically accurate results if you also tell AI what medications you're taking.

Put all this together and you might create a prompt like the following:

**I'm a [age] year-old [gender]. I weigh [weight] pounds and am [height] tall. I don't always have time to cook my own meals, so I eat out a lot. Can you create a meal plan to help me lose 20 pounds in the next 6 months?**

I fed this prompt into ChatGPT and got the recommendations you see in Figure 11.2, along with sample meal plans for each meal and tips for eating out more wisely.

## BEWARE OF UNSAFE GOALS

AI seems to have limited guardrails built in to ensure that its advice is safe. For instance, when I asked ChatGPT for a plan to lose 20 pounds in 10 days, it responded: "Losing 20 pounds in 10 days is an extreme goal that is generally not considered safe or sustainable. A more realistic and healthy weight loss rate is about 1-2 pounds per week. Rapid weight loss can lead to muscle loss, nutritional deficiencies, and other health problems. However, I can suggest a more gradual and sustainable plan to help you lose weight effectively and healthily." Still, it is always advisable to consult an expert before starting a new regime.

To achieve a weight loss of 20 pounds over six months, we'll aim for a gradual reduction in weight that focuses on a balanced diet and incorporates options from restaurants, since you eat out frequently. Given your stats, a moderate calorie deficit that allows for safe and sustainable weight loss would be ideal.

Here's a tailored meal plan that considers your age, weight, height, and lifestyle:

### Estimated Calorie Needs

Based on your age, weight, and height, your estimated daily caloric needs for maintenance (not weight loss) are approximately 1700 calories. To lose weight safely, a reduction of about 500 calories per day is recommended, which would lead to about a pound of weight loss per week. This puts your target at about 1200-1300 calories per day. However, this is just an estimate, and I'd recommend consulting a dietitian for a precise calculation tailored to your metabolism and activity level.

### Sample Meal Plan

**Breakfast (Choose one)**

- **Greek Yogurt & Fruit:** A cup of low-fat Greek yogurt with a half-cup of mixed berries.

- **Oatmeal:** A small bowl of oatmeal topped with a sliced apple and cinnamon.

**FIGURE 11.2**

*A personalized nutrition plan from ChatGPT.*

# Using AI-Powered Fitness and Nutrition Tools

All-purpose AI tools do a good job of creating personalized fitness and nutrition plans, but specialized fitness and nutrition tools can do even better. These tools not only provide personalized plans but also monitor your progress and, often, serve as virtual coaches for your workout routines.

These tools all work in similar fashion. You input your vital statistics and your goals, answer some questions about your lifestyle and preferences, and get back a personalized plan. Some of these tools interface with personal fitness devices, such as smartwatches and fitness trackers, to monitor your performance in real time. They then track your progress and adjust your routines as necessary.

Most of these AI-powered fitness and nutrition tools are mobile apps you use with your smartphone. This way you always have the tool with you when you're eating out or working out. Some of the more popular of these AI-powered apps include

- ArtiFit (https://artifit.app) creates personal workout plans, uses your phone's camera to track body movement, and provides real-time feedback.

- Coachify.AI (https://coachify.ai), which is tailored for fitness enthusiasts, provides personalized workout experiences, tracks progress, and ensures proper exercise technique.

- Fitbod (https://fitbod.me) creates personalized workouts and learns from each workout to enhance your continuing progress.

- FitnessAI (www.fitnessai.com), which is designed for weight training, optimizes sets, reps, and weight each time you work out.

- GymBuddy AI (www.gymbuddy.ai) creates personalized workout programs tailored your fitness level and goals.

- Lifesum (https://lifesum.com) lets you track your meals (including carbs, protein, and fat) versus your personal meal plan and uses AI to identify foods via image recognition.

- MikeAI (www.mikeai.co) offers personalized AI-generated fitness assessments, workout plans, and meal plans.

- MyFit-AI (https://myfit-ai.com) creates personalized fitness programs and meal plans.

- MyFitnessPal (www.myfitnesspal.com) is an all-in-one fitness, food, and calorie tracker.

- Noom (www.noom.com) is another all-in-one app that creates personalized meal plans and tracks meals and exercise; it provides statistics and insights to help you stay motivated over time.

- Planfit (https://planfit.ai) has personalized workout plans and access to a personal AI trainer.

- TempoFit (https://tempo.fit) offers personalized weight training plans that work with your smartphone camera to monitor your form and progress.

While some of these apps are free, most offer some sort of subscription plan with monthly or yearly payment options.

# Using AI for Your Mental Health

AI isn't just for your physical health. You can use AI to help maintain and improve your mental health. This section covers some of the ways you can use AI in this fashion. But always work with your healthcare provider if you have mental health concerns. AI is not a substitute for professional guidance.

**WARNING**   ChatGPT, Google Gemini, Microsoft Copilot, and other all-purpose AI tools were not specifically designed to address mental health needs. They can lack diagnostic accuracy and often misinterpret symptoms. While these tools can provide useful assistance, they should not be used as a substitute for professional counseling and psychotherapy.

## Providing Information and Resources

The first way that AI can assist your mental health needs is by providing information about mental health disorders, coping strategies, and resources. Just ask any all-purpose AI tools questions such as

- **What are the symptoms of depression?**
- **What causes bipolar disorder?**
- **How can I cope with anxiety?**
- **What resources are there to help with eating disorders?**

## Encouraging Journal Writing

One approach to better mental health is to keep a daily journal about your feelings, thoughts, and experiences. Journal writing can help you process confusing emotions and gain self-awareness.

All-purpose AI tools can help you start journaling and continue with it on a regular basis. Just prompt an AI tool with something along the following lines:

**Can you help me start writing a mental health journal?**

Once you get started, you may have trouble putting your thoughts into words. This is another area where AI can help. Just prompt the AI that you need to create a daily journal entry and then enter some of what you felt or experienced that day. You might start with something like this:

**I need to create a daily journal entry.**

Figure 11.3 shows how Claude AI responded. Just continue answering the AI's questions and you'll have your entry.

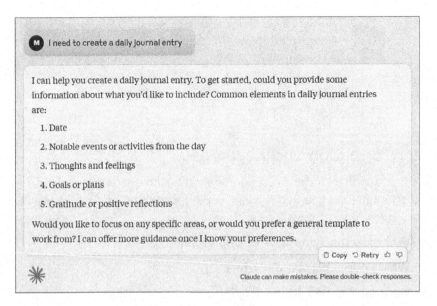

**FIGURE 11.3**

*How Claude AI can help you create a journal entry.*

## Guiding Cognitive Behavioral Therapy Exercises

Cognitive Behavioral Therapy (CBT) can help you identify and deal with negative thought patterns that may be causing stress and affecting your mental health. Any all-purpose AI tool can lead you through CBT exercises with a prompt like this:

**Guide me through some CBT exercises.**

Figure 11.4 shows how Google Gemini responded.

CBT, or Cognitive Behavioral Therapy, is a form of therapy that helps you change unhelpful thinking patterns that can contribute to negative emotions and behaviors. Here are a couple of exercises you can try yourself:

**1. Thought Challenging:**

- **Identify your triggers:** Pay attention to situations or events that cause you to feel anxious, sad, angry, or overwhelmed.
- **Catch the negative thought:** Once you notice a negative emotion, write down the automatic thought that popped into your head.
- **Challenge the thought:**
  - Ask yourself: Is this thought entirely accurate? Is there evidence to support it?
  - What's an alternative, more balanced way of looking at this situation?
- **Reframe the thought:** Rewrite your negative thought into a more realistic and helpful one.

**2. The ABC Model:**

This model helps you identify the connection between events (A), your beliefs (B),

**FIGURE 11.4**

*Letting Google Gemini guide you through CBT exercises.*

## Guiding Relaxation Exercises

Similarly, all-purpose AI tools can provide instructions for various relaxation techniques that can help improve your mental health. Here are some example prompts:

**Guide me through some relaxation exercises**

or

**Help me relax**

Figure 11.5 shows what Microsoft Copilot recommended.

**Copilot**

Certainly! Here are a few relaxation techniques you can try:

1. **Deep Breathing**: Find a quiet spot, sit or lie down comfortably, and take slow, deep breaths. Inhale deeply through your nose, hold for a few seconds, and then exhale slowly through your mouth. Repeat this several times.

2. **Progressive Muscle Relaxation**: Start from your toes and work your way up. Tense each muscle group for a few seconds, then release. Focus on the sensation of relaxation as you let go of tension.

3. **Visualization**: Close your eyes and imagine a peaceful scene, such as a beach, forest, or mountaintop. Picture the details vividly—the colors, sounds, and smells.

4. **Listen to Calming Music**: Choose soothing music or nature sounds. Let the melodies wash over you and help you unwind.

5. **Mindfulness Meditation**: Sit quietly and focus on your breath or a specific sensation. When your mind wanders, gently bring it back to the present moment.

Remember, relaxation is personal, so find what works best for you. 😊

**FIGURE 11.5**

*Getting relaxation advice from Microsoft Copilot.*

## Using Chatbots for Automated "Therapy"

While interfacing with an AI chatbot will never replace facetime with a human counselor or therapist, you can still get some value by talking about your problems with AI. For people who might otherwise be hesitant about seeing a therapist, AI chatbots, such as those offered by most all-purpose AI tools, can serve as a gateway to in-person therapy. In addition, some younger people may be more comfortable with a technological solution than talking to someone in person.

You can initiate a discussion with an AI chatbot with a simple prompt, such as

**I'd like to talk about a problem I'm having.**

The chatbot should respond, asking for more information. You then respond to that response and continue the conversation. (Figure 11.6 shows the start of such a conversation with ChatGPT.) It's not the same level of counseling you'd get from a trained professional, but it might be enough to help a little.

**NOTE**   If having a text-based discussion with an AI chatbot feels too impersonal, consider a chatbot from a multimodal AI tool, such as that offered by the ChatGPT mobile app. These voice-activated chatbots let you talk to the AI and then respond via computer-generated voices. It's a lot more natural approach that some people will appreciate.

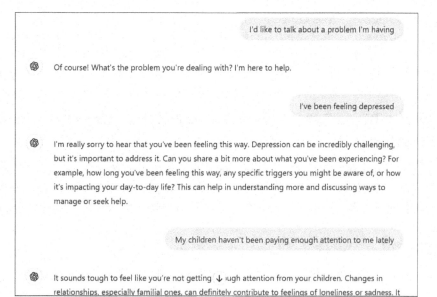

**FIGURE 11.6**

*Starting a "counseling" session with ChatGPT.*

## Using Purpose-Built AI for Mental Health

In addition to the functionality offered by all-purpose AI tools, several AI apps are designed especially for mental health needs. Some of the more popular apps include

- Calm (www.calm.com) offers stress relief, breathing and grounding exercises, and other tools to relieve anxiety.

- Happify (www.happify.com) provides exercises, activities, and games to improve your emotional well-being.

- MindDoc (https://minddoc.com) offers real-time mood tracking and analyzing patterns to provide useful insights into your emotional well-being.

- Replika (https://replika.com) is an AI chatbot that many use to share their thoughts and emotions.

- Rootd (www.rootd.io) is designed to help individuals deal with panic attacks.

- Youper (www.youper.ai) uses CBT and AI chatbots to provide mental health assessments, monitoring, and support.

In addition to these consumer-focused apps, many healthcare systems and employers offer AI-based mental health solutions for their enrollees and employees. Check with your employer or healthcare provider to see what's available to you.

# Using AI to Understand Health and Wellness Information

One of the challenges in dealing with your health and wellness is understanding symptoms, disorders, diagnoses, and the like. There's always technical medical lingo involved, and it isn't always easy to understand. AI, fortunately, can help.

## Researching Medical Conditions and Diagnoses

You can use AI to find out a lot of useful information before you contact your physician or healthcare provider. Sometimes this information can save you a trip to the doctor or clinic—or convince you that you need an in-person appointment.

In this regard, any all-purpose AI tool can do the job. Simply prompt the AI with your symptoms and receive a list of what could be causing your problem. For example, you might use one of these prompts:

**I'm experiencing neck and upper back pain when I wake up in the morning. What could be causing this?**

or

**I get stomach cramps and nausea after I eat ice cream. What could cause this?**

ChatGPT's response to the latter prompt is shown in Figure 11.7.

AI can also help you learn more about specific conditions—causes, common symptoms, seriousness, treatment, and the like. Just use a prompt like this:

**Tell me about bone spurs**

Figure 11.8 shows what Meta AI knows about that condition.

Stomach cramps and nausea after eating ice cream could be caused by a few different issues:

1. **Lactose Intolerance**: This is a common condition where your body lacks enough of the enzyme lactase, which is needed to digest lactose, the sugar found in milk and dairy products. Consuming dairy can lead to symptoms like cramps, nausea, bloating, gas, and diarrhea.

2. **Dairy Allergy**: Unlike lactose intolerance, a dairy allergy involves the immune system. If you're allergic to dairy, consuming milk-based products like ice cream can trigger a range of symptoms, including stomach cramps, nausea, hives, and even severe reactions.

3. **Cold-Induced Reactions**: Some people experience stomach pain or nausea from the cold temperature of ice cream, though this is less common.

4. **Overeating or Fat Content**: Sometimes, the simple act of overeating or the high fat content in some types of ice cream can lead to digestive discomfort.

If you consistently experience these symptoms after eating ice cream, it might be helpful to avoid dairy products and see if your symptoms improve. Additionally, consulting with a healthcare provider can help you determine whether you have a food intolerance or allergy and guide you on how to manage it.

**FIGURE 11.7**

*ChatGPT's analysis of some distressing symptoms.*

**Meta AI**
**What are Bone Spurs?**

Bone spurs, also known as osteophytes, are small, abnormal growths of bone that can develop on the edges of joints or on the surface of bones. They are usually smooth and hard, and can occur in various parts of the body, such as the:

- Spine (cervical, thoracic, or lumbar regions)
- Hips
- Knees
- Shoulders
- Hands and feet

**Causes of Bone Spurs:**

Bone spurs can occur due to various reasons, including:

- Osteoarthritis (wear and tear on joints)
- Inflammation or injury
- Poor posture or body mechanics
- Genetic predisposition
- Age-related wear and tear

**Symptoms of Bone Spurs:**

Bone spurs may not always cause symptoms, but can lead to:

- Pain or stiffness in the affected joint or area
- Limited range of motion or flexibility

**FIGURE 11.8**

*Learning about a given condition from Meta AI.*
*source: www.meta.ai*

You can also ask AI how to treat a specific condition. Use a simple prompt like this one:

**How can I treat an ingrown toenail?**

Figure 11.9 shows what Google Gemini recommends.

Ingrown toenails can be quite painful, but luckily there are home treatment options that can often resolve the issue. Here are some steps you can take:

- **Soaking:** Soak your feet in warm, soapy water for 10-20 minutes, 3-4 times a day. This helps reduce swelling and soften the nail.

- **Cotton or floss:** After soaking, gently lift the ingrown edge of the nail and place a small piece of cotton or dental floss under it. This will hopefully nudge the nail to grow in the right direction.

- **Antibiotics and bandaging:** Apply a thin layer of antibiotic ointment and bandage the toe to prevent infection.

- **Pain relievers:** Over-the-counter pain relievers like acetaminophen or ibuprofen can help manage discomfort.

- **Footwear:** Wear loose-fitting shoes or sandals to avoid putting pressure on the toe.

**FIGURE 11.9**

*Treatment advice from Google Gemini.*

## USE AI HEALTH ADVICE WITH CAUTION

As with all things AI, you should treat AI's medical advice with caution. Just as with any other online research, AI sometimes serves up all scenarios and not just likely ones. So don't panic if AI brings up extreme conditions or diseases in offering possible causes of your symptoms—you should focus on the most common causes, not the extremely rare ones.

This is why it's essential to verify any health-related information you receive from AI with what's available from trusted healthcare websites, such as Healthline (www.healthline.com), Mayo Clinic (www.mayoclinic.org), and WebMD (www.webmd.com). Just as important, you should always discuss vital health issues with your physician or clinician before taking any action on your own. AI isn't a trained medical professional; your doctor is.

## Researching Medications

You can also use AI to research medications. If you simply want to find out more about a given medication, ask AI a question like this:

**Tell me about [medication]**

Maybe you want to know the risks and side effects of a given medication, in which case you'd use a prompt like

**What are the side effects of [medication]?**

(Figure 11.10 shows such a response from Microsoft Copilot.)

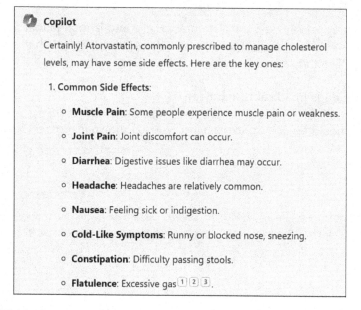

**FIGURE 11.10**

*Researching medication side effects with Microsoft Copilot.*

You can also use AI to uncover unfavorable interactions between medications with a prompt like this:

**Can I take [medication 1] along with [medication 2]?**

If you want to find some alternatives to a given medication (maybe you're allergic to the original or it's not covered by your health insurance), use the prompt

**What are some alternatives to [medication]?**

Finally, if you just want to find out what drugs are used to treat a given condition, use the prompt:

**What medications are used to treat [condition]?**

## Interpreting Medical Results

We depend on physicians and clinicians to keep us healthy, but sometimes they use medical jargon, acronyms, and language we don't understand. It's becoming increasingly common for test results to be sent home to you via a letter or patient portal without a call to explain the results. It's even worse when you examine your invoices or insurance documents; it's often difficult to figure out just what your results were or what you're paying for.

Fortunately, AI can help translate medicalese into language that anyone can understand. Enter confusing terms into the AI tool, along with the appropriate prompt, like this:

**What does [medical term] mean?**

The AI should be able to explain it to you, as shown in Figure 11.11.

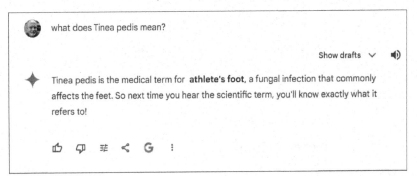

**FIGURE 11.11**

*Google Gemini translates a fancy medical term into plain English.*

Even better, ask AI to explain medical lingo or your doctor's instructions in plain English. Consider this prompt:

**Explain hypertension to me like I'm an 8th grader.**

When prompted in this fashion, Meta AI provided the easy-to-understand description shown in Figure 11.12.

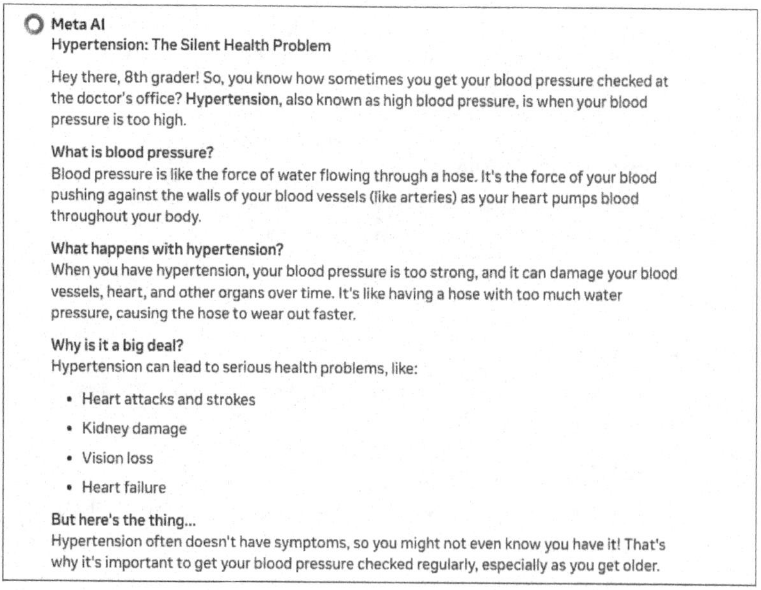

○ Meta AI
Hypertension: The Silent Health Problem

Hey there, 8th grader! So, you know how sometimes you get your blood pressure checked at the doctor's office? **Hypertension**, also known as high blood pressure, is when your blood pressure is too high.

What is blood pressure?
Blood pressure is like the force of water flowing through a hose. It's the force of your blood pushing against the walls of your blood vessels (like arteries) as your heart pumps blood throughout your body.

What happens with hypertension?
When you have hypertension, your blood pressure is too strong, and it can damage your blood vessels, heart, and other organs over time. It's like having a hose with too much water pressure, causing the hose to wear out faster.

Why is it a big deal?
Hypertension can lead to serious health problems, like:

- Heart attacks and strokes
- Kidney damage
- Vision loss
- Heart failure

But here's the thing...
Hypertension often doesn't have symptoms, so you might not even know you have it! That's why it's important to get your blood pressure checked regularly, especially as you get older.

**FIGURE 11.12**

*How Meta AI explains hypertension to an 8th grader.*

## Communicating with Healthcare Providers

You can use all your AI-based research to better communicate with your healthcare providers. Based on what you find out from AI, you can prepare more intelligent and targeted questions to ask your providers, as well as direct their attention to specific issues identified by AI.

For example, if your doctor says you need to cut back on carbohydrates, you can ask AI for help, like this:

> **My doctor told me I need to cut back on carbs. I don't know what this means. What do I need to do?**

Figure 11.13 shows how ChatGPT responds.

Similarly, if you're facing a surgical procedure and have some qualms and questions, ask AI for assistance:

> **I am preparing for sinus surgery. Can you give me some questions for me to ask my doctor about the surgery?**

Cutting back on carbs means reducing your intake of carbohydrates, which are found in foods like bread, pasta, rice, sugary snacks, and some fruits and vegetables. Carbohydrates can impact your blood sugar levels and weight, so managing their intake can be beneficial for your overall health. Here are some tips on how to cut back on carbs effectively:

**1. Understand Carbohydrates:**

- **Simple Carbs:** Found in sugary foods, white bread, pastries, and sodas. They are quickly absorbed by the body and can cause spikes in blood sugar.
- **Complex Carbs:** Found in whole grains, legumes, and vegetables. They are digested more slowly and provide a steady source of energy.

**2. Read Labels:**

- Check nutritional labels for carbohydrate content. Pay attention to both total carbohydrates and sugars.

**3. Choose Whole Grains:**

- Opt for whole grain versions of bread, pasta, and rice. Whole grains are higher in fiber and

**FIGURE 11.13**

*How ChatGPT explains a doctor's instructions.*

Figure 11.14 shows the questions Google Gemini provided.

 Absolutely, here are some important questions to ask your doctor in preparation for your sinus surgery:

**Before the Surgery:**

- **What type of sinus surgery will I be having and why?** (There are different procedures for different sinus issues)
- **What are the risks and complications associated with this surgery?**
- **What is the success rate of this surgery for my specific condition?**
- **How long will the surgery take?**
- **Will I need to stay overnight in the hospital?**
- **What kind of anesthesia will be used?**
- **What medications will I need to take before and after surgery?**
- **Are there any foods or drinks I should avoid before surgery?**

**Recovery:**

- **What can I expect for pain after surgery?**
- How long will it take to recover?

**FIGURE 11.14**

*Google Gemini prepares you for an upcoming surgery.*

# HOW THE HEALTHCARE INDUSTRY IS INCORPORATING AI

Not surprisingly, AI is being adopted throughout the healthcare industry for a variety of tasks. Don't be surprised if you find yourself interfacing with AI the next time you schedule a visit.

Medical professionals are currently using or evaluating the use of AI for

- Scheduling appointments
- Checking in for appointments
- Assisting providers
- Managing medications
- Remotely monitoring patients
- Analyzing patient data
- Enhancing online patient portals
- Answering patient questions
- Assisting in diagnosing conditions and recommending treatments
- Automating billing and other administrative tasks

In short, expect AI to touch just about every aspect of your future healthcare. Ideally, this will help provide more efficient and accurate care—and reduce frustrating wait times!

## Summary

In this chapter, you learned many of the ways you use AI to improve your physical and mental health. You learned how to use AI tools to create personal fitness and nutrition plans, relieve stress, and better understand medical conditions, diagnoses, and medications.

AI promises to be a boon to the medical profession and those of us who rely on it for our health and well-being. Providing quality healthcare is a complex proposition that can benefit from the "intelligence" and automation provided by AI technology. AI will help you better manage your own care and improve the care you receive from medical professionals.

# 12

# USING AI TO HELP CAREGIVERS

As you learned in the previous chapter, AI can be a boon for your personal health and wellness. Not surprisingly, AI can also help family caregivers in navigating their daily tasks, monitoring those in their care, and even providing companionship for those in care.

# Using AI to Help Caregivers with Health Tasks

Generative AI can be a real help to family caregivers. Although caregiving can be rewarding, it is often something new and quite stressful for family members, and they have lots of questions about what to and what not to do. AI can provide the answers.

If you're a caregiver and not sure what to do in a given situation, an all-purpose AI tool such as ChatGPT, Google Gemini, or Microsoft Copilot can help. When you run into any of the following situations, here are some prompts to help.

## Getting Smarter about Medical Information

As discussed in Chapter 11, "Using AI for Health and Wellness," AI can be a boon for anyone trying to understand medical conditions and medical terminology. You can use AI much like an encyclopedia, asking it questions about various topics or having it explain complex medicalese in everyday terms.

This capability helps caregivers better understand the medical conditions of those receiving care and the medical implications of the care they receive. It also helps caregivers make more informed decisions and improve their caregiving skills.

Extracting useful medical information from an all-purpose AI tool is as easy as asking the right questions. For example, if you want to learn more about a specific medical condition, you might use the prompt

**Tell me more about [condition].**

If you're having trouble comprehending a doctor's care instructions, use the prompt

**Please explain the following instructions in language a child would understand [include instructions].**

You can even ask AI for advice on what to do in a given situation, such as when a person appears confused or has fallen and bruised a hip. Use the following prompt:

**The person in my care has [describe condition or situation]. What should I do?**

 **WARNING** Remember, AI cannot substitute for advice from a trained medical professional. Asking AI for help is a good first step, but always consult a physician for all important medical matters. Remember, AI makes mistakes.

## Working with Doctors

As you also learned in Chapter 11, AI can help you prepare those in your care for upcoming doctor's visits or hospital stays. Before accompanying someone to an upcoming visit, use AI to prepare a list of questions for the doctor with a prompt like this:

> **The person in my care is [describe the patient's age, weight, and other vitals] and has been experiencing [describe any current health issues or conditions]. What questions should we ask the doctor during an upcoming visit?**

Also, as stated previously, you can use AI to translate anything the doctor says that you don't grasp into easier-to-understand language.

## Providing Personalized Care Plans

AI can analyze the data you provide about the person for which you're caring to create a personalized care plan. This plan might include daily schedules, medication maintenance, dietary guides, and exercise routines. Just provide the AI tool with key information about the person and ask for a care plan:

> **Please create a personalized care plan for a person for whom I'm caring. They are [describe the patient's age, weight, and other vitals] and have the following conditions: [describe any current health issues or conditions]. They are in generally [excellent/good/fair/poor] health and require [constant/intermittent] care. Include information about [any or all of the following: daily schedules, medication maintenance, diet, and exercise].**

Again, be wary of sharing personal information because it will feed into AI's learning database. And verify AI's output, since it's not always accurate.

## Monitoring Health Conditions and Identifying Trends and Issues

AI excels at analyzing data, identifying trends, and predicting future outcomes. This capability can prove useful to caregivers monitoring the well-being of those in their care.

If you track the person's vitals on a regular basis, you can enter that information into an all-purpose AI tool and ask the tool to identify trends or predict possible oncoming medical conditions. You can do this for the person's weight, blood pressure, blood sugar, heart rate, and other key metrics. Just use the following prompt (and be prepared to either cut and paste data from another application or enter it manually):

> **Analyze the following [metric] data for a [enter the person's age, weight, and other vitals] individual. Please identify any trends and alert me to any possible developing conditions.**

Note that you don't have to track this information manually. Most smartwatches, such as the Apple Watch (www.apple.com/watch/), Google Pixel Watch (store. google.com/us/category/watches_trackers), and Samsung Galaxy Watch (www. samsung.com/us/watches/), can monitor heart rate, blood oxygen level, and other vitals and report results back to caregivers or medical professionals.

There are also numerous wearable personal pendants and other safety devices designed with caregivers in mind. These devices typically include much of the functionality of a smartwatch paired with remote functionality so a caregiver can access the device from their smartphone. Some of these devices also include two-way audio so the caregiver can communicate with the person in their care.

Companies offering these personal safety devices include

- Alert 1 (www.alert-1.com)

- Bay Alarm Medical (www.bayalarmmedical.com)

- LifeAlert (www.lifealert.com)

- Lifeline (www.lifeline.com) (learn about discounts for AARP members at www.aarp.org/membership/benefits/)

- Medical Guardian (www.medicalguardian.com)

- MobileHelp (www.mobilehelp.com)

- Theora Care (https://theoracare.com)

- UnaliWear (www.unaliwear.com)

 **NOTE** Some of these devices require a paid subscription to a monitoring service for full functionality. There are many health apps available for your smartphone that track an individual's vitals, including some that tie into a smartwatch or personal monitoring device to obtain key information. You can find these apps in your phone's app store.

Then there's the Together app, shown in Figure 12.1, that uses your smartphone to video selfies of a person to determine their vitals and share that information with caregivers or loved ones. It's easy to use; just have the individual stare into the phone's camera for 60 seconds or so and it uses AI technology to determine their blood pressure, pulse rate, heart rate variability, and respiratory rate. It's pretty nifty. Learn more at www.togetherapp.com.

**FIGURE 12.1**

*Taking heart pulse and respiratory rate via selfie with the Together app.*

## Improving Nutrition

As also discussed in Chapter 11, you can use all-purpose AI tools to provide nutrition advice or meal plans for the person in your care. Just prompt the AI with information about that individual, any dietary restriction they have, and any health goals they may want to achieve. Use a prompt like the following:

**Please provide a seven-day meal plan for a [describe person's age, weight, and other vitals] [male/female] with [describe any health conditions]. This person needs to restrict carb consumption and is allergic to soy. They'd like to maintain or increase their weight by a few pounds over the next month.**

# Using AI to Help Caregivers with Financial and Legal Matters

AI can help caregivers with more than just health-related issues. AI can also be a good source of information and advice about the financial and legal issues facing those caring for family members.

## Managing the Financial Waters

One of the most challenging parts of being a family caregiver concerns finances. Fortunately, AI is able to help answer a lot of financial questions.

Here are some prompts you may want to try to help you navigate healthcare costs, insurance claims, and financial planning related to the person in your care; some of these prompts should result in the AI tool asking you additional questions:

- **Create a budget for managing caregiving expenses for a [describe age and gender] living on their own with minimal care**
- **What financial assistance programs are available for caregivers?**
- **How do I apply for Medicaid or other government aid for caregiving?**
- **How do I claim caregiving expenses on my taxes?**
- **What strategies can I use to manage my [enter age] father's medical expenses?**
- **What is the best type of long-term care insurance for my [enter age] father?**
- **Are there any employer benefits or support programs available for caregivers?**
- **How much should I set aside in an emergency fund for caregiving expenses?**

## Understanding Legal Issues

There are a plethora of legal issues surrounding long-term care. As a family caregiver, you can use any all-purpose AI tool to ask questions such as these:

- **What legal documents should I have in place as a caregiver?**
- **What do I need to know about estate planning for my [enter age] parents?**
- **My parent has approximately [enter dollar amount] in savings. How can I best manage her finances on a weekly basis?**

- I'm on a fixed budget and my mother needs long-term care. How can we manage this?

- How do I obtain power of attorney for my elderly parent?

- What is a healthcare proxy and how do I designate one for my father?

- What is a living will, and how do I create one for my mother?

- What are advance directives, and why are they important in caregiving?

- What is guardianship, and when is it necessary for a caregiver to seek it?

- How do I become a legal guardian for my elderly parent?

- What legal steps should I take to manage my parent's finances responsibly?

 **WARNING**  AI cannot substitute for professional legal or financial advice. Check with a professional who can review your unique circumstances.

## Receiving Useful Tips and Personalized Advice

You can ask any AI tool for caregiving tips. Use a prompt like this:

**Can you give me some useful tips for caregiving for a family member?**

When you enter information about the person receiving care, AI can provide personalized care advice. Use a prompt like this:

**I'm caring for my father. He's [age] years old and living by himself in a [house/apartment]. He has trouble walking and is no longer capable of driving. His mind is still sharp, but his memory is starting to fade. He doesn't like people looking after him but needs assistance with many things. Can you give me some advice on caring for him?**

You can also ask for personalized advice for dealing with specific situations. For example:

**My mother is no longer capable of maintaining her house and yard by herself. We're afraid she'd react adversely to being put into an assisted care facility. What options do we have in dealing with this situation?**

## Discovering Other Resources

Want to know more about resources available to you as a caregiver? AI can locate and recommend local resources, support groups, specialists, and more, based on your specific needs and the needs of the person receiving care. All you have to do is ask:

- **What resources are available to caregivers in the [enter your location] area?**

- **Are there any local support groups for children caring for parents with Alzheimer's?**

- **My [enter age] mother is having foot problems. Can you recommend a specialist in our area?**

- **Can you recommend someone to help me navigate Medicare options for my [enter age] mother?**

- **I'm a caregiver for my parents and I need more help, especially when I'm at work. What can you recommend?**

Just ask the AI tool for whatever you need wherever you may be.

# Using AI for Emotional Support for Caregivers

AI can provide caregivers a sympathetic ear and can help reduce stress and avoid burnout. AI chatbots can provide some of the emotional support caregivers might need.

Most all-purpose AI tools provide interactive chat capability. Some, like ChatGPT, provide voice chat, so you can talk with the AI instead of just typing text messages. Sometimes after a long, frustrating day of caregiving, you just need to talk a little bit about how it's affecting you.

 **WARNING** AI chat tools should never replace genuine human contact and conversation. If caregiving is really getting you down, consider engaging the services of a therapist or counselor, or finding a support network to help you get through the tough times. Learn about AARP's caregiving resources and support at aarp.org/caregiving.

## SMART TECHNOLOGY FOR CAREGIVING

You can use various smart home devices to make your tasks easier and automate tasks for the person in your care. While most of these smart devices don't currently use AI (or, if they do, only rudimentarily via predictive AI), expect companies to more fully integrate generative AI in the future. Future smart home technology can potentially use AI to better predict user behavior and integrate information between devices to enhance remote caregiving.

Consider the following:

- Smart lighting helps turn lights on or off without having to get off the couch.
- Smart thermostats control temperature on a preconfigured schedule or learn an individual's heating/cooling needs.
- Smart doorbells let those in care see who's at the door without having to open it.
- Smart door locks control who can enter a house or apartment—and notify caregivers when a resident leaves unexpectedly.
- Smart cameras let caregivers or family members monitor loved ones from a distance.

These smart devices can be operated on preconfigured schedules, via smartphone apps, or via voice-controlled smart speakers, such as the Amazon Echo or Google Nest devices. Smartphone operation lets caregivers operate these devices remotely, which is useful for when you can't be there in person. Smart speakers also let caregivers communicate with and remotely listen in on those receiving care.

# Using AI to Provide Virtual Companionship and Assistance

A newer and perhaps more significant use of AI in caregiving is the ability to provide virtual companionship. Being able to converse with an AI chatbot can help relieve loneliness and boredom.

As you learned in Chapter 11, virtual companionship is available today. Most all-purpose AI tools enable text-based conversations if the person receiving care is able to use a computer keyboard.

With other generative AI tools, such as ChatGPT, an individual can speak to the AI tool and have the AI respond in a human-like voice. This enables more natural conversation, especially as AI gets better at reading a person's mood and emotions and can respond with some semblance of empathy and personality.

Expect AI-enabled chatbots to get more human-like over time and be integrated into more and different physical devices. For example, the ElliQ "AI sidekick" is a device with a tablet-based display, speaker, and microphone that uses AI technology to carry on real-time conversations. Think of it as a very smart Amazon Echo Show fine-tuned for an older market. Figure 12.2 shows ElliQ in action; learn more at https://elliq.com.

**FIGURE 12.2**

*ElliQ providing AI-powered companionship. (Photo courtesy of ElliQ.)*

You can also expect future versions of Amazon Alexa, Apple Siri, and Google Assistant to provide more realistic and sophisticated conversations. The current versions of these voice assistants use predictive AI to guess at what you want or ask for; newer versions will incorporate generative AI to provide true one-on-one conversations.

# Examining Other AI Tools for Caregivers

In addition to the apps and devices discussed elsewhere in this chapter, there are a handful of AI-powered tools designed specifically for caregivers that bear further examination, including

- **Arti** is a home healthcare platform that integrates with third-party devices and healthcare organizations to provide caregivers and assisted living facilities with a variety of useful services. The Arti platform enables remote monitoring and can also predict and uncover previously hidden health problems. (Learn more at www.caredaily.ai.)

- **CareFlick** is an AI-powered management platform for assisted living organizations. It includes Yana, an AI-powered co-pilot that offers advice and insights to caregivers, as well as care monitoring and insightful reporting. (Learn more at www.careflick.com.)

- **CarePredict** is a wearable device that uses AI to learn a person's daily activity patterns and alerts caregivers to changes that might indicate health issues. (Learn more at www.carepredict.com.)

- **Medisafe** is a medication management app that uses AI to provide personalized medication reminders and tracks adherence. (Learn more at www.medisafe.com/download-medisafe-app/.)

- **Vera** is a smartphone app that uses AI-tailored music to improve memory care. (Learn more at www.veramusic.com.)

While some of these tools, such as Arti and CareFlick, are targeted at larger facilities and organizations, it's likely that much of the functionality they offer will filter down to individual caregivers in the future. The other tools are available to individual caregivers today.

## THE FUTURE OF AI IN CAREGIVING

The potential impact of AI on caregiving is enormous. It's all a matter of integrating advanced AI models into easy-to-use tools and devices.

In some ways, generative AI will make current devices better. Instead of merely tracking a person's heartrate and breathing, for example, AI will enable health and fitness trackers to analyze a person's health over the long term and suggest needed care. Instead of requiring caregivers to physically monitor surveillance cameras and audio feeds, generative AI will automate the monitoring and know when a human caregiver needs to intervene. Instead of just responding to simple questions (such as "what's the weather today?"), generative AI will turn today's voice assistants into humanlike companions.

Generative AI will do all this and more, naturally and unobtrusively. Those receiving care will interface with these apps and devices via natural-language voice commands, just like talking with a human caregiver. Caregivers, loved ones, and healthcare professionals will be able not only to monitor the individual but also respond to subtle trends and provide more personalized care. The changes are likely to be incremental but significant.

It's important, then, to keep abreast of new developments in AI-assisted caregiving. We're likely to see a lot of new products, services, and functionality over the next few years that promise to make easier the lives of caregivers and those they care for. And for certain tasks, people may come to prefer a robot to a human to help maintain a level of dignity or privacy.

# Summary

In this chapter, you learned ways that AI, however peripherally, is used in caregiving today. In particular, you learned all the different ways caregivers can use AI to help them navigate their daily tasks, from better understanding medical information to managing legal and financial issues.

In addition, you learned how generative AI chatbots can be used to provide virtual companionship and assistance. You also learned about a few other AI-assisted tools available to caregivers today.

While AI won't singularly relieve the growing caregiver crisis, it will help caregivers to do more with their limited time—and enable those receiving care to live more independently without the need for in-person care. AI will change the dynamics of caregiving—with major developments expected over the next several years.

## IN THIS CHAPTER

- What's next for AI?
- How will AI impact your life in the future?
- What risks lie ahead?

# 13

# THE FUTURE OF AI

If you've made it this far through this book, you've learned a lot about artificial intelligence and how to use it in everyday life. What we haven't yet examined is what's next for AI, what it's likely to look like and do in the near and not so near future.

The reality is that AI today is in its infancy, not unlike how the Internet was in the mid-90s. Back then we had no idea that the Internet would lead to a boom in online shopping (and the corresponding decline in physical retail stores), personalized news feeds and all the information in the world at our fingertips (including a new universe of disinformation), and the domination of social media (often at the expense of real-world connections).

That's where we are with AI today. We know it's here, we know it's evolving, we know its initial impact, but we have no idea where it's going to be five, ten, or more years in the future. What we do know is that AI is going to have a big impact—and how people use AI will inevitably evolve as it becomes more a part of our everyday lives.

# What's Next for AI?

If you had a crystal ball back in 1965, you would have bought shares in IBM at about $1.50 per share. Today that stock is going for almost $200 per share.

That same crystal ball, at different times, might have predicted the advent of global communications satellites, humans walking on the moon, the rise of the Internet, and the end of the Cold War. Think what you could have done with any of that information if you had it.

And if you had a crystal ball today and were looking at the AI market, you'd... well, what would you do? What does the crystal ball say about what's next for artificial intelligence?

AI technology is advancing so rapidly that it's impossible to know what directions it might take in the months and years ahead. But let's take a guess.

## AI Gets Smarter, Faster, and Less Expensive

It's safe to say that AI technology will continue to advance. Maybe not at today's accelerated rates, but still rapidly, at least for the foreseeable future.

We can also predict that AI will get smarter and more accurate over time, due to increases in computing power, the amount and quality of data fed into large language models, and the sophistication of the algorithms and programming behind the technology. The more data AI has to work with, the more informed—and at least apparently "smarter"—it will become.

In practical terms, this means you can expect AI models to provide more accurate answers to questions when queried for information. For example, AI-aided healthcare may provide more personalized health recommendations. Movies and TV shows are likely to take advantage of faster, better, and lower-priced special effects, leading to onscreen fantasy elements that put today's computer-generated imagery to shame. And AI image generators will no doubt inundate us with fantastic images that look as real as a photograph but picture places and characters that only existed in our imagination.

In addition, the way we interact with AI will become more natural. Instead of typing text into a prompt box, we'll talk with devices that can see and hear everything around them. You'll speak to these AI-powered devices and they'll respond, sounding as real as your neighbor next door. You won't be able to tell the difference between an AI chatbot and a human being. And, as conversational-AI assistants can access calendars and other real-time data, they can become even more helpful.

You can also safely predict that AI will get faster as computing power continues to increase. Big AI tasks, like creating visually sophisticated images, will be completed in the blink of an eye, instead of waiting minutes to generate results. Complex mathematical and scientific calculations will be completed as soon as you hit the Enter button.

How fast AI will evolve is less predictable. Will it be twice as smart or twice as fast in one year, two years, or longer? There are too many variables to even venture a prediction. Just know that history shows that technology always gets faster and smarter and cheaper. The same will happen with AI.

## From Artificial Intelligence to Artificial Superintelligence

Today's artificial intelligence has not yet advanced to the level of human intelligence. That's the next step in AI development, to match and, ultimately, exceed that of human beings.

Experts consider today's artificial intelligence to be weak AI, or what some call *narrow artificial intelligence* (ANI). AI that works like and performs at the level of human intelligence is called strong AI or *artificial general intelligence* (AGI). AI that exceeds the constraints of human intelligence is called superintelligent AI or *artificial superintelligence* (ASI).

Put another way, ANI is typified by machines that imitate human behavior, typically one task at a time. AGI involves machines that can continuously learn from their experiences and thus approach true human intelligence. ASI builds on that to create machines that are smarter than humans in all aspects and measurement of intelligence.

ANI is what we have today and AGI could be achieved in the near future—some say within the next few years. ASI, however, may take a lot longer to achieve, if it can be achieved at all. ASI machines would have enormous capabilities and the ability to learn and grow in an exponential fashion, eventually achieving what some call the technological singularity. (We'll talk more about the singularity later in this chapter—and there's a lot to talk about.)

Bottom line: When betting on AI growth, it's artificial general intelligence that's next up to bat—AI systems that approach and match that of us flesh and blood humans. It's likely that we'll achieve AGI in our lifetimes, but what happens after that is nearly impossible to predict. Figure 13.1 shows one estimate of how AI will progress in the future, based on information presented in philosopher Nick Bostrom's book *Superintelligence: Paths, Dangers, Strategies*.

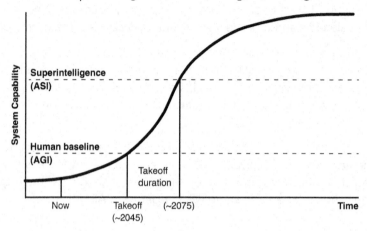

**FIGURE 13.1**

*A possible timeline to AGI and ASI. (Based on* Superintelligence: Paths, Dangers, Strategies *by Nick Bostrom. Estimates of the timing and duration of takeoff were not included on Bostrom's original graph.)*

## AI Gets Embedded in Other Devices

Today, most of us use AI on dedicated websites or smartphone apps. Going forward, AI will become part of other devices, either used seamlessly by the device or easily accessible by users.

Consider, for example, self-flying delivery drones. Instead of having to be remotely piloted at the source, embedded AI will help the drone navigate to the desired address while dealing with any real-world obstacles that might appear in flight. You won't see the technology in use but will experience its benefits.

Microsoft, as another example, is introducing a new generation of personal computers that include a neural processing chip and embedded AI capabilities. These Copilot+ PCs, as Microsoft is calling them, will be able to enhance available lighting and visual effects for better-looking video calls, provide real-time live captions and subtitles when playing videos, and recall anything and everything you've ever done on that device. Plus you'll be able to use the embedded AI to generate any text or images you imagine.

What other devices might include embedded AI? A short list might include smartphones, smart watches, fitness trackers, televisions and streaming media players, smart home devices, and self-driving cars. The longer list includes just about any device you can think of. (Yes, there will be—and, in fact, already is—an AI-enabled toaster. It apparently makes perfect toast, every time.)

# AI AND SELF-DRIVING CARS

One of the most anticipated uses of AI is in self-driving vehicles. While there are various AI-assisted features in cars today (such as adaptive cruise control, lane-keeping assistance, and automatic emergency braking), most of us aren't quite ready to jump into a self-driving vehicle—at least not yet.

Experts refer to a vehicle that can operate without any human intervention under all possible driving conditions—no steering wheel or other driving controls needed—as a Level 5 autonomous vehicle. Unfortunately, the industry isn't quite there yet.

Whenever the auto industry develops the first practical Level 5 autonomous vehicle, expect the initial uses to be for fleet vehicles. The trucking industry, for example, is likely to be upended by self-driving vehicles that replace the current ranks of long-haul truck drivers. The ridesharing industry is also likely to replace human drivers with autonomous vehicles, thus significantly impacting the millions of individuals currently driving for Lyft, Uber, Via, and other ridesharing services.

The technical challenges in developing a true self-driving vehicle are daunting and beyond what the tech and auto industries can accomplish today. Most experts predict that we won't see widespread use of Level 5 autonomous vehicles until the year 2040 or later.

## AI Merges with Other Technologies and Services

Embedding AI in freestanding devices is just the first step. Experts are also working on how to integrate AI with other technologies to improve their operation and efficiency.

One potential merging of technologies involves AI and robotics. By themselves, current-generation robots are pretty dumb; they have to be guided by an external human operator. In contrast, AI-enabled robots (what some call autonomous mobile robots, or AMRs) can learn to "think" on their own in real time, freely navigating their environment and performing more advanced tasks.

For example, Ameca (www.engineeredarts.co.uk/robot/ameca/) is an autonomous humanoid robot (see Figure 13.2) that its manufacturer bills as "the world's most advanced human shaped robot." Ameca merges artificial intelligence with a human-like artificial body, enabling it to respond to commands and questions in real time with lifelike facial expressions.

**FIGURE 13.2**

*The Ameca AI-powered humanoid robot. (Photo courtesy Engineered Arts.)*

Imagine an AI-enabled robot like Ameca in a retail store or restaurant. The robot could greet customers by name, direct them to what they're seeking, and prepare and deliver fancy cocktails or coffee drinks—all without human intervention. An AI-enabled robot could even make small talk with customers and recommend specific products or specials based on their conversations.

 **NOTE** AI-enabled robots also have a future in caregiving, as discussed in Chapter 12, "Using AI to Help Caregivers."

What other technologies can benefit from using AI? How about these:

- AI and the Internet of Things—devices with sensors and software—which could improve existing smart home technologies

- AI with health trackers that could detect critical health issues

- AI with digital assistants—which is already happening, with Amazon planning to release an AI-powered version of Alexa and Google integrating Google Gemini AI into its Google Assistant technology

- AI with virtual reality (VR), such as AI-powered characters that appear in your field of vision and interact with you when you're wearing VR glasses

- AI with videogame tech, to create more lifelike characters that interact with you in real time

- AI with holographic technology, to put a face and a body to your AI assistant's voice—and show you how to do things, just like a real person in the room would

And there's more. AI can merge with both technologies and services to provide additional benefit to individuals.

For example, AI and robotics can merge with health coaching to create empathetic artificial companions or with mental health therapy to provide 24/7 support and care. Both of these advancements could significantly improve patient care, especially in a field that is already experiencing a shortage of qualified workers.

Predicting this future is easy. AI becomes even more useful when it works together with these and other technologies.

## AI Gets Personalized

One other expected path for AI going forward is in creating personalized experiences of all sizes and shapes. As AI advances, it will obtain more personal data about each and every one of us. While this raises some privacy concerns, it also opens up the potential to create products, services, and experiences that are tailored to your individual likes and needs.

Imagine a world that is crafted just for you—not just your Internet newsfeed or streaming video recommendations, but all your entertainment, shopping, and education needs. You'll literally experience a world of your own, created by AI for your enjoyment.

# How Will AI Impact Your Life in the Future?

How will all these possible developments affect you directly? It's a given that AI will touch many aspects of your life, whatever your job or social standing. How you take advantage of AI's benefits are totally up to you.

## AI and You at Home

It's a few years from now. You're woken up at the designated time by the soothing voice of your personal AI assistant coming to you from a nearby speaker or in a holographic image. (Think of Amazon's Alexa or the Google Assistant, except much more advanced.) Your AI assistant provides the weather forecast and your schedule for the day and recommends what clothes to wear. It has also started cooking your breakfast to be ready when you're done in the shower, which is already running at your desired temperature.

AI has already planned out your day and programmed your self-driving car to take you where you need to go. Not a moment is wasted; everything is ready for you at the exact moment you need it. If something new crops up—maybe the carpool fails and one of your children needs to be picked up from school—AI automatically adjusts everything in real time to compensate.

Perhaps midway through the day you begin to feel unwell. You tell AI your symptoms, and your AI assistant automatically diagnoses the problem. If it's something simple, like a cold, AI tells you how to treat it. If it's more serious, AI schedules a virtual visit with your doctor and transmits its diagnosis to the physician's office. The doctor uses AI tools to confirm the diagnosis and prescribe the proper treatment; if a prescription is needed, it is automatically transmitted to your pharmacy and delivered to your home via AI-powered drone.

While you're out doing things, your AI is busy making sure your home is running in tip-top order. Your AI-powered self-driving lawn mower is cutting the grass in perfect patterns, the house is automatically heated or cooled to the right temperature in each room for whomever is (or isn't) in it, and every square inch of your floors are being cleaned by your AI-powered robotic vacuum cleaner.

That evening, after a dinner planned by AI (but still prepared by you), you settle down for some relaxing entertainment. AI knows what you like to watch and puts it onscreen for you. It knows not to interrupt you while you're watching, but gently reminds you the best time to go to bed for your personal sleep cycle.

And that's a day with AI in the home.

## AI and You at Work

In the future, AI will do a lot of your old work for you. If your responsibilities include a lot of repetitive, time-consuming tasks, AI will be a blessing.

For example, if you currently sit around all day plugging numbers into a spreadsheet, AI can do that boring work for you. If you sit in front of a computer screen conducting research or retrieving information, AI can do it for you—much faster than you can. If you spend most of your day trying to come up with new marketing or product ideas, AI can generate a number of new ideas for you to choose from.

A lot of what you do will be directed by AI systems. AI will essentially be running the day-to-day aspects of your company, only pulling people in when they're necessary. You'll get your assignments from AI, so your work will be targeted precisely where you're needed.

Not only will AI help you get your work done faster, but it will help you be more accurate. Run your work through an AI tool, and it will find any mistakes you might have made. It will even find factual and logical inconsistencies. Not that you can ever achieve perfection, but AI will help you get close.

If you're on the road, AI will plan the perfect routes and make all necessary reservations. You probably won't be on the road a lot, however, because you'll be conducting most of your meetings virtually. AI will make it look and sound like everyone is in the same room, even though you're all in separate locations. Initially you'll see a conference room onscreen with everyone around the same virtual table; in time, your colleagues will appear together holographically in 3D space.

For upper management, AI will monitor key metrics in real time and determine when certain actions need to be taken. AI will feed the right information to the C-suite so that executives can make better-informed decisions. In fact, AI will recommend certain strategies and courses of action, and those recommendations are likely to be followed. AI will, in many ways, know more about the business than management does.

Bottom line (and business is all about the bottom line), AI will take over all the mundane, routine, utterly mind-numbing manual tasks common in businesses today. It will help run the business and make decisions for the future. That will result in higher productivity and higher profits.

On the other side of the equation, some workers may get left behind in the upcoming AI revolution. AI will replace some existing workers if their skills are no longer needed. If AI can do what you currently do better and cheaper, your workday may consist of training and searching for a new job—which AI can also help you do.

## AI and You at Play

All work and no play makes AI a dull technology, so it's a good thing that AI will play a significant role in your extracurricular life.

I've never considered myself an artist. In fact, I can't draw a perfect circle, and I have trouble coloring inside the lines. But with generative AI, I'll be able to create all sorts of images in all manner of styles just by telling it what I want. That's exciting.

AI will let you be creative in all sorts of ways. Want to create a new piece of artwork to hang on your wall? AI can do it. Want to write a short story, or your family's memoirs? AI can do it. Want to compose that perfect piece of music that's been banging around your head for years? AI can do that, too.

With generative AI, you no longer need innate skills to be creative. AI can take your ideas and run with them, in whatever medium you desire. Thanks to AI, we could be on the cusp of a new creative era, one that enables individuals of all types to pursue their creative muses.

And that's not all. AI will help you get better at your favorite sports by observing your performance and offering personalized advice. Want to improve your golf swing? AI will show you how. Want your kids to be better at baseball or soccer? AI will help train them. Have a free half hour and want to get a little exercise? AI will come up with the perfect exercise routine on the spot.

Let's not forget more passive entertainment. As previously noted, AI knows your viewing and listening habits and will recommend new movies, TV shows, and music for your entertainment pleasure. You'll get personalized playlists and viewing queues, with really good recommendations for new stuff you'll probably like.

## AI and You All Day, Every Day

Look forward even just a few years and you can see how AI will integrate with almost all facets of your daily life. You'll use AI to plan your day, to communicate with others, to assist in work, and to help entertain you. If all goes as it could, AI will improve your life in a multitude of both small and big ways. It will be everywhere.

# What Risks Lie Ahead?

The future of AI may not be altogether rosy. There are many ways that artificial intelligence can be used for evil as well as for good—and many experts fear that out-of-control AI could pose significant risks to our society.

Some people are already using AI-generated images to mock, to taunt, to sexualize, to ridicule, and to poke fun at both public and private figures. AI makes it easier for people to violate others' privacy and exploit biases; it also makes it difficult to determine what is real and what is a deepfake. While AI has the potential to create wonderful changes in our daily lives and societies, it's important to be aware of some of the large-scale risks connected with letting the technology get too far ahead of regulators and law.

## We Lose Oversight and Control

As AI systems become more autonomous and capable of making decisions on their own, there is a very real risk that we'll lose oversight and control of that technology and other systems. When we let AI make too many decisions for us, we might come to rely on AI too much and lose the capacity to make our own decisions—and the accompanying accountability.

Along the same lines, as we let AI manage more and more activities, our own skills required to perform those activities may atrophy. This could be as simple as not being able to add, subtract, multiply, and divide in our heads (already a problem since the advent of the handheld calculator) or as worrisome as diminishing interpersonal skills because we don't interact with real live human beings as often as before. And after years of blindly following your GPS app, can you still read a map? If this happens, it won't necessarily be AI's fault but rather our own, for letting AI take over too much of our lives.

## We Let AI Become Weaponized

It is an unfortunate fact: many of society's most important technological advancements have either come about as part of a war effort or been enlisted to support a war effort. One need look no further than the use of motorized vehicles and airplanes in World War I, radar and nuclear weapons in World War II, and spy satellites during the Cold War.

Knowing this, it's quite likely that AI will be co-opted by the military for both defensive and offensive purposes. Consider these potential uses of AI by domestic and foreign militaries—some of which are already in use:

- Using swarm intelligence technology to guide hundreds of decentralized drones in coordinated attacks to overwhelm an enemy's defense systems

- Using AI to make targeting decisions in warfare

- Transferring attack decisions from humans to Lethal Autonomous Weapons Systems (LAWS)

- Developing armies of autonomous, so-called killer robots to fight on the battlefield

Okay, that last one may seem a little far-fetched—until, that is, you realize that the Marines have already tested an autonomous utility robot equipped with an anti-tank weapon for battlefield use. It shouldn't surprise you to discover that the United States and China are currently in a LAWS arms race, each side aggressively pursuing research and development of AI systems for military purposes.

The possible weaponization of AI isn't the sole purview of the world's militaries, however. Hackers can use (and are probably already using) AI to develop sophisticated and dangerous malware to use in cyberattacks. Machine learning can help hackers more quickly develop malicious code, thus staying a step ahead of legitimate cybersecurity efforts. AI can help automate cyberattacks, increasing their speed and scale. And AI can assist malicious individuals in developing more targeted and effective phishing scams.

Malicious actors may also be able to use AI to manipulate essential systems for their own purposes. Imagine AI being used to infiltrate and disrupt critical infrastructure, such as a nation's power grid or water supply. Whatever bad things humans can do, chances are AI can do it even better.

## The Ultimate AI Risk: Achieving the Singularity

Many scientists and AI experts believe that, based on continuing increases in computing power and advancements in AI models, at some point in the future, AI will reach and surpass the level of human intelligence and become cognizant. This point, where AI exceeds the intelligence of humans, is called the *singularity*—and it could bode ill for us humans left behind.

Although some experts fear that a truly sentient AI could turn against its human creators, others dismiss the entire concept of the singularity as either implausible, improbable, or not quite as dire as others predict. To ease any concerns you might have, know that there are just as many arguments against the singularity occurring as there are for it happening. The chief arguments against the singularity occurring include the following:

- **Technological advancements tend to level off over time.** AI is experiencing significant growth now, but that growth is likely to slow in the coming years, meaning artificial intelligence will never become artificial superintelligence.

- **AI will never be as smart as humans—because it isn't human.** Artificial intelligence today relies almost totally on a few discrete forms of input—essentially text, images, audio, and video fed into large language models. Human intelligence, in contrast, is informed by a range of sensory inputs that aren't available to today's AI models, including touch, taste, smell, and other senses. Computers simply don't and can't experience the world in the many ways that humans do and thus won't become human.

- **Resources are not unlimited.** The fact that all resources are limited includes those resources necessary to develop and power AI. We may simply run out of the raw materials required to build enough powerful servers—or not have enough electricity available—to reach the singularity.

- **A single, large, universal artificial superintelligence is unlikely.** A singularity event requires a huge, universal AI model. It's more likely that AI will evolve into multiple smaller, more task- or industry-specific models rather than a single model that tries to serve everyone and everything. In addition, it's highly unlikely that multiple countries will link their AI models to those of their enemies.

- **Human intelligence can evolve, too.** Other experts think that the singularity can be avoided by advancements in human intelligence. Continuing developments in bioengineering, genetic engineering, and mind-altering drugs could lead to an explosion in human intelligence levels, tapping into previously unused or underused brain capacity.

- **We can pull the plug.** Some believe the simplest defense against a universal ASI model that might try to take over the world is to simply turn it off—if, indeed, that's possible. When experts sense that a given ASI model might be edging close to desiring world domination, they can figuratively flip the switch or pull the plug. AI needs power to work. Deprive the computers that drive AI of that power and they quit working—and AI isn't very smart at all when its brains shut down.

All that said, it's important to know that many experts in the field are seriously concerned about the possibility of the singularity and how it might possibly affect humankind. While the probability of the singularity occurring may be low, it's not something to be taken lightly.

# Summary

The precise future of artificial intelligence is difficult to predict, other than it will continue to get smarter, faster, and cheaper. The path of evolution will likely move from today's weak narrow artificial intelligence to stronger human-like artificial general intelligence to the ultimate artificial superintelligence—although at what speed remains to be seen.

So far we've only tapped the surface as to how we can use artificial intelligence technology. Going forward, we'll discover new and currently unimagined uses for AI. As with any developing technology, how we envision AI today is likely to be much different than how it actually ends up being used.

We know that AI can automate repetitive operations. We know it can conduct research and inform decision-making. We know it can generate text, images, audio, and video to inspire creativity.

We don't know what else AI can do or how we can use it. We will eventually discover new and exciting uses for AI that will make our lives better. We just don't yet know what those uses might be. That will come with time and experience, of which we'll have much. As I know you'll discover on your own, the more you use AI, the more ways you'll think of to use it.

Whatever the future holds, AI will continue to develop and to become smarter. How much smarter is up to us humans, as is how we choose to use everything AI promises to deliver.

# Glossary

**AGI**   See *artificial general intelligence.*

**AI**   See *artificial intelligence.*

**AI generator**   A software or service that uses generative AI to generate content—text, images, video, audio, code, or other media.

**AI image generator**   A type of AI software or service designed to create visual imagery from textual or other forms of input.

**algorithm**   A set of rules or instructions that perform a task or solve a problem, commonly used by AI.

**all-purpose AI tool**   A versatile AI generator designed to perform a wide variety of tasks. Popular all-purpose AI tools include ChatGPT, Claude AI, Google Gemini, Meta AI, and Microsoft Copilot.

**ANI**   See *artificial narrow intelligence.*

**artificial general intelligence (AGI)**   An AI system that works like and performs at the level of human intelligence.

**artificial intelligence (AI)**   The ability of a computer or machine to mimic human intelligence.

**artificial narrow intelligence (ANI)**   AI systems designed to address specific tasks but that do not meet human capabilities.

**artificial superintelligence (ASI)**   A hypothetical AI that exceeds the constraints of human intelligence.

**ASI**   See *artificial superintelligence.*

**automation**   The use of technology or processes to perform a task or activity with minimal human input.

**autonomous vehicle**   A self-driving car or other vehicle, powered by AI technology, that can navigate and operate without human intervention.

**chatbot**   A program designed to simulate conversations with human users; AI-powered chatbots employ conversational AI (either written or spoken).

**computer vision**   A technology that teaches computers to extract meaningful information from images.

**conversational AI**   A type of AI that enables machines to understand, process, and generate human language in the form of a conversation.

**data training set**   A collection of information and other inputs used to teach an AI model.

**deep learning**   A type of machine learning that uses artificial neural networks to simulate human thought.

**deepfake**   Artificially created media in which people's likenesses—including their voice, image, or statements—have been manipulated without their permission, typically using AI.

**digital assistant**   An app or service designed to assist users by answering simple questions and performing simple tasks on demand.

**GenAI**   See *generative AI.*

**generative AI**   A newer type of AI designed specifically to generate or create new content.

**GPT**   Generative pretrained transformer, a type of AI language model trained to answer questions and generate new content.

**hallucination**   In the world of AI, an incorrect response to a prompt.

**large language model (LLM)**   An extensive deep learning computational model  trained on large amounts of data.

**LLM**   See *large language model.*

**machine learning (ML)**   A subset of AI that uses algorithms to autonomously learn processes without specific human programming.

**ML**   See *machine learning*

**multimodal AI**   An AI system that can process and integrate information from multiple data types, such as text, sound, and images.

**narrow AI**   See *artificial narrow intelligence.*

**natural language processing (NLP)**   The subset of AI that enables computers to analyze, understand, and derive meaning from human language.

**neural network**   A type of machine learning program that works in a similar fashion to the human brain.

**NLP**   See *natural language processing.*

**personalization**   The act of designing something to meet a person's individual requirements or desires.

**predictive AI**   AI designed to predict trends and based on past patterns and algorithms; predictive AI has been around for a while.

**prompt**   Text-based input given to an AI system to generate a specific output or response.

**sentiment analysis**   The process of identifying whether the emotional tone of a message is positive, negative, or neutral.

**singularity**   A hypothetical future point at which AI gains sentience and technological growth and becomes uncontrollable and irreversible, resulting in unforeseeable changes to human civilization.

**smart devices**   Devices that can be controlled remotely via Internet-connected apps or AI algorithms.

**smart home**   A home equipped with multiple smart devices.

**smart speaker**   A type of speaker and voice command device with an integrated virtual assistant that offers interactive actions and hands-free activation. Today's most popular smart speakers include the Amazon Echo and Google Nest devices.

**speech-to-text (STT)**   A technology that translates the spoken word into written text.

**strong AI**   See *generative AI.*

**STT**   See *speech-to-text.*

**technical singularity**   See *singularity.*

**text-to-speech (TTS)**   The process of translating written text into spoken word.

**TTS**   See *text-to-speech.*

**voice assistant**   A digital assistant that interacts with users through voice recognition and natural language processing.

**weak AI**   See *predictive AI.*

# Index

# D

# G

# H

# N

# O

# P

# V

Valet EZ, 244
Vasco Translator, 242
Vera, 277
verifying AI-generated content, 46, 93
Via, 244
video games, AI in, 285
videos, identifying AI-generated content, 44
virtual companionship, 256-257, 275-276
virtual reality (VR), 284
virtual travel assistants, AI as, 229
voice, talking with AI via, 161-164
von Kemplelen, Wolfgang, 7
VR (virtual reality), 284

# W

watermarks, 39
Watson, 9
Waymo, 9
Waze, 241
weak AI, 281. See also predictive AI
weaponization of AI, 289-290
weather predictions with AI, 239
web pages, summarizing, 71
web search. See search engines
WebMD, 260
weight-loss plans, creating with AI, 250-251, 271
Westworld (film/television series), 10
WhatToPack, 239
white fonting, 211
Winston AI, 43
Wonderplan, 230, 235-236
Wordtune, 112, 122-123
Wordvice AI, 220
workout plans, creating
 with AI, 248-249
 for caregivers, 269

workplace, future impact of AI, 286-287
work-related AI usage
 for improving productivity, 216-222
  communication and collaboration, 219
  creating presentations, 220-222
  generating content, 216
  managing projects, 217-218
  translation tools, 220
 for managing meetings, 222-226
  scheduling meetings, 223-224
  taking notes and summarizing meetings, 224-226
Wray, Christopher, 32
Wrike, 218
writing
 AI's impact in, 21, 30, 36, 97. See also AI generators
 ethics of AI-generated content, 98-99
 identifying AI-generated content, 38-40
 improving with AI, 107-112
  editing content, 111-112
  Grammarly, 112-114
  Hemingway Editor, 114-116
  HyperWrite, 116-117
  outlining content, 109-110
  ProWritingAid, 118-119
  QuillBot, 119-120
  resumes and LinkedIn profiles, 206
  rewriting content, 110-111
  Sudowrite, 121-122
  suggesting topics, 108-109
  Wordtune, 122-123
 types of, 99-107
  business letters, 103-104
  cover letters, 210-211
  email messages, 101-102
  journal writing, 253-254
  memoirs, 104-105
  personal letters, 101

# Register Your Product at informit.com/register

## Access additional benefits and save up to 65%* on your next purchase

- Automatically receive a coupon for 35% off books, eBooks, and web editions and 65% off video courses, valid for 30 days. Look for your code in your InformIT cart or the Manage Codes section of your account page.

- Download available product updates.

- Access bonus material if available.**

- Check the box to hear from us and receive exclusive offers on new editions and related products.

---

## InformIT—The Trusted Technology Learning Source

InformIT is the online home of information technology brands at Pearson, the world's leading learning company. At informit.com, you can

- Shop our books, eBooks, and video training. Most eBooks are DRM-Free and include PDF and EPUB files.

- Take advantage of our special offers and promotions (informit.com/promotions).

- Sign up for special offers and content newsletter (informit.com/newsletters).

- Access thousands of free chapters and video lessons.

- Enjoy free ground shipping on U.S. orders.*

*\* Offers subject to change.*

*\*\* Registration benefits vary by product. Benefits will be listed on your account page under Registered Products.*

## Connect with InformIT—Visit informit.com/community

 twitter.com/informit

 Pearson

Addison-Wesley • Adobe Press • Cisco Press • Microsoft Press • Oracle Press • Peachpit Press • Pearson IT Certification • Que